*Poe Abroad*

# Poe
## *Abroad*

INFLUENCE, REPUTATION, AFFINITIES

*Edited by* LOIS DAVIS VINES

University of Iowa Press, Iowa City

University of Iowa Press, Iowa City 52242

Copyright © 1999 by the University of Iowa Press

Printed in the United States of America

http://www.uiowa.edu/~uipress

The publication of this book was generously supported by the
University of Iowa Foundation.

Printed on acid-free paper

Library of Congress Cataloging-in-Publication Data
Poe abroad : influence, reputation, affinities / edited by Lois Davis
Vines.
p.     cm.
Includes bibliographical references and index.
ISBN 0-87745-697-6
1. Poe, Edgar Allan, 1809–1849—Appreciation—Foreign
countries.    2. Poe, Edgar Allan, 1809–1849—Translations—
History and criticism.    3. Fantasy literature, American—
Translations—History and criticism.    4. Fantasy literature,
American—Appreciation—Foreign countries.    5. Literature,
Modern—American influences.    6. Poe, Edgar Allan, 1809–
1849—Influence.    I. Vines, Lois.
PS2638.P62   1999
818'.309—dc21                                                99-36989

99   00   01   02   03   C   5   4   3   2   1

# Contents

PART II:

# *Preface & Acknowledgments*

Throughout this volume titles are given in the original language first. In cases where there is a known translation in English, the English title is given in italics for books and between quotation marks for poems, short stories, and essays. If there is no known English version of the work, the title is translated literally without italics or quotation marks. Titles in Latin are not translated.

The term "Spanish America" is used instead of "Latin America" to refer to countries in Central and South America where Spanish is the dominant language. Portugese-speaking Brazil is treated in a separate chapter.

The preparation of this volume has involved the collaboration of many scholars from around the world. In addition to those who contributed chapters, I would also like to thank others for their help and suggestions: Eric W. Carlson, Kent Ljungquist, Robert Burchfield, Dean McWilliams, James Thompson, Janice Thompson, Walter Grünzweig, Elvira Osipova, and Reet Sool. For permission to use altered or updated versions of articles appearing earlier, I am grateful to *Comparative Literature*, *Review of Contemporary Fiction*, *Polish Review*, and *University of Mississippi Studies in English*.

# Introduction

The French poet and essayist Paul Valéry remarked in 1924 that Poe "would today be completely forgotten if Baudelaire had not taken up the task of introducing him into European literature."[1] Valéry's observation is both an exaggeration and an understatement. Poe certainly would not have been completely forgotten. Although the French are loath to admit it, he was read and admired by Americans during his lifetime and afterward. But the importance of Baudelaire's contribution to Poe's renown goes far beyond Valéry's estimation. Not only did Baudelaire's translations and essays introduce Poe into European literature, they also played a major role in his becoming known throughout the world, especially in Asia and Latin America.

Nineteen ninety-eight marked the 150th anniversary of the publication of Baudelaire's first Poe translation, an event that inspired him to produce five volumes of Poe in French. The names Baudelaire and Poe are linked in literary circles worldwide. Before Poe died in 1849, he learned that his tales were being translated in France but was unaware that his work had the good fortune of falling into the hands of a writer who would become one of France's greatest poets. To commemorate the 150th anniversary of Poe's death in 1999, *Poe Abroad* offers a tribute to his extraordinary international influence and reputation.

*Poe Abroad* is the first attempt to bring together in one volume an account of Poe's effect on literatures around the world and to present analyses of his influence on major foreign writers. Several years ago Eric W. Carlson invited me to contribute a chapter on Poe's influence abroad to his book *A Companion to Poe Studies* (1997). Since my work on Poe in France gave me a head start, I set out to do the research with an enthusiasm that soon turned into amazement at the complexity of the subject and then into despair. How would it be possible to present a study of Poe's worldwide influence within the strict limits of a forty-page manuscript? After coming to grips with the fact that I could present only the tip of the iceberg, I completed the chapter, "Edgar Allan Poe: A Writer for the World," with the promise to myself to publish a more in-depth study that would do justice to the subject. My present editor kindly offered me four hundred manuscript pages. Again, elation was followed by despair. As I explored the subject further, I was constantly reminded of Joyce Carol Oates's question: "Who has *not* been influenced by Poe?"[2] Now I am convinced that four thousand pages might not even suffice, especially if foreign texts written about Poe were included.

Part I of *Poe Abroad* offers the reader an overview of Poe's influence and reputation in specific countries and regions of the world.[3] The purpose of this historical approach is to give an idea of when Poe was first introduced to general readers and the effect he had on literary figures and movements in the various cultures. Part II explores his direct influence on writers who have gained an international reputation. The selection of countries, regions, and authors included in *Poe Abroad* was determined, in part, by my being able to identify scholars with a knowledge of the specific literatures in the foreign languages who were also interested in research on Poe and capable of presenting their work in English. In cases where studies on Poe in certain foreign countries have already been done, I asked the contributors to give an overview of the earlier work, then present more recent research.

Baudelaire's translations and articles on Poe, along with E.-D. Forgues's 1846 essay describing Poe as having "a peculiar lucidity of intellect," set the tone for admiration that spread quickly to other countries. One of the striking aspects of Poe's worldwide influence is the effect his work has had on vastly different areas of literary endeavor. He inspired Symbolism, Surrealism, Modernism, the detective story, the pseudoscientific novel, several types of short stories, and approaches to literary criticism. In Baudelaire's translation of "The Philosophy of Composition" and "The Poetic Principle," budding poets found the encouragement to steer their efforts toward "*The Rhythmical Creation of Beauty*" and away from "the Heresy of *The Didactic*," to use Poe's phrases. The French Symbolist poets discovered in Poe their high priest, and poets in other countries were soon influenced by the movement. The Chinese poet Yu Geng-yu, who became a Poe devotee in the 1920s, argued in his own essays that the poet should write poems "solely for the poem's sake," citing "The Raven" as a model. Movements that were called "young" and "new" in various countries found their inspiration in Poe. In the 1880s the generation referred to as La Jeune Belgique [Young Belgium] was guided in aesthetic matters by Poe and Baudelaire. In the early twentieth century the intellectuals and writers in the Young Estonia movement considered Poe their guide as they attempted to Europeanize Estonian culture and literature. In Latin America the Modernistas brought Poe's life and work into the literary consciousness of a new generation of writers.

"The Raven," one of the earliest of Poe's works to be translated into a number of foreign languages, inspired lively debates on poetics and how poems should be translated. At least sixteen versions of the poem have been published in Czech, including a Communist rendition in which the poet asks the bird to fly to the White House and say "nevermore" to Harry Truman. Silvia Campanini collected and evaluated twenty-two versions of "The Raven" in Italian that appeared between 1881 and 1986. Translators' skills and aesthetic principles were put to the test by rendering "The Raven" into Estonian, the subject of a detailed examination by Reet Sool.

Poe initiated the detective story with the creation of C. Auguste Dupin, the shrewd crime solver in three tales, "The Murders in the Rue Morgue," "The Mystery of Marie Rogêt," and "The Purloined Letter." Dupin is endowed with remarkable analytical powers, brilliant reasoning, and a keen imagination that allows him to enter the mind of the criminal. Although aloof from the police and other lesser mortals, Dupin takes pleasure in demonstrating his extraordinary intellectual faculties by solving the most baffling crimes. Poe's character inspired a number of detectives possessing similar traits: Sir Arthur Conan Doyle's Sherlock Holmes, the French sleuth Monsieur Lecoq created by Emile Gaboriau, and Feodor Dostoevsky's detective Porfiry Petrovitch in *Crime and Punishment*. Valéry used Dupin as a model for his intellectual superbrain Monsieur Teste, who attempts to apply the famous detective's strategies to solving the mystery of how his own mind functions. In Japan Hirai Taro read Poe's "The Murders in the Rue Morgue" at the age of twenty-one, adopted the pen name Edogawa Rampo (the Japanese pronunciation of Edgar Allan Poe), and began publishing stories inspired by Poe's tales of crime and detection.

Poe had an enormous influence on the short story in many countries. In the 1920s he was often mentioned in leading Chinese periodicals, where he was described as "the founder of the short story"and "an extraordinary genius." From Uruguay to Japan there are many examples of tales that can be directly connected to Poe's. Jules Verne openly admired Poe and incorporated elements from his tales into a new genre, the pseudoscientific novel, which proved to be highly successful for the French writer.

As we read the chapters in Part II dealing with Poe's influence on individual authors, we cannot help but be moved by the close affinity certain writers felt with Poe's sad life as recounted by Baudelaire, who saw Poe as his double. The Nicaraguan writer Rubén Darío discovered his soul mate in Poe. In Croatia

Antun Gustav Matoš felt such a strong affinity throughout his adult life that he adopted the title of Poe's tale "Hop-Frog" as one of his pseudonyms. Writers recognized in Poe a fellow sufferer who had the courage of his literary convictions in spite of disapprobation in his own country. The Swedish writer Ola Hansson's devotion to Poe helped him overcome the negative criticism of his early published work and provided him with arguments for the value of "psychological-artistic" literature.

Even for writers who did not identify with Poe's personal life, there was a deep intellectual affinity. Valéry's life was very different from Poe's. He went to law school and lived a bourgeois existence in Paris but nonetheless experienced an intellectual and artistic bond with the American writer that influenced his writing and deepened his friendship with Stéphane Mallarmé, who also admired Poe. A similar link developed between August Strindberg and Ola Hansson, who played a major role in introducing his fellow Swede to Poe. In Russia a passion for Poe was shared by Valery Brjusov and Konstantin Bal'mont, for whom Poe was an obsession in his everyday life and literary endeavors.

In some cases the connection between a specific author's work and Poe's is an obvious imitation. Examples of influence (as opposed to imitation) are much more difficult to discern because the writer has taken the precursor's work in a new direction. Valéry's view of influence describes accurately the effect Poe has had on writers throughout the world: "It is when a book or an author's collected work acts on someone not with all its qualities, but with one or a few of them, that influence assumes its most remarkable values. The development of a single quality of one person by the full talent of another seldom fails to produce results marked by an *extreme originality*." [4] We are still discovering this "extreme originality" in the creative endeavors of writers in many countries who fell under the spell of Edgar Allan Poe.

*Poe Abroad* is in no way an exhaustive study. On the contrary, it is a gold mine for future research on national literatures and specific authors. For example, Poe's influence in Scandinavia has been well researched, but we do not have an account of Poe in Finland. A contributor who was committed to doing research on Poe in Arabic became ill and was not able to complete the project. Excellent research on Poe in Estonia is included in the present volume, but we are left to wonder if he had similar influence in the other Baltic countries. In Brazil Poe's name is linked with a number of authors, although in-depth research on the specifics is lacking. Poe's influence on the African continent remains to be explored. In short, *Poe Abroad* begs a second volume.

NOTES

1. *The Collected Works of Paul Valéry*, 15 vols., ed. Jackson Mathews (Princeton, N.J.: Princeton UP, 1956–1975), vol. 8, p. 204.

2. In the "Afterword" to her collection of short stories *Haunted: Tales of the Grotesque* (New York: Dutton, 1994), Oates talks about her debt to Poe.

3. Burton R. Pollin compiled a catalog of illustrated editions of Poe's work in thirty-three countries. See Burton R. Pollin, *Images of Poe's Works: A Comprehensive Descriptive Catalogue of Illustrations* (Westport, Conn.: Greenwood, 1989). The volume includes "Filmography," pp. 323–361. *Poe Abroad* does not attempt to evaluate Poe's influence on art, music, film, or theater.

4. *The Collected Works of Paul Valéry*, vol. 8, p. 242.

PART ONE

*Poe's Influence in Countries and Regions Around the World*

# Poe in France

LOIS DAVIS VINES

Poe's influence in France has been extensive and profound. From 1847 to 1945 three of the greatest French poets, Charles Baudelaire, Stéphane Mallarmé, and Paul Valéry, sang his praises and were influenced by his work. Poe played a major role in the development of Symbolism, the short story, the pseudoscientific novel, and the detective genre in France. In the twentieth century he has inspired psychoanalytic studies, literary debates, and a work by the New Novelist Michel Butor. Poe's influence on French prose writers, poets, and critics is impressive by its diversity and its effects on new initiatives in literature.

Baudelaire is the best-known translator of Poe into French, although he was not the first. W. T. Bandy, a Baudelaire scholar who was equally captivated by Poe's early appearance on the international scene, conducted much of the detective work that was needed to identify the earliest translations in France. Bandy corrected the mistaken belief, repeated by Yarmolinsky, that Poe was translated into Russian before he made his debut in France.[1] According to Bandy, at least four French translators published versions of Poe's tales before Baudelaire's rendition of "Magnetic Revelation" in 1848.[2] The first published evidence that Poe was known outside the English-speaking world is an imitation of his "William Wilson" that appeared in *La Quotidienne* in December 1844 signed G.B., whom Bandy identified as Gustave Brunet. The first translation into French with Poe indicated as the original author was a version of "The Gold-Bug," which came out in the *Revue britannique* in November 1845. The translator was noted simply as A.B.; Bandy's meticulous research revealed that the initials stand for Alphonse Borghers, a pseudonym of Amédée Pichot (B xiii). But it was the five translations by Isabelle Meunier that probably brought Poe to the attention of Baudelaire. Her version of "The Black Cat," one of Baudelaire's favorite tales, appeared in *La Démocratie pacifique* in January 1847.

Poe was aware that his work was becoming known in France, although his knowledge of the details has proven to be incorrect. In a letter to the literary entrepreneur Evert Duyckinck dated December 30, 1846, he wrote: "Mrs. Clemm mentioned to me, this morning, that some of the Parisian papers had been speaking about my "Murders in the Rue Morgue."[3] Poe believed he had been mentioned in the Paris paper *Charivari*, which turned out not to be the case (B xi). The event that brought his name to the attention of Parisian newspaper readers in 1846 was a lawsuit involving plagiarism. E.-D. Forgues, a French journalist whose interest in literature inspired him to translate stories from British and American sources, published in *Le Commerce* a version of "The Murders in the Rue Morgue" similar to one that had appeared earlier by another translator in the Paris daily *La Quotidienne*. Although this newspaper raised no objection, a rival paper, *La Presse*, which Forgues had once accused of plagiarism, accused him of the same. When *La Presse* refused to give Forgues the opportunity to respond in their pages, he brought suit for libel. The most significant outcome of the case was that it made Poe's name known in Paris and probably inspired more translations of his tales.

Forgues was to play an even greater role in making Poe known in France. A couple of months after the trial, he wrote a long article based on twelve tales in the Wiley and Putnam edition (1845), thus becoming the first critic to publish a review of Poe's work in a foreign language. The twenty-page article, which appeared in the prestigious *Revue des deux Mondes* on October 15, 1846, recognized Poe as a "logician, a pursuer of abstract truth,"and a "lover of the most eccentric hypotheses and the strictest calculations."[4] Forgues compared the American writer's ideas to those of Pascal and Laplace, thus emphasizing the intellectual qualities that were to have a great appeal to French readers and writers. There is no evidence that Poe ever saw this article, which would have brought him enormous pleasure and satisfaction during a period when his literary reputation at home was on the wane.

Bandy surmises that Baudelaire most likely discovered Poe through Meurnier's translations and Forgues's article. Baudelaire's "singular shock" when he first read Poe has become legend in literary history. He discovered in Poe's family history uncanny parallels with his own life and in Poe's work ideas he had already considered. Baudelaire's strong feelings of identity with Poe were based on a number of similarities. They had both lost their biological fathers at an early age and had to deal with surrogates, a stern stepfather in Baudelaire's case and a foster father in Poe's. As a consequence, their mothers played a major role in their lives, creating a source of both conflict and comfort. Although Poe had three mother figures — Elizabeth Arnold Poe (his biological mother whom he lost at age two), Frances Allan (his foster mother), and Maria Poe Clemm (his aunt and mother-in-law) — it was Clemm whom Baudelaire idolized. In the dedication to his first volume of Poe translations, he paid tribute to her: "I owe this public homage to a mother whose greatness and goodness honor the World of Letters as much as the marvelous creations of her son."[5] Each writer sought his mother's approval and encouragement as he confronted a day-to-day existence that was resolutely hostile, or at least indifferent, to literary aspirations.

Poe and Baudelaire were brought up in well-to-do families but were later condemned to live hand-to-mouth because of their determination to establish themselves as writers. Their unusual lifestyles brought reprobation from family and society, especially in regard to abuses of alcohol and drugs. Even though the two men lived in different cultures, they shared the status of personae non grata, a fate bestowed upon poets in Baudelaire's opinion. The bond of sympathy these similarities inspired motivated Baudelaire's determination to establish Poe as a great writer and literary prophet whose voice was ridiculed or ignored in his own country (see Part II, "Charles Baudelaire").

After publishing his first Poe translation, "Mesmeric Revelation," in 1848, Baudelaire prepared a major article on Poe's life and work, which appeared in 1852 in the *Revue de Paris*[6] and was later used as the preface (with some revision) to his first volume of Poe tales, *Histoires extraordinaires*, in 1856. A revised and condensed version became the preface to the second volume of tales, *Nouvelles Histoires extraordinaires* (1857).[7] The version of Poe's biography handed down from one generation to the next in France (and to readers and writers in other countries) was for a long time based on Baudelaire's account, which, through no fault of his own, contained a few errors. In totally fictitious accounts, Baudelaire relates that Poe ran away from home to participate in the Greek Revolution after a violent argument with his foster father. Having survived the Greek experience, Poe supposedly went to Russia, where, after getting into trouble, he was saved from exile to Siberia by the American consul's intervention.[8] Baudelaire's account makes for good reading but, unfortunately, contains elements of fiction that went undetected.

Even more important than Baudelaire's Poe biography are his comments on Poe as a literary innovator. Baudelaire saw in his American mentor a literary genius who understood the mechanism of artistic creation. In the brief introduction to his translation of "The Philosophy of Composition," Baudelaire remarks that even for a genius such as Poe, inspiration and enthusiasm do not produce a poem. Poe gives the reader, according to Baudelaire, a glimpse of "the benefits that art can gain from deliberation" and a more precise idea of "the labor that this luxury called Poetry demands."[9] For Baudelaire and his successors, it was of little importance whether Poe, in truth, composed "The Raven" the way he described in "The Philosophy of Composition." They were excited that Poe presented a new dimension to the art of writing poetry. They agreed with Poe that subjects better treated in prose, such as history, politics, and morality, have no place in poetry. Poe recommends that the poem be short and that all the elements going into its creation be carefully calculated to have a specific effect on the reader. Poe's views on the relationship between poetry and music set forth in "The Poetic Principle" were basic concepts for the French Symbolist poets. Baudelaire's translation of this essay contains the vital word "correspondence," which took on such important meaning in Symbolist poetry. When we examine Poe's original text, the word "correspondence" cannot be found, although the idea of transcending the physical world and discovering a spiritual realm revealed through the senses is explicitly stated.

While Mallarmé admired the emphasis Poe placed on the calculated use of language in poetry, his own aesthetics went far beyond Poe's goal of creating a state of pleasure. Mallarmé envisioned a poetic language that would be purified of everyday meaning through the creation of new usage, rhythms, rhymes, and even the positioning of the words on the page (see Part II, "Stéphane Mallarmé and Paul Valéry"). In Poe's literary essays, Baudelaire and Mallarmé found ideas that confirmed their own beliefs and inspired the Symbolist movement. From Mallarmé on, the effect of Poe on French writers diverges radically. The Symbolists (Mallarmé, Kahn, de Gourmont, Moréas, Vielé-Griffin, and Valéry) admired the Poe of ordered thought, the master of artistic calculation. In contrast, the Decadents (Huysmans and Villiers de l'Isle-Adam) and the pre-Surrealists (Rimbaud, Lautréamont, Jarry, and Apollinaire) were inspired by the horror, mystery, dreams, and explorations of the disordered mind, what André Breton later called the "convulsive beauty."[10]

During the second half of the nineteenth century, Poe also had a major influence on French prose writers. The most obvious examples can be seen in the stories of Auguste Villiers de l'Isle-Adam (1838–1889). In his tale "Véra" there are many similarities to Poe's "Ligeia," especially when the main character, Véra, after a death as mysterious as Ligeia's, seems to be constantly present, not only in the memory of her lover but in a half-human, half-spiritual form. Other tales from his *Contes cruels* [Cruel stories] (1883) appear to be directly inspired by Poe's stories. Joris-Karl Huysmans (1848–1907), a French Decadent writer, mentions Poe in his novel *A rebours* [*Against the Grain*] (1884), in which the main character, Des Esseintes, remarks that Poe is one of the few writers he can bear to read. In his description of Des Esseintes, Huysmans reveals his own admiration for Poe: "To enjoy a literature uniting, as he desired, with an incisive style, a penetrating, feline power of analysis, he must resort to that master of Induction, that strange, profound thinker, Edgar Allan Poe."[11]

Guy de Maupassant (1850–1893), one of France's greatest short story writers, read Poe and applied Poe's "unity of effect" to the creation of his own tales. In addition to his interest in Poe's theoretical writing about the genre, Maupassant was influenced by themes in Poe's tales. "Apparition," for example, is reminiscent of "The Fall of the House of Usher," with the narrator recounting a visit to an old castle, the apparition of a beautiful wife who had died earlier, and the description of the woman in a mysterious, gloomy setting. Richard Fusco in his *Maupassant and the American Short Story* analyzes additional connections between Poe and the French writer. Fusco points out that in "Fou?" ["Mad?"] (1892), "a crazed husband recounts, in a narrative reminiscent of Poe's tales, his descent into maniacal jealousy."[12]

Alexandre Dumas (1802–1870), well known for his adventure novels including *Le Comte de Monte-Cristo* [*The Count of Monte Cristo*], claimed to have lived with Poe in Paris in 1832, a ficticious account that has inspired several articles.[13] Two novelists and art critics who were contemporaries of Dumas, the Goncourt brothers (Edmond, 1822–1896, and Jules, 1830–1870), praised Poe's innovative techniques in creating short stories.

With the publication of "The Murders in the Rue Morgue," Poe initiated the detective story, a genre that has been widely imitated, most notably by Sir Arthur Conan Doyle in England and Emile Gaboriau (1832–1873) in France. The resemblances between Gaboriau's amateur detective Monsieur Lecoq and Poe's Dupin are striking. Both men have amazing powers of deduction and induction, love books, are considered somewhat bizarre, and arouse jealousy in the heart of the Paris police chief. Gaboriau's methods of using ratiocination and deciphering to solve crimes remind the reader of Poe's detective stories and other tales.[14]

Jules Verne (1828–1905), initiator of the pseudoscientific novel in France, openly admired Poe and incorporated elements from the American writer's tales into his own works, which proved to be highly successful. Verne's "Cinq semaines en ballon" ["Five Weeks in a Balloon"] derives directly from Poe's "The Balloon Hoax." In *Le Tour du monde en 80 jours* [*Around the World in Eighty Days*] Verne takes an idea from "Three Sundays in a Week" to create suspense just at the moment when the reader thinks the story is over. Verne wrote *Le Sphinx des glaces* [*The Sphinx of the Icefields*] (1897) as a sequel to *The Narrative of Arthur Gordon Pym*, dedicating his tale to "the memory of Edgar

Poe, and my friends in America." Verne contributed an essay on Poe to the April 1864 issue of *Musée des Familles* in which he discussed several Poe tales, concluding that "Poe, through a few inventions, could have made his stories more believable."[15] In a recent Verne biography, Herbert Lottman emphasizes the importance of Poe: "In an armchair, there could be no better company than Edgar Allan Poe: his tales help to explain the aura of mystery enveloping so many Verne stories. The difference between the two writers is that Jules Verne began by puncturing mystery, scattering the aura, in quest of rational explanations; Poe left readers with his hallucinations."[16]

During the first half of the twentieth century, Paul Valéry carried the banner for Poe, which had been passed to him by his predecessors Baudelaire and Mallarmé. When Mallarmé and Valéry first met in Paris in 1891, the subject of Poe brought the two of them together in a close relationship, which lasted until Mallarmé's death in 1898. But they got an essentially different message from their common mentor. Impressed by Poe's devotion to the technique of writing verse, Mallarmé dreamed of perfecting the art of writing and of giving it a universal value to be realized in a book. Poe's effect on Valéry was, in one sense, just the opposite. Although he, too, was intrigued by poetic technique, for him it was not a means to the same end. Valéry's ultimate goal was not to create a supreme work but rather to understand the mind, his own mind, during the act of artistic creation. This particular effect of extreme intellectual self-consciousness distinguishes Poe's influence on Valéry from that of his predecessors (see Part II, "Stéphane Mallarmé and Paul Valéry ").

In 1927 Célestin Pierre Cambiaire published the first study that attempted to give an account of Poe's influence in France during the previous eighty years. Reprinted in 1970, *The Influence of Edgar Allan Poe in France* still serves as a valuable reference work on the subject.[17] Six years later a major psychoanalytical study on Poe came out in France. Marie Bonaparte (1882–1962) was a French psychoanalyst trained by Sigmund Freud, who graciously wrote the foreword to her influential study *Edgar Poe, sa vie — son oeuvre: Etude analytique* [*Life and Works of Edgar Allan Poe*] (1933). Translated into German (1934), English (1949), Italian (1976), and possibly other languages, the study examines Poe's work as manifestations of a victim who suffered major childhood traumas, mainly sickness and the death of his mother. The theme of the Oedipus complex dominates her analyses, but we also find the fear of premature burial and of sexual encounters. In his critique of the Bonaparte study, Roger Forclaz objects to the "suppression of contradictions" as one of the "cardinal principles" of the work.[18]

Poe's influence and reputation entered the world of the French theater through Aurélien-Marie Lugné (1869–1940). An important actor, writer, and director, Lugné became so captivated by Poe that he changed his last name to Lugné-Poe, which is how he is known today.

After Valéry's death in 1945, no other major French writer continued the Poe cult. T. S. Eliot, who knew Valéry well, wrote one of the best essays on Poe's influence in France, "From Poe to Valéry," first published in 1949.[19] Although Eliot had ambivalent feelings about Poe as a writer, describing him as having "the intellect of a highly gifted young person before puberty," his appraisal of Poe's influence on French poets is very perceptive. He recognized that Valéry's interest in observing himself creating a poem comes from his reading of "The Philosophy of Composition" and that his concept of pure poetry derives from Poe's idea that "a poem should have nothing in view but itself." After pointing out the basic weaknesses of several of Poe's poems, Eliot observes that while Mallarmé's translations are an improvement over the originals, "the rhythms, in which we find so much of the originality of Poe, are lost."[20] Eliot did not believe that the French overrated Poe because of their imperfect knowledge of English, but he remarked that they were not aware of the weaknesses that bother anglophones.

Poe's work has attracted the attention of literary critics and creative writers in France during the latter half of the twentieth century. In the 1960s "The Purloined Letter" became the focus of a major literary theory debate initiated by Jacques Lacan's seminar on this tale. All of the relevant texts have been brought together in *The Purloined Poe*, edited by John P. Muller and William J. Richardson.[21] Lacan's psychoanalytic interpretation challenged literary theorists and provoked a response from the French philosopher Jacques Derrida. Their opposing views inspired other critics to engage in a lively debate that seems less concerned with Poe and more preoccupied with the "act of analysis" and the "act of analysis of the act of analysis," as Barbara Johnson describes the exchange of views.[22]

Other contemporary French intellectuals have used Poe's work to demonstrate a particular point of view. Roland Barthes applied his system of textual analysis to "The Facts in the Case of M. Valdemar"; Jean Ricardou wrote a lengthy discussion of "The Gold-Bug"; and Gaston Bachelard included references to Poe in his study *The Psychoanalysis of Fire* and prepared the introduction to a new edition of Baudelaire's translation of *The Narrative of Arthur Gordon Pym*.[23]

Poe studies in France have been carried out by Claude Richard, who has attempted to replace the image of Poe as Baudelaire's *poète maudit* with a more accurate portrayal of him as a lucid writer. Richard's 962-page tome offers an in-depth study of Poe as journalist and critic.[24] Other French scholars who have made significant contributions to Poe studies include Georges Poulet, Roger Asselineau, Maurice Lévy, and Henri Justin.[25]

Michel Butor (b. 1926), an important proponent of the New Novel, wrote a strange work called *Histoire extraordinaire* (1961) that deals with Poe and Baudelaire.[26] Based on a dream Baudelaire had in 1856, the book-length essay links various points in the dream to works by Poe and to Baudelaire's writings about Poe. Although not a very interesting literary creation, it shows that Butor had a detailed knowledge of Poe's work and used various aspects of it in his own creative endeavors.

From the precursors of Symbolism to the New Novel, Poe has had an influence on the major literary movements in France for a century and a half. Since Paris is a literary mecca, aspiring writers from many countries have come to the French capital to hone their craft by learning from the masters, most of whom paid homage to their high priest, Edgar Allan Poe. Speaking of Baudelaire, Valéry once remarked that in exchange for what he had taken, Baudelaire "gave Poe's thought an infinite expanse. He offered it to future generations." [27] The torch of admiration for Poe has been passed to generations of writers throughout the world. Jorge Luis Borges, who admired both Poe and Valéry, noted that Valéry passed on "the lucid pleasures of thought and the secret adventures of order," the legacy of Poe.[28]

Poe's popularity among general readers in France has never waned, judging from the many critical works and new editions produced by French publishing houses each year. I was particularly struck by Poe's importance among French readers during a visit to Paris in July 1989 when the Bicentennial celebration was in full swing and bookshops were crammed with historical works. In the forefront of an elegant shop window was a new edition of Poe, displayed as the focal point with the historical tomes relegated to the background. Poe still occupied center stage, even during the two hundredth anniversary of the French Revolution.

NOTES

1. W. T. Bandy, "Were the Russians the First to Translate Poe?" *American Literature* 31 (1960): 479–480.

2. W. T. Bandy, *Edgar Allan Poe: Sa Vie et ses ouvrages* (Toronto: U of Toronto P, 1973), pp. xi–xvi; hereafter cited as B. For detailed discussions of Poe translations in French, see Haskell M. Block, "Poe, Baudelaire and His Rival Translators," in *Trans-*

*lation in the Humanities*, ed. Marilyn Gaddis Rose (Binghamton, N.Y.: SUNY Binghamton Translation and Research Instruction Program, 1977), pp. 59–66; Haskell M. Block, "Poe, Baudelaire, Mallarmé and the Problem of the Untranslatable," in *Translation Perspectives*, ed. Marilyn Gaddis Rose (Binghamton, N.Y.: SUNY Binghamton Translation and Research Instruction Program, 1984), pp. 104–112.

3. *The Letters of Edgar Allan Poe*, 2 vols, ed. John Ward Ostrom (Cambridge: Harvard UP, 1948), vol. 2, p. 336.

4. The complete article translated into English can be found in Jean Alexander, *Affidavits of Genius: Edgar Allan Poe and the French Critics, 1847–1924* (Port Washington, N.Y.: Kennikat P, 1971), pp. 79–98.

5. Charles Baudelaire, *Baudelaire on Poe*, ed. and trans. Lois Hyslop and Francis E. Hyslop Jr. (State College, Penn.: Bald Eagle, 1952), p. 164.

6. English translations are included in Baudelaire, *Baudelaire on Poe*, pp. 37–86, and in Alexander, *Affidavits of Genius*, pp. 99–121. Alexander includes many texts by French critics too numerous to describe here.

7. Baudelaire also translated *The Narrative of Arthur Gordon Pym* (1858), *Eureka* (1863), and a third collection of tales, *Histoires grotesques et sérieuses* (1865).

8. See Baudelaire's 1852 article, "Edgar Allan Poe, sa vie et ses ouvrages," in *Oeuvres en prose d'Edgar Allan Poe*, trans. Charles Baudelaire (Paris: Gallimard, 1951), p. 1007; English translation in Baudelaire, *Baudelaire on Poe*, pp. 47–48.

9. Baudelaire, *Baudelaire on Poe*, p. 156.

10. See Claude Richard, "André Breton et Edgar Poe," *Nouvelle Revue Française* 172 (April 1967): 926–936.

11. Joris-Karl Huysmans, *Against the Grain*, trans. Havelock Ellis (New York: Dover, 1969), p. 178. The passages dealing with Poe from this novel are found in Alexander, *Affidavits of Genius*, pp. 203–205. Frederick Garber presents an analysis of Poe and Huysmans in *The Autonomy of the Self from Richardson to Huysmans* (Princeton, N.J.: Princeton UP, 1982).

12. Richard Fusco, *Maupassant and the American Short Story* (University Park: Pennsylvania State UP, 1994), p. 37.

13. See Andrew DeTernant, "Edgar Allan Poe and Alexandre Dumas," *Notes & Queries* 162 (December 28, 1929): 456; W. Roberts, "A Dumas Manuscript. Did Edgar Allan Poe Visit Paris?" *Times Literary Supplement*, November 21, 1929, p. 978; Thomas Ollive Mabbott, "Dumas and Poe," *Times Literary Supplement*, January 2, 1930, p. 12; H. D. MacPherson, "Poe and Dumas Again," *Saturday Review of Literature*, February 22, 1930, p. 760.

14. Célestin Pierre Cambiaire, *The Influence of Edgar Allan Poe in France* (New York: Stechert, 1927; rpt. 1970), pp. 257–280. See translation of *Monsieur Lecoq* (New York: Charles Scribner's Sons, 1904).

15. Jules Verne, "Edgard [*sic*] Poe et ses oeuvres," *Musée des Familles* 30 (April 1864): 193–208. A translation of this article is in *The Edgar Allan Poe Scrapbook*, ed. Peter Haining (New York: Schocken Books, 1978), pp. 56–73.

16. Herbert R. Lottman, *Jules Verne: An Exploratory Biography* (New York: St. Martin's P, 1996), p. 106.

17. Cambiaire, *The Influence of Edgar Allan Poe*.

18. Roger Forclaz, "Psychoanalysis and Edgar Allan Poe: A Critique of the Bonaparte Thesis" in *Critical Essays on Edgar Allan Poe*, ed. Eric W. Carlson (Boston: G. K. Hall, 1987), pp. 187–195. Even before the Bonaparte study was published, Poe was the subject of psychoanalytical criticism in France, most notably in Emile Lauvrière, *Edgar Poe, sa vie et son oeuvre: Etude de psychologie pathologique* (Paris: F. Alcan, 1904).

19. T. S. Eliot, "From Poe to Valéry," *Hudson Review* 2 (1949): 327–342. rpt. in Eric W. Carlson, ed., *The Recognition of Edgar Allan Poe: Selected Criticism since 1829* (Ann Arbor: U Michigan P, 1966), pp. 205–219.

20. T. S. Eliot, "From Poe to Valéry"; rpt. in Carlson, *Recognition*, p. 214.

21. John P. Muller and William J. Richardson, eds., *The Purloined Poe: Lacan, Derrida & Psychoanalytic Reading* (Baltimore: Johns Hopkins UP, 1988).

22. Ibid., p. 213.

23. See Roland Barthes, "Textual Analysis of Poe's 'Valdemar,'" in *Untying the Text: A Post-Structuralist Reader*, ed. Robert Young (London: Routledge, 1981; rpt. 1987), pp. 133–161. A different translation of the same text was published in *Poe Studies* 10.1 (June 1977): 1–12. Tracy Ware discusses Barthes's analysis in "The 'Salutary Discomfort' in the Case of M. Valdemar," *Studies in Short Fiction* 31 (1994): 471–480. Jean Ricardou, "Gold in the Bug," *Poe Studies* 9.2 (December 1976): 33–39. Gaston Bachelard, *La Psychanalyse du feu* (Paris: Gallimard, 1938); Gaston Bachelard, *The Psychoanalysis of Fire*, trans. Alan C. M. Ross (Boston: Beacon P, 1964); Gaston Bachelard, "Introduction," in *Aventures d'Arthur Gordon Pym*, trans. Charles Baudelaire (Paris: Stock, 1944).

24. Claude Richard, *Poe: Journaliste et critique* (Paris: Klincksieck, 1978). Richard is also the author of *Cahier: Edgar Allan Poe* (Paris: Herne, 1974).

25. For a presentation of the work of Poulet, Asselineau, and Lévy, see Patrick F. Quinn, *Poe and France: The Last Twenty Years* (Baltimore: Enoch Pratt Free Library, 1970).

26. Michel Butor, *Histoire extraordinaire* (Paris: Gallimard, 1961).

27. *The Collected Works of Paul Valéry*, 15 vols., ed. Jackson Mathews (Princeton, N.J.: Princeton UP, 1956–75) vol. 8, p. 204.

28. Jorge Luis Borges, "Valéry as Symbol," in *Labyrinths*, ed. Donald Yates and James Irby (New York: New Directions, 1964), p. 198.

# Poe in Russia

ELOISE M. BOYLE

Of all American writers adopted by and beloved of the Russian people, Edgar Allan Poe best captures the Russian imagination and satisfies the Slavic taste for the absurd, macabre, and bizarre. Poe's presence in Russia, strong for more than a century, has elicited passionate reactions in writers from Feodor Dostoevsky to Vladimir Nabokov. Some of them adopted Poe's "imp of the perverse," while others patterned their poetry, translations, even lifestyles after the American's example. Dostoevsky, the Russian Symbolists and Decadents, and Nabokov stand out among the dozens of writers in whom one can discern Poe's influence. The American author played such an important role in the lives of Konstantin Bal'mont and Valery Brjusov that a separate chapter is devoted to them (see Part II).

A comprehensive study of Poe's influence in Russia until 1958 was published by Joan Grossman in 1973. According to her, the first authenticated translation of Poe into Russian dates to 1847, when a version of "The Gold-Bug" appeared in *Novaja biblioteka dlja vospitanija* [The new library for education].[1] There is no question that Poe came to Russia via the French Symbolists, especially through Baudelaire. The most significant translations of Poe's works into Russian were a version of "The Raven" in 1878, Bal'mont's collection of Poe's tales in 1895, and his collected edition of Poe's work in 1901.[2] Poe continues to be popular in Russia, as evidenced by a number of recent translations of his works and ongoing scholarly interest.

While the first translations of Poe into Russian were mostly limited to his prose fiction, his poetry remains the preferred genre for Russian readers. Without a doubt, "The Raven" is the most popular of Poe's poems in Russian, with "The Bells" following close behind. Of all his short stories, "The Fall of the House of Usher" best retains its ghastly grip on the Russian imagination.

Poe's transition into Russian was not without problems, however. Complicating the reception of Poe in Russia was the fact that occasional translations from English in the 1850s were often excruciatingly bad, with the translators "adjusting" the text to fit their command of the language. In 1906

Aleksandr Blok wrote that Poe was damaged by "the imperfection in the translations. . . . [A translator of Poe] certainly must be a poet, very sensitive to the music of words and to style. Bal'mont's translation satisfies all these requirements . . . [he] succeeds completely in translating the 'depths' and 'melodiousness' of Poe."[3]

Bal'mont's enthusiasm and avowed affinity contributed to the image and reputation of Edgar Poe (as the Russians usually call him) in Russia. The Russian Symbolists were deeply influenced by Baudelaire. A close study of Bal'mont's 1895 collection of Poe's work in Russian reveals evidence that the translations were rendered not from the original English (as were the earliest Russian translations of Poe from the late 1840s and early 1850s) but were in fact translations from Baudelaire's French versions of Poe.[4] Furthermore, the choice of Poe's stories that appeared in Russian journals was highly selective and particular to each individual editor. In other words, the combination of personal interpretations of Poe by each of his poet-translators and the rather didactic selection standards employed by journal editors of the nineteenth century (much of Poe's more horrifying prose was omitted from the Russian editions) makes his appearance in Russian literature more than just that of a best-selling horror writer.

Poe's literary reputation and his image as a mystic and a seer grew steadily throughout the nineteenth century, with his popularity peaking during the Symbolist/Decadent movement of the 1890s. Baudelaire's portrait of Poe as a literary outcast fascinated Bal'mont, who became Poe's devoted translator and created an image of the American "mad genius" that may be the most lasting of Bal'mont's legacies in Russia. Grossman rightly points out that "avid translating of French prose into Russian is thus another channel by which Poe's presence in Russian was enhanced, through a sort of multiplier effect" (G 94). Yet interest in Poe was limited to a very select audience in Russia during the time he was so overwhelmingly popular in France. What accounts for this disparity? An examination of the extent to which the Poe cult was adopted in Russia, and by whom, will yield an answer to this question.

Dostoevsky read Poe and wrote critical articles on his short prose.[5] Although he had a technical and intellectual affinity with Poe, no true spiritual attraction existed between the two writers. (Dostoevsky considered Poe's use of the fantastic "strangely material.") As Grossman points out, there are parallels between Poe's detective Dupin and Porfiry Petrovich in *Crime and Punishment* as well as between the murderer in this novel and in "The Tell-Tale Heart" (G 45). Both authors devote a great deal of description to their characters' motivations and the planning of the crimes. While Dostoevsky scholars have long associated him with Poe in terms of plot and motivation, there is also a deep intellectual kinship shared by the two writers, which can been seen in Dostoevsky's own observation: "[Poe] describes the inner state of [a] person with marvelous acumen and amazing realism."[6] One need only recall Dostoevsky's own heroes (Raskolnikov, Stravrogin, and Ivan and the other Karamazov brothers) and their sharply delineated thought processes, along with the demonic plots they hatch, to see that he and Poe shared more than a mere love of the detective genre.

Throughout the great prose of the second half of the nineteenth century, certain themes and motifs from Poe stand out in Russian literature: the "imp of the perverse," the linkage of love and death, and the exploration of a person's inner life. Dostoevsky, Ivan Turgenev, and Feodor Sologub are three of the authors analyzed by Grossman in this regard. Still, it was not until the rebirth of Russian poetry at the end of the century that a consistent, complete portrait of Poe emerges in Russia. The image of the perverse genius surrounded by a melodramatic Gothic aura had a special appeal to adherents of the Russian Decadent and Symbolist movements.

Comprising two separate and autonomous circles of writers based in Moscow and St. Petersburg, the Decadent and Symbolist schools nonetheless shared many of the same innovators of Russian poetry. The Decadents were attracted equally to the physical (erotic) and the spiritual worlds. Like the Symbolists, they were writers who paid careful attention to the mechanics of poetry. In this sense they helped to breathe new life into Russian poetry, which had languished through much of the nineteenth century.

The Symbolists, on the other hand, were much more responsive to the spiritual world. The principal figures of this circle, Vjačeslav Ivanov, Andrei Belyj, and Aleksandr Blok, all revered Vladimir Solov'ev (1853–1900), an idealist and apocalyptic thinker. Solov'ev's belief in poetry as the ultimate tool of "vision" had a profound effect on the development of Russian versification early in the twentieth century: poetry was believed to be the ultimate instrument of revelation. It was through the combined efforts of the Symbolists and Decadents in getting translations of Poe's works into print that Poe, the poet and the man, achieved the status of an American writer whom, according to Yarmolinsky, "the Slav has taken . . . to heart with all his unearthliness and morbidity."[7]

Valery Brjusov, along with other lesser-known poets and critics, founded journals in order to present a steady flow of modern literature to the Russian reading public. The editors of these journals not only introduced European, especially French, writers to Russian readers but also nurtured Russians' own avant-garde literary talents. The Symbolists found a soul mate in Poe, a genius who had decades earlier also thrown off the mantle of "usefulness" and didacticism in poetry and strove to create "art for art's sake." The Symbolists created a Poe out of carefully selected traits: they delved into his inner psychology, explored (and in some cases imitated) his drinking and drug habits, and celebrated the madness at the heart of his genius. For many, Poe the man was inseparable from Poe the artist. The psychological impact of Poe on Russian writers is unquestionable, as Grossman notes.

From a technical standpoint, the preeminent place rhyme occupied in the Symbolists' verse drew them to the melodiousness of Poe's poetry. Rhyme is an organic part of Symbolist poetry, and the translations of Poe's works into Russian preserve and sometimes improve on the American's mastery of this device. The Symbolists sought a "musicality" in verse, a creation of music through new combinations of sounds and rhymes. In this particular quality, Grossman states that evidence of Poe's influence is "easily traced in the obvious devices of rhythm, internal rhyme, and repetition" (G 166). Krystyna Pomorska, in her study of Russian poetics, emphasizes the importance of music for the Symbolists: "'Music' in poetry means its special organization. . . . [The] crucial problems were the following: 1) the saturation of poetry with sound repetition; and 2) a special choice of phonemes, namely those which were believed to have 'melodic' values."[8] This principle accounts for the tremendous popularity of Poe's "The Bells" among Russians. Thematically, too, the Russian Symbolists felt a close kinship with Poe, as Pomorska points out: the "well known Symbolist theme of the struggle between darkness and light" can be found in numerous manifestations in Poe's own poetry and prose.[9]

Although the Symbolist elite wholeheartedly embraced Poe as a genius worthy of Russian admiration, general readers were somewhat less enthusiastic. According to Blok, "among the Russian public . . . Poe was only an 'aesthete' [who] entertained and frightened, [and] in general, amused the public."[10] By all accounts, his most popular work in Russian is "The Raven." It may well be that the Russian suspicion of things foreign or the inability to comprehend some of the darker aspects of Poe's literary output limited his appeal to the average reader, a fact that carries more serious consequences after the Russian Revolution of 1917 and the ascendancy of the Bolsheviks, who advocated a "proletarian culture."

Symbolism in Russia was followed by two avant-garde schools of literary criticism: Futurism and Formalism. Around 1914–1915 the Russian Formalists, led by Roman Jakobson, Viktor Shklovsky, Yury Tynyanov, and Boris Eikhenbaum, flourished in the experimental early days of the Soviet Union in the

1920s and disbanded during the Stalinism of the 1930s. The Formalists believed that a literary work is the sum total of its parts, and they advocated a close reading of a literary text independent of the biographical or historical conditions of its creation. To the Formalists, the essence of a literary work lies in the process of transforming "verbal material" into a work of art. If this "verbal material" — words, rhymes, literary devices — achieves an aesthetic effect, then the reader accepts the work of art as life. Given these philosophical and critical beliefs, it is not surprising that many of the Russian Formalists greatly appreciated Poe's essay "The Philosophy of Composition." Jakobson, in particular, considered Poe a genius. In his essay "Language in Operation," he analyzes Poe's "The Raven" in terms of the connections between sound and meaning.[11]

What was Poe's fate during the years of the Communist regime? Grossman traces the literary and mythical influence of Poe, waning to be sure, throughout the early years of Soviet literature, through Socialist Realism, and into the "thaw" period of the 1950s. Although Brjusov continued his critical studies of Poe for several years after the Revolution, nowhere during the first sixty-five years of the Soviet Union did Poe's reputation or influence manifest itself as it had during its flowering under the Symbolists. The lack of interest is not surprising, given the Soviets' distrust of the mystical and the occult and their rejection of psychological fiction altogether during the years of Stalinist censorship. The psychological and futuristic novels of Aleksandr Grin (1880–1932) and the tepid detective fiction of Venjamin Kaverin (b. 1902) contain glancing references to Poe, but it is not until later in the century, in the writings of Vladimir Nabokov (1899–1977), who produced works in both Russian and English, that we again clearly see the influence of Poe on a writer of Russian origin.

Nabokov's most notorious novel, *Lolita*, is filled with references to Poe. Within the first paragraph of the work we find a restatement of the famous opening lines of Poe's "Annabel Lee": "In point of fact, there might have been no Lolita at all had I not loved, one summer, a certain initial girlchild. In a princedom by the sea."[12] The main character, Humbert Humbert, refers to himself more than once as "Dr. Edgar H. Humbert." "Lenore," "The Raven," and Virginia Clemm herself all make cameo appearances in the novel.

As Dale Peterson points out, Nabokov in his early poetry shares Poe's quest for an eidolon (an unreal image, a phantom, an ideal), and his poetry is imbued with a tragic atmosphere reminiscent of Poe's love poetry.[13] Peterson sees in Nabokov the "lyrical commemoration of what has been lost" and the "unforgotten yet inaccessible moments of time" that characterize Poe's nostalgia for the past. The eidolon of the recently deceased wife hovers over Nabokov's story "The Return of Chorb," in which the author incorporates many of the motifs found in Poe's tales of obsession, "Berenice," "Morella," and "Ligeia."

New editions of works by Bal'mont, Brjusov, and Dostoevsky that include essays on Poe have been published in the 1970s and 1980s. Scholars, among them Elvira Osipova, are now free in postglasnost Russia to explore Poe once again, unconstrained by the censorship and literary conservatism that characterized the Soviet years.[14]

One of the most recent additions to Poe scholarship in Russia comes from Kuban University in Krasnodar. Yuri Luchinsky and Vladimir Cherednichenko, in *Edgar Allan Po: Esse, materialy, issledovanija* [Edgar Allan Poe: Essays, papers, reviews] (1995), have collected for the first time in Russian material on Poe's life and works that was previously unavailable to Russian readers.[15]

Edgar Allan Poe captured and for 150 years has held the Russian imagination more than any other American writer. For Russians there are two Poes: the man — the tortured genius, the dark, decadent figure — and the visionary poet whose creations translate into Russian with a clarity and beauty that rival the original. While his personal life fascinates readers, it is his poetry that has entered the Russian heart and soul.

NOTES

1. Joan Delaney Grossman, *Edgar Allan Poe in Russia: A Study in Legend and Literary Influence* (Wurzburg: Jal-Verlag, 1973), p. 24. Hereafter cited as G.

2. "The Raven" appeared in *Vestnik Evropy* 3 (1878): 121–127. Bal'mont's two early volumes of Poe translations are *Ballady i fantazii* (Moscow: F. Bogdavov, 1895) and *Sobranie sočinenij* (Moscow: Skorpion, 1901).

3. Aleksandr Blok, *Polnoe sobranie sočinenij* (Moscow: Xudožestvennaja literatura, 1962), vol. 5, p. 618.

4. Abraham Yarmolinsky mistakenly reported that Poe was translated into Russian even before his works appeared in French. W. T. Bandy corrected this error through meticulous research. See Abraham Yarmolinsky, "The Russian View of American Literature," *Bookman* 44.1 (1916): 44–48; W. T. Bandy, "Were the Russians the First to Translate Poe?" *American Literature* 31 (1960): 479–480.

5. Dostoevsky's essay "Three Tales of Edgar Poe" is included in *Critical Essays on Edgar Allan Poe*, ed. Eric W. Carlson (Boston: G. K. Hall, 1987), pp. 77–79.

6. Feodor Dostoevsky, *Polnoe sobranie xudožestvennyx sočinenij*, 13 vols., ed. B. Tomashevsky and K. Khalabaev (Leningrad: 1926–1930), vol. 13, p. 524.

7. Yarmolinsky, "The Russian View of American Literature," p. 44.

8. Krystyna Pomorska, *Russian Formalist Theory and Its Poetic Ambience* (The Hague: Mouton, 1968), p. 73.

9. Ibid., p. 62.

10. Blok, *Polnoe sobranie sočinenij*, vol. 5, pp. 617–618.

11. Roman Jakobson, *Language in Literature*, ed. Krystyna Pomorska and Stephen Rudy (Cambridge: Harvard UP, 1987).

12. Vladimir Nabokov, *Lolita* (New York: G. P. Putnam's Sons, 1955), p. 11.

13. Dale Peterson, "Nabokov and the Poe-etics of Composition," *Slavic and East European Journal* 33 (1989): 95–107.

14. Elvira Osipova, "Rasskaz Edgara Poe 'Ligeija': Problemy interpretacii," *Filologičeskienauki* 4 (1990): 102–109.

15. *Edgar Allan Po: Essen, materialy, issledovanija*, comp. Yuri Luchinsky and Vladimir Cherednichenko (Krasnodar: Kuban State University, 1995).

# Poe in Estonia

TIINA AUNIN

Edgar Allan Poe's role in shaping modern Estonian culture has only recently been duly estimated. Three aspects of the influence of his works are particularly important: their effect on the popular imagination, the direct link between words in Poe's texts and neologisms in Estonian, and the inspiration his works provided for Estonian writers.

No other American author has occupied the Estonian reader's attention more than Poe. The first reference to a translation of his work into Estonian dates to 1879, when a free adaptation of "The Gold-Bug" was written by P. Undritz.[1] After Poe's stories appeared in various periodicals in the 1890s, they quickly became the modern equivalent of myths. The earliest literary review was a short anonymous piece published in a newspaper in 1903. More significant in making Poe known in literary circles was the 1918 article by Friedebert Tuglas (1886–1971), who later became a well-known Estonian author. He acknowledged the impact of Poe's translations on the "Noor Eesti" ["Young Estonia"] literary movement and on the "enrichment of the Estonian language and literature as a whole."[2] A measure of Poe's popularity among general readers can be seen in the forty-nine translations of his work published between 1891 and 1940, all cataloged at the Estonian Museum of Literature.[3]

A master of creating suspense, a writer with a special talent for raising the reader's gooseflesh, Poe has modeled new cultural images of fear for twentieth-century Estonians. This reaction is best summed up in Martin Tropp's remark that "disillusionment and fear of the future" are the hallmarks of our era. In the twentieth century "horror fiction and real terror coincided; the same audience read and reacted to both."[4] As Freud pointed out, even a dream can be considered a work of art, depending on its degree of adjustment to reality. Similarly, horror stories are not nightmares transcribed but rather fears recast into safe and communicable forms. Popular fiction often responds to the shared dreams and hidden fears of its audience and vice versa. Since the beginning of the twentieth century, Poe's poems and especially his "dark tales" have helped Estonians adjust to the absurdities of social realism, the barbarisms of cultural purification, the realities of corruption, and anonymous crimes. His stories literally became part of the popular subconsciousness, thus preparing it for the cataclysmic disaster of the Second World War and the mass deportations that followed.

These anxieties are reflected in Karl Ristikivi's novel *Ei Juhtunud Midagi* [Nothing happened] (1947), in which the main character's experiences and thoughts are echoed by the sinister tapping motif, clearly borrowed from "The Raven." In the novel, everything essential has been reduced or moved to the background, as the author describes a multitude of details taking place or being said. What he does not describe are the political determinants causing these minutiae. The nightmarish refrain "nothing happened" only deepens the reader's conviction that a real catastrophe has taken place.

The second aspect of Poe's influence on Estonian culture is linked to the neologistic movement introduced by Johannes Aavik (1880–1973), a distinguished Estonian linguist, polyglot, and translator. Aavik's fascination with Poe goes back to 1903, when his translation of "The Tell-Tale Heart" was published in the newspaper *Postimees* [Postman]. With a fervor similar to Baudelaire's, Aavik continued to produce translations of Poe that are unique in the Estonian language. His goal was to modernize the language and make it more flexible. Although Aavik's invention of words is not limited to his Poe translations, his 1937 collection of twenty tales has a glossary of 386 new words in Estonian. For example, to translate the noun "dream" he invented *ulm* to replace *unenägu*, which means "what one sees in a dream"; for "garment" he created *rõivas* to replace *riidematerjal*, referring to the material of the cloth; to express "delicious" he preferred the sound of *sulnis* rather than the existing word combination *magus-armas*, meaning "sweetly nice."

Aavik created neologisms because he believed that the old words did not have the right vowels, consonants, or rhyme or did not convey the right mood or emotion. In many cases, he found the existing Estonian descriptive notions too awkward to render the meaning of the original. In current usage, Aavik's invented words are used along with the old ones, thus making one's speech more varied, interesting, and up-to-date. Since the neologisms frequently appear in fiction, the reader has to learn the new words in order to read translations of Poe. The second volume of Aavik's Poe translations, published in Sweden in 1955 on the occasion of his seventy-fifth birthday, is accompanied by a glossary of 1,050 neologisms.[5] From this elaborate vocabulary used to translate Poe, it is estimated that more than a third of the words have come into current Estonian usage. While the modern reader might have to refer to the glossary, Aavik never forgot a word and never created the same one twice. His linguistic intuition for certain shades and coloring seemed to be faultless, thus enriching both literary Estonian and everyday usage.

Translators' skills and aesthetic principles were put to the test by rendering "The Raven" into Estonian. Aavik tried to promote and cultivate the beauty of his native tongue by expressing its finer shades of meaning through stylistic devices as well as through new words. His translation of "The Raven" in 1929 was followed a year later by a version by Ants Oras (1900–1982), an outstanding Poe scholar and translator in his own right. In a separate essay on Poe, Oras explains his choice of the poem, analyzes the hardships of the translation process, and describes his own mood when rendering the music and rhythm of Poe's verse. A subtle piece of literary analysis, this essay along with the first translation of "The Philosophy of Composition" appeared with Oras's *Valik Luuletisi* [Selected poems] (1931), a collection of Poe's poetry translated into Estonian.

Estonian critics are especially attracted by the phrase "poetry of nerves," which in Poe's case refers to the hidden soul or core of the poem, generally thought to be untranslatable. This very soul might be recaptured through the meticulous imitation of the metrical pattern but above all "by taking into account the deepest meaning of the original and presenting it gently and sparingly," according to Reet Sool, a literary scholar who made a detailed comparison of translations of "The Raven" by Oras, Aavik, and G. Kajak, who based his 1915 translation on Bal'mont's well-known Russian version.[6] Sool is convinced that translating poetry can never be considered a mere technical problem, such as she sees in the analysis of Johannes Silvet (1895–1979). Sool prefers to place emphasis on subtle reading and interpreting as the most important aspects of translating poetry, especially "The Raven." Both critics observe that Oras is more carried away by his own poetic impulses than are the other translators; contrary to Oras's heightened tone, Aavik chooses to keep his version sober by omitting Poe's exclamation marks; Aavik often misses dramatic points, whereas Oras retains a sinister implication with the bird saying "nevermore"; and while Oras is careful to preserve internal rhymes, Aavik omits them occasionally. After the translations of "The Raven" by Oras and Aavik were published in 1929 and 1930, respectively, only two more Estonian versions were attempted under Soviet domination.

The third aspect of Poe's influence on Estonian culture can be seen in numerous motifs recurring in the works of Estonian authors. Admiration for Poe in literary circles goes back to the Young Estonia movement in the early twentieth century. First created as a secret student society in 1903, Young Estonia became a powerful joint effort of young intellectuals to Europeanize Estonian culture and literature. Before it disbanded in 1915, the group published five literary albums and two journals, *Noor-Eesti* [Young Estonia] and *Vaba Sōna* [Free word]. Through the French Symbolists, they became familiar with Poe's poetry, tales, and literary essays. They considered the symbol to be a primary means of aesthetic cognition and expression while rejecting national heroic Romanticism as well as critical Realism. Although there is no direct evidence that the Young Estonians analyzed Poe's literary theories, his work represented a model of synthesis. Tuglas summed up this view in his 1918 article: "As to the origin of Poe's work and his cultural background, his writing was a conglomeration of many different substances. He presented a harmonious cultural unity of Old Europe and the New World, being one of the greatest talents Europe has forwarded and, without any doubt, the greatest that America has ever produced." Tuglas goes on to observe that Poe's tales reflect "the same nightmarish experience that our epoch [First World War] so abundantly offers — the mood of horror and irrational fantasy."[7] It was this aspect of Poe's work that attracted the general reader and Estonian writers.

In addition to Ristikivi's novel mentioned earlier, Poe's influence can be seen in Tuglas's story "Popi and Huhuu" (1917), in which dreaming is better than living, the conception of the value of objects is peculiar, and good and evil become confused in the character's mind.[8] Creating an absurd universe consisting of two ownerless animals (a dog and a monkey), Tuglas persuades the reader that the visible situation is merely a threshold to fearful revelation. What happened to the master of the house is never revealed; it can only be guessed. A major emphasis is placed on the Gothic element, which, as in Poe's work, has important implications for Tuglas's tale.

The motifs of death, decay, and destruction in Poe's work presented a strong contrast to the generally optimistic spirit of Estonian national life before the Second World War. Poe, it might seem, belonged completely to another epoch. Nevertheless, Estonians have always had an unfaltering admiration for the eccentricities of Poe's genius. In 1989 Helga Kross, the first female translator of Poe in Estonian, produced a collection of twenty tales that set new standards for translators by skillfully rendering the subtle ways in which Poe imprinted his dark designs of horror on the fabric of reality. The power of his images and his violent suspense can be irritating — even shocking — to the sober Estonian mind, but his works never prove dull.

NOTES

1. P. Undritz, *Kuldpõrnik* (Tartu: Laakmann, 1879).

2. Friedebert Tuglas, "Edgar Allan Poe: Valitud novellid," *Postimees* 10 (1918): 1.

3. The Museum of Literature is located in Tartu, Estonia.

4. Martin Tropp, *Images of Fear: How Horror Stories Helped Shape Modern Culture (1818–1918)* (Jefferson, N.C.: McFarland, 1990), p. 2.

5. E. A. Poe, *Enneaegne Matmine Ja Teisi Jutustusi* (Stockholm: Kirjastus Vaba Eesti, 1955).

6. Reet Sool, "Edgar Allan Poe in Estonian, Notes on Critical Reception and Method," *Uchenie Zapiski Tartuskogo Universiteta* 792 (1988): 77–86.

7. Tuglas, "Edgar Allan Poe," p. 1.

8. An English translation of this story can be found in *Tales from Far and Near*, ed. Ernest Rhys and C. A. Dawson-Scott (New York: D. Appleton, 1930), pp. 105–129.

# Poe in Scandinavia

JAN NORDBY GRETLUND,

ELISABETH HERION-SARAFIDIS,

AND HANS H. SKEI

Poe's introduction to Scandinavia came through Denmark, where an edition of seven of his tales was published in 1855. As more translations appeared, interest in his life and work was awakened, kindled by the French enthusiasm expressed in Baudelaire's anguished account of Poe's life. The Scandinavian interest, triggered by the Neoromantic and Symbolist reaction to Naturalism, peaked in the 1890s, when echoes of a Poesque influence can be distinguished in both poetry and fiction. Although Scandinavian authors read, discussed, and wrote about Poe, his influence was never as obvious as among French writers.

A comprehensive study of the first century of Poe's influence in Denmark, Norway, and Sweden is found in Carl L. Anderson's *Poe in Northlight: The Scandinavian Response to His Life and Work* (1973).[1] Anderson's contention that Poe's broadest appeal has been as a writer of horror stories and murder mysteries seems to hold true also for the period since the publication of his book. As Anderson points out, the early interest in Poe's poetry and tales coincided with the reaction to Naturalism. Writers who were later called Lyricists and Symbolists were dedicated to the exploration of the mysteries of the human soul and the ideal of beauty. The new Scandinavian poetry, concerned with sentiment and mood, found a reading public in 1893 through the Danish publication *Taarnet* [*The Tower*], which welcomed Symbolism as the "poetic means of renewing a reverence for life and restoring profundity to the arts" (A 31). Poe's life and art provided valuable insights, and he was regarded as the "priest of Beauty and the prophet of the autonomy of art."

Twelve years after the 1855 edition of Poe's tales came out in Denmark, another Danish translator, Robert Watt, produced a collection of stories that included an introduction with biographical details based mainly on Baudelaire's account. Anderson suggests that J. P. Jacobsen discovered Poe through Watt's volume and was influenced by the American writer. Jacobsen's poem "En arabesk" is reminiscent of "The Tell-Tale Heart" and "Ligeia." But it was the poet and critic Johannes Jørgensen (1866–1956) who made the greatest contribution to Poe's popularity in Denmark by translating his work and writing an introduction to *The Narrative of Arthur Gordon Pym* in which he brought out some of the characteristics of Poe's fiction. The most knowledgeable Danish critic on the subject of Poe in the 1890s was Niels Møller, whose familiarity with the studies of Baudelaire, George E. Woodberry, and John Henry Ingram gave him a perspective that offered a balance to the traditional view of Poe as the martyred poet.

As Anderson explains, interest in Poe in Norway was not as strong as in Denmark, perhaps due to the lukewarm attitude toward Decadence and Symbolism. The only Norwegian essay on Poe during the 1890s was written by Nils Kjær, a newspaper literary critic who, like Møller in Denmark, was familiar with Woodberry's work. Comparing Poe to Emerson, Kjær remarked that Poe's "soul is impassioned, agitated, subjective, and above all, rich in fantasy" (A 50). He praised the musical effects and the symbolic nature of Poe's poems. Contrary to Baudelaire's view, Kjær did not see Poe as a martyr of American materialism, arguing that Poe's loneliness and alienation would have been the same wherever he lived.

In contrast to the rather tepid reception of Poe in Norway, Swedish appreciation was at its height in the 1890s, largely because of Ola Hansson and August Strindberg (see Part II,"Ola Hansson and August Strindberg"). Hansson, who was well versed in contemporary French literature, read Poe in English in 1888 and soon after published three essays on the American writer. The most important essay, translated by Anderson and included in the appendix to *Poe in Northlight*, was also an attack on the main proponents of Realistic and Naturalistic fiction. Declaring war on the rule of reason in literature, Hansson regarded Poe as the epitome of a "psychological-artistic" principle, the ideal fusion of the perceptive and the conscious artist that he envisioned for himself. For Hansson, Poe's work indicated the "direction that the future course of literature would take" (A 68).

Anderson's chapter on Strindberg ties into the chapter on Hansson, who first brought Poe to Strindberg's attention. The relationship between the two Swedish writers was complex, but early on they were united in their admiration for Poe and in their conviction that the writing of the future lay in the direction he had charted. Of Poe's tales, it seems to have been "The Gold-Bug" that particularly caught Strindberg's fancy. A story by Hansson, "En Paria," dramatized by Strindberg, shows clear signs of Strindberg's readings of Poe. At that time — the late 1880s — the power of suggestion, the occult, mesmerism, and the triumph of mind and will over darkly suspected threats were themes of intense interest to Strindberg, as they had been to Poe.

The Scandinavian interest in Poe peaked in the 1890s, but, as Anderson points out, the translations and essays produced during this period assured Poe's renown for subsequent generations. In 1916 Gunnar Bjurman wrote a thirty-chapter Swedish dissertation that covers most aspects of Poe's poetry, prose, sources, and reputation (A 143). The Norwegian Egil Rasmussen published a Poe biography that was, according to Anderson, "deeply concerned with the psychological basis and social function of artistic creativity" (A 154– 158). Thorkild Bjørnvig wrote two major essays in Danish dealing with Poe's aesthetics and his contributions as a critic (A 158–160).

In Sweden during the past twenty years, the many editions, reprints, and new translations of Poe's tales of the fantastic bear witness to the resilience of the interest in Poe as a mystery writer. His well-known tales are continuously reprinted in magazines and selected editions, some directly aimed at a younger audience, others addressed to crime fiction buffs. In 1985, for example, "The Murders in the Rue Morgue" appeared in the series "Entimmesboken" [The one-hour book], in which a short story classic was published biweekly as an inexpensive booklet. A new translation of "The Fall of the House of Usher" by Sam J. Lundwall came out as a booklet in 1993. Numerous short essays and articles of an introductory nature addressing various aspects of Poe's work have also appeared during the last two decades, thus guiding new generations of readers.

The Swedish magazine *Jury*, a publication dedicated to mystery stories and detective fiction, featured a special issue on Poe in 1991 containing articles on diverse aspects of the writer and his work. The main subjects were the "armchair detective" Dupin, Poe as the creator of the classic "whodunit," and the many films based on Poe's tales. Also included was an excerpt from Lars-Erik Nygren's yet to be published but much anticipated bibliography of Poe's detective stories and other tales.[2]

In Sweden very little attention has been paid to Poe's criticism and writings on aesthetics, and these texts have not been readily available in translation. Seeking to redress this state of affairs, Leif Furhammar published a selection of Poe's essays on poetics along with his own annotated translation of "The Philosophy of Composition," "The Poetic Principle," and "How to Write a Blackwood Article," as well as Poe's review of *Twice-Told Tales* and a selection from his "Marginalia" with a lengthy explanatory postscript.[3]

Scholarly and critical reflection on Poe's texts has produced some interesting articles in Sweden. Åke Gustafsson's collection of poetic essays (1980) was inspired by the poetry and prose poems of Poe and Gustav Fröding as well as by the lives of these poets.[4] In an original blend of essay and fiction, in one sense a study of the mystery of a person's creative capacity, he suggests links between Poe and Fröding. Gustafsson is intrigued by the way in which the "tormented men of genius" created mesmerizing poems and texts, a complex mixture of the sane and the crazed, of the truly great and the destructive, of the cruel and the hauntingly beautiful.

Olof Hägerstrand's 1985 article "Massa och vanmakt i speglarnas sal" [Masses and powerlessness in the hall of mirrors] is a somber meditation on the new breed of human being, produced by mass civilization, who suffers the disease of the dissolution of the self.[5] Hägerstrand uses "The Man of the Crowd" to show that while Poe was surely not the first to observe the state of soullessness brought on by megalopolis, no one before him had noted the effects on the psyche of mass existence and the way in which the city and the masses cause a "thinning of the inner self." Bringing in David Riesman's *The Lonely Crowd* and Christopher Lasch's *The Culture of Narcissism*, Hägerstrand discusses the nature of the forces in contemporary society that corrode an authentic life. In Hägerstrand's view, Poe's haunted night-wanderer is a shadowy yet persistent presence, the personification of the emptiness of modern life.

In 1994 Horace Engdahl included Poe in a collection of essays in which the critic attempts to re-create the elusive "voice" of the author, an element of style that leaves its indelible imprint on the reader.[6] In "The Facts in the Case of M. Valdemar," Engdahl focuses on voice in Romantic poetry, on the fascination of the Romantics with the relationship between the soul and the soulless — the territory of the tales of the fantastic. Engdahl argues that the voice of the deceased M. Valdemar should, ultimately, be considered an allegory of Poe's own text, the "text itself."

In Norway Poe is a mystical and mythical figure looming somewhere in the minds of most well-educated readers. Although he did not have an advocate among writers, such as Hansson and Strindberg in Sweden, Poe is clearly visible in Norway as the creator of the detective story and as a writer who helped define the short story. When the association for crime writers in Norway, *Rivertonklubben*, celebrated the 150th anniversary of Poe's birth, Hans H. Skei presented a lecture in which he praised Poe as the writer who laid down formulaic principles for literary detection that are still valid, with certain modifications.[7] In a chapter on the detective story, Skei uses Poe's definition of the short story and his crime tales to show that the first real detective was a fiction created by Poe.[8]

Norwegian editions of Poe's work in recent years seem to have been determined by market expectations and popular appeal. With few exceptions, the books are often edited with little care and printed in cheap paperback editions. Since 1970 six different collections of Poe's tales have been published in Norway, thus indicating the predilection for his prose fiction. Many poets and translators have translated individual poems over the years, some of which can be found in the comprehensive edition of world poetry published in Norwegian.[9] A new translation of "The Raven" appeared in the young poet Alexander G. Rubio's 1994 collection of his own and translated poems, *Betonghagen* [The concrete garden].[10]

In Denmark every decade seems to call for its own selection of Poe's short stories and for a different critical angle on the American writer. A traditional selection of Poe's detective tales was translated by Ole Storm in 1975, thus confirming the old claim that for Danish readers the perennial Poe is the father of crime and detective stories.[11]

The poet Thorkild Bjørnvig wrote two important essays on Poe at the end of the 1950s, as Anderson notes, but Bjørnvig's most important contribution to Poe studies is a 1973 article in which he makes a clean break with most traditional approaches to Poe by arguing that many of the so-called short stories are also essays.[12] An important work published in 1978 elucidates this idea. Erik A. Nielsen's *Fortolkningens veje* [Modes of interpretation], subtitled "A Didactic Essay on Edgar Allan Poe," is concerned with Poe's interpretation of reality.[13] Nielsen argues that Poe's central quest was for clarity and truth; the focus on the clarity of the creative moment is a common denominator in several stories. In this sense "The Gold-Bug" is primarily about the glorious moment when the interpreter's calculations seem confirmed by experience. Poe's focus is on the need for intuition in a search for a meaningful order even in a so-called rationalistic world. Nielsen argues convincingly that Poe's detective stories are fully compatible with the rest of his work. Like the narrators of "The Tell-Tale Heart" and "The Black Cat," C. Auguste Dupin is simply trying to sort out what really happened. He acts as a poet seeking the moment of truth. Nielsen's book develops into a study in religious Modernism as he emphasizes the fall of humanity and the leap of faith in a Kierkegaardian sense. In a final appreciation, Poe is compared to Dostoevsky, although placed a step below the Russian writer on a ladder of religious achievement.

In 1981 Nielsen published another selection of Poe's stories and essays, *Ned i malstrømmen* [Into the maelstrom] translated by Christian Kock.[14] There is an obvious emphasis on stories of doom, tales that are possibly moralizing or perhaps even religious. Nevertheless, the main critical emphasis on Poe's work in Denmark during the 1980s constitutes a return to the traditional view of Poe as a writer of detective and crime stories. The spokesperson for this view is Jørgen Holmgaard, whose long essays "Krimiens historie og socialpsykologi" [The history of the crime story and social psychology] and "Poe og mordene i Rue Morgue" [Poe and the murders in Rue Morgue] appeared in *Lystmord* [Premeditated murders], subtitled "Studies in the Literature of Crime from Poe to Sjöwall/Wahlöö."[15] Holmgaard's latter essay takes its point of departure in Poe's work and places him in the company of Conan Doyle, Agatha Christie, Dorothy L. Sayers, Dashiell Hammett, Raymond Chandler, Ross MacDonald, Georges Simenon, and contemporaries such as Patricia Highsmith, Poul Ørum, Maj Sjöwall, and Per Wahlöö.

Perhaps as a reaction to Holmgaard's traditional view of Poe, the 1990s began with a critical book that considers quite a different Poe. Henning Goldbæk's *Grænsens filosofi* [The philosophy of limits], subtitled "Reason and Utopia in Edgar Allan Poe," praises the American writer for treating such issues as idealism, progress, the American Dream, optimism, materialism, mass culture, and freedom — that is, most of what makes up the identity of modern Western civilization.[16] Goldbæk claims that Poe "expresses the fear and fragmentation of a post-idealistic reality" and tries to master fear. The book is an attempt to see Poe as a post-Romantic, a man caught between Romanticism and Modernism straining against the limitations of the only aesthetics available to his time and place. Goldbæk sees Poe as a man who wrote of the gray area between the known and the unknown, which he invoked by means of his intuitive reasoning. The constant presence of the unknown in his work, argues Goldbæk, saves Poe from being a mere writer for effect. Detailing Poe's reception in France, Germany, and the United States, Goldbæk criticizes American scholars for their failure to see that Poe, rooted in his contemporary society and popular culture, was more critical of what he saw than were other writers of the American Renaissance. Goldbæk concludes that it is time for Poe criticism to steer away from purely ideological reactions so that Poe will not remain forever adrift between the continents in his hot air balloon.

While Poe's role as an inspiration and model for Scandinavian writers seems to be a thing of the past, his short stories and essays live on, often clad in contemporary linguistic garb, and they continue to inspire and enthrall new generations of Scandinavian readers. As the situation appears to have been for more than 150 years, Poe's position in Denmark, Norway, and Sweden is still visible, and his reputation remains secure.

NOTES

1. Carl L. Anderson, *Poe in Northlight: The Scandinavian Response to His Life and Work* (Durham, N.C.: Duke UP, 1973); hereafter cited as A.

2. Lars-Erik Nygren, "Edgar Allan Poe. En bibliografi. Detektivhistorier, hemlighetsfulla och sällsamma berättelser på svenska, 1862–1986." Unpublished manuscript.

3. Leif Furhammar, *Den okände Poe: Edgar Allan Poes estetiska skrifter* (Uppsala: Bokgillet, 1963).

4. Åke Gustafsson, *Fröding är inte död: genier lever alltid* (Stockholm: Bonniers, 1980).

5. Olof Hägerstrand, "Massa och vanmakt: speglarnas sal," *Horisont* 5 (1985): 1–6.

6. Horace Engdahl, *Beröringens ABC: En essä om rösten i litteraturen* (Stockholm: Bonniers, 1994).

7. Hans H. Skei, "Fascinasjonen ved den leselige teksten," *Samtiden* 3 (1992): 47–55.

8. Hans H. Skei, "Kriminalnovellen," in *Under lupen*, ed. Alexander Elgurén and Audun Engelstad (Oslo: Cappelen, 1995), pp. 121–132.

9. Hartvig Kiran, Halldis Moren Vesaas, and Sigmund Skard, eds., *Framande dikt frå firetusen år* (Oslo: Det Norske Samlaget, 1968).

10. Alexander G. Rubio, *Betonghagen* (Oslo: Gyldendal, 1994).

11. *Mordene i Rue Morgue: Auguste Dupins kriminalsager*, ed. and trans. Ole Storm, (Copenhagen: Spectrum, 1974).

12. Thorkild Bjørnvig, "Essay/novellen hos Poe," in *Virkeligheden er til: Litterære Essays* (Copenhagen: Gyldendal, 1973), pp. 134–154.

13. Erik A. Nielsen, *Fortolkningens veje* (Copenhagen: Gyldendal, 1978).

14. *Ned i malstrømmen*, ed. Erik A. Nielsen, trans. Christian Kock (Copenhagen: Centrum, 1981).

15. Jørgen Holmgaard, ed., *Lystmord* (Copenhagen: Medusa, 1984).

16. Henning Goldbæk, *Grænsens filosofi* (Copenhagen: Akademisk Forlag, 1991). A summary in English of this book is found in Henning Goldbæk, "Poe in Progress: A Reappraisal," *American Studies in Scandinavia* 23 (1991): 105–120. Goldbæk translated into Danish his own selection of Poe's short stories, *Noveller af Edgar Allan Poe* (Copenhagen: Dansklærerforeningen, 1993).

# Poe in Germany and Austria

ROGER FORCLAZ

Poe's reception by readers of German has been the subject of contradictory assessments. Haldeen Braddy wrote in 1953 that "Teutonic appreciation of Poe, except in the realm of literary research, has lagged behind that of the other major countries of Europe."[1] Other studies give quite a different picture with a more positive image. Harro Heinz Kühnelt considers Poe as the American writer who is the most read and discussed in Germany, while Klaus Lubbers claims that Poe has always been more appreciated by German readers than by Americans.[2] An example of Poe's German popularity is the fact that he is the only American writer included in a collection of world classics published in 1980 for the general reader of German.[3] Frank Zumbach's seven hundred–page biography (1986) also testifies to the continuing interest in Poe in Germany. As a poet, writer of fiction, and theoretician of literature, Poe has enjoyed a lasting reputation in Germany and in other German-speaking countries, attracting both popular and academic attention.[4] English-language assessments of Poe's reception in Germany were scanty before Gerhard Hoffmann's detailed account came out in 1983.[5]

Until recently, the earliest known translations of Poe into German dated from 1853, when "The Raven," "The Pit and the Pendulum," and "Three Sundays in a Week" were published in two magazines.[6] In 1993 Ewald Brahms discovered a German translation of "A Descent into the Maelström" that dates back to 1846 (three years before Poe died), thus placing Poe's introduction into the German language at about the same time he was being translated into French.[7] The first edition in book form of a selection of Poe's tales in German was published in 1853.[8] As early as 1849 Poe had been mentioned in a magazine article devoted to foreign literature, and four years later the author of an anonymous article published in a leading German journal declared that Poe's name was bound to live in the annals of American literature.[9] Selections from his work continued to appear in the 1850s. He became known among German American readers after a German version of "A Descent into the Maelström" was published in New York in 1855.[10] Poe found a wide readership in the second half of the nineteenth century when about a dozen editions of his selected works were published in German. By the early twentieth century his popularity in Germany even began to outstrip that of James Fenimore Cooper and other well-known American writers.

Credit for introducing Poe to German readers is generally attributed to the novelist and short story writer Friedrich Spielhagen (1829–1911), who in 1859 included some of Poe's poems in his anthology *Amerikanische Gedichte* [American poems] and in an 1860 article called Poe "the greatest American poet." [11] Spielhagen wrote several articles in which he praised Poe's aesthetic theories, particularly in his analysis of "The Philosophy of Composition." While preferring Poe's poetry to his prose fiction, Spielhagen refers to Poe in his own stories and novels, one of which, *Mesmerismus*, reveals the direct influence of the American writer.

Spielhagen was not alone in his preference for the poet rather than the tale-writer. During the second half of the nineteenth century, Poe's reputation in Germany was based mainly on his poems, which were published in numerous translations between 1853 and 1910. In 1913 Fritz Hippe compared the existing translations and compiled a bibliography that includes German translations of Poe's poems and prose as well as articles about the writer.[12] Poe did not exert a direct influence on nineteenth-century German literature anything like the strong effect he had on the Symbolists in France, although through those writers he had an indirect influence on poets such as Rainer Maria Rilke (1875–1926), Hugo von Hofmannsthal (1874–1929), and Stefan George (1868–1933). His influence on the Expressionist poet Georg Trakl (1887–1914) also deserves to be mentioned.

Before the twentieth century, with the exception of Spielhagen, the recognition of Poe as a short story writer was chiefly restricted to authors of popular fiction, especially detective stories. He was, for example, hailed as the pioneer of the genre and influenced the Austrian writer and journalist Heinrich Levitschnigg (1810–1862), author of *Die Leiche im Koffer* [*The Corpse in the Chest*] and two other detective novels in which he anticipated Conan Doyle.

Poe's influence on Thomas Mann (1875–1955) has been examined in detail by Burton Pollin, who brings to light the similarities between Mann's novel *Buddenbrooks. Verfall einer Familie* [*Buddenbrooks: The Decline of a Family*] (1901) and Poe's "The Fall of the House of Usher." [13] Not only is the overall theme similar to "Usher," but Mann also repeats the most important motifs of disintegration, decay, and death. Like Poe's protagonist, the young aristocrat Kai, a decadent artist haunted by a sense of his own early death, is endowed with a morbid sensibility as he faces a clearly impending doom. Kai admires

Poe as a Symbolist and praises "The Fall of the House of Usher" as the best example of this Symbolism, calling Roderick Usher "the most remarkable character ever conceived" and exclaiming, "If ever I could write a tale like that!"[14] As in Poe's story, the vulnerability of the artistic temperament is an outstanding feature of Mann's novel. Pollin points out that apart from *Buddenbrooks*, Mann's interest in Poe as a theoretician and writer of fiction can be seen in several of his statements throughout his life, and traces of Poe are evident in Mann's "Tristan" (1903), "Tonio Kröger" (1903), and *Der Tod in Venedig* [*Death in Venice*] (1912).

During the first decade of the twentieth century, Poe's reputation in Germany was at a high point. The publication of the first comprehensive German edition of Poe started in 1901, and in 1902 the Swiss scholar Louis P. Betz wrote a study about Poe's relationship with Baudelaire and French literature.[15] In 1909 the centenary of Poe's birth was marked by the publication of thirty articles in German-language literary journals and newspapers. Fascination with the writer's personality still predominated, reflecting the interest of the age in biographical details. Following the characterization given by Baudelaire, Poe was popularly considered a romantic figure who was a victim of the materialistic world in which he lived. The historical perspective was finally superseded by the psychoanalytical approach, which focused on the medical and psychiatric aspects of Poe's works and his character. Karl F. van Vleuten, for example, argued in 1903 (and was later echoed by Ferdinand Probst) that epilepsy was the key to Poe's genius. This reductive approach to Poe's creative talent laid the groundwork for Marie Bonaparte's psychoanalytic interpretation thirty years later. Her book, which appeared in German with a preface by Sigmund Freud in 1934, found wide acclaim in Germany, as it had in France.[16]

The medical interpretation of Poe was energetically countered by the novelist and short story writer Hanns Heinz Ewers (1871–1943), an ardent admirer of Poe. Ewers's small but influential book about Poe promotes a view of the poet akin to Baudelaire's.[17] Alcohol was thought to be a source of inspiration for Poe, whom Ewers represents as a literary saint, a "poet martyr" living in a hostile world utterly divorced from his surroundings. Along with Karl Hans Strobl (1877–1946), editor of a Poe anthology, Ewers initiated the modern Poe cult in Germany and Austria. They were the first German writers to discover symbolic features in Poe's fiction and to stress the creative element and the visionary mysticism in his work. As writers of the fantastic mode of literature in the early twentieth century, Ewers and Strobl looked to Poe's fiction for the literary merit that legitimized their own creative efforts. Strobl justified the recourse to terror as a source of aesthetic emotion in a reference to E.T.A.

Hoffmann and Poe: like humor, terror is "the expression of the masculine and sovereign will of domination over life."[18] Alfred Kubin (1877–1959), best known as an artist but also the author of a fantastic novel, *Die andere Seite* [*The Other Side*], and Gustav Meyrink (1868–1932), author of *Der Golem* [*The Golem*], incorporated elements of Poe's work into their own.

Gerhard Hoffmann observes that Poe's most important influence was on the role of the imagination and on the dreamlike character of German fiction, the duality between the natural and the supernatural, the cyclical patterns of thought, symbolism, and complexes of motifs.[19] The fundamental difference between Poe's fiction and that of his German and Austrian disciples lies, according to Hoffmann, in the quasimythical or supernatural component of later fantastic fiction, its overall symbolic reference to a mystic realm of the supernatural, and the systematization of the duality between the natural and the supernatural. Contrary to his German followers, whose fiction was based on an ideological spiritual concept, Poe concentrates on the fictional possibilities of the fantastic and only plays with the supernatural.

The recognition of the modernity of Poe's work is one of the striking features of his reception in Germany. In 1957 Günter Blöcker (b. 1913), for instance, praised Poe as a precursor of our age who heralded "new realities."[20] Going beyond the traditional identification between the author's life and his literary production, some German writers and critics directed their attention to the importance of Poe's work in relation to the problems of the modern age. As early as 1904 Arthur Moeller-Bruck stressed Poe's modernity in descriptions of criminals and urban life that anticipated Dostoevsky and Zola. Poe was celebrated as the explorer of the dark side of the human soul. Rilke, for example, was attracted to Poe's depiction of the alien, the perverse, the unexplainable, and the mysterious as parts of the totality of human existence. Rilke saw "The Pit and the Pendulum" as a parable of the plight of modern people. In a passage from his *Briefe an einen jungen Dichter* [*Letters to a Young Poet*] (1904), Rilke speaks of "that dangerous uncertainty which impels the prisoners in Poe's stories to feel the contours of their terrible prison and not to remain strangers to the inexpressible horrors of their confinement."[21]

In his use of fear as a literary technique and by the exploration of the uncanny, Poe anticipates Franz Kafka (1883–1924), whose works have been compared to those of his American predecessor. Hoffmann analyzes the similarities in theme, structure, and technique in tales by the two authors while observing an interesting difference: Poe begins with a natural situation then progresses to the unnatural, while Kafka introduces an unnatural incident which he then works out rationally (see Part II, "Franz Kafka").[22]

Following Rilke and Kafka, other writers have found particular relevance for the modern age in Poe's archetypal situations and existential discourse. Ernst Jünger (b. 1895), one of the most important interpreters of Poe's work in Germany, is the best example of this existentialist view. For Jünger, Poe embodies the crisis of our age by describing the "terror of the soul" so characteristic of modernity. Poe's stories are for Jünger apocalyptic symbols and hieroglyphs of truth. The symbolic force of the maelstrom particularly attracted him. He mentions Poe's story several times, calling it "one of the great visions prefiguring the catastrophe of our times."[23]

Poe's influence on Arno Schmidt (1914–1979) is one of the most interesting cases of a twentieth-century writer being attracted to the American author's life and work. Thomas S. Hansen's in-depth study reveals that Schmidt had a personal affinity with Poe and was influenced by the American writer to the point of imitation in his early works.[24] Later on, in his novel *Zettels Traum* [Bottom's dream] (1970), Schmidt, who had done some startling Poe translations, incorporated Poe into his creative work in a very unusual way (see Part II, "Arno Schmidt").

Poe has also had an influence on modern German literature as a theoretician. Even though his literary essays had been relatively neglected before 1965, contemporary writers and critics have found Poe's literary theories to be as important as his poetry or short stories. Franz H. Link's 1968 study sees Poe's fiction, poetry, and literary theory as a transition between what the critic calls Romantic and Modern.[25] The German writer and critic Walter Benjamin (1892–1940) regards Poe as "one of the great technicians in world literature."[26] Poe became one of the models for poets in the mainstream of experimental modern poetry, his role being acknowledged by Rilke, Hofmannsthal, and Stefan George, who participated in the new approach to literary form. Hofmannsthal mentions Poe along with Baudelaire, Mallarmé, and Valéry as having an influence on his poetry, calling him "one of the great artists."[27] Poe also influenced Stefan George's aesthetic theories, which reflect the American poet's conception of the reader's response to beauty as an "artistic excitement."

As in France, major writers have played an important part in establishing Poe's status as a great American author in Germany. Although his influence in German-speaking countries has not been as extensive as in France, his importance for German literature lies in the fact that he suggested ideas and opened new fields to literature, leading in particular to the growing interest in the irrational. Another characteristic of Poe's German reception lies in the important contribution of German scholars and critics to Poe studies. Not only did they open the door to a psychological understanding of Poe's genius, they also rightly evaluated the mood of Poe's modern art as essentially American.

NOTES

1. Haldeen Braddy, *Glorious Incense: The Fulfillment of Edgar Allan Poe*, 2nd ed. (Port Washington, N.Y.: Kennikat, 1953; rpt. 1968), p. 130.

2. Harro Heinz Kühnelt, "Die Aufnahme und Verbreitung von E. A. Poes Werken im Deutschen," in *Festschrift für Walther Fischer*, ed. Horst Oppel (Heidelberg: Carl Winter, 1959), p. 195; Klaus Lubbers, "Zur Rezeption der amerikanischen Kurzgeschichte in Deutschland nach 1945," in *Nordamerikanische Literatur im deutschen Sprachraum seit 1945*, ed. Horst Frenz and Hans-Joachim Lang (Munich: Winkler, 1973), p. 52.

3. *Edgar Allan Poe*, presented by Kurt Möser in the series "Die grossen Klassiker — Literatur der Welt in Bildern, Texten, Daten" (Salzburg: Andreas, 1980).

4. For descriptions of German criticism on Poe and a major German edition of his works, see Roger Forclaz, "Poe in Europe — Recent German Criticism," *Poe Studies* 11.2 (December 1978): 49–55, 21.1 (June 1988): 1–10. See also Roger Forclaz, "A German Edition of Poe," *Poe Studies* 9.1 (June 1976): 24–26.

5. Gerhard Hoffmann, "Edgar Allan Poe and German Literature," in *American-German Literary Interrelations in the Nineteenth Century*, ed. Christoph Wecker (Munich: Wilhelm Fink Verlag, 1983), pp. 52–104. Earlier studies in English that attempted to survey Poe's influence abroad include only a few pages on Poe in Germany. See, for example, C. Alphonso Smith, *Edgar Allan Poe, How to Know Him* (Garden City, N.Y.: Garden City Publishing, 1921); John C. French, *Poe in Foreign Lands and Tongues* (Baltimore: Johns Hopkins UP, 1941); and W. T. Bandy, *The Influence and Reputation of Edgar Allan Poe in Europe* (Baltimore: F. T. Cimino, 1962). For an overview in German, see Liliane Weissberg, *Edgar Allan Poe* (Stuttgart: J. B. Metzlersche Verlagsbuchhandlung, 1991), pp. 198–204.

6. Elise von Hohenhausen, "Literarische Symptome in den Vereinigten Staaten," *Magazin für die Literatur des Auslandes* 70 (November 6, 1853): 278–280; Elise von Hohenhausen, "Der Brunnen und der Pendel. Nach dem Englischen des Edgar Poe, von H. du Roi. Drei Sonntage in einer Woche. Novelle von Edgar Poe," *Bremer Sonntagsblatt* 17 (April 24, 1853): 132–133, 18 (May 1, 1953): 139–140, 25 (June 19, 1953): 188–190.

7. Ewald Brahms, "Edgar Allan Poe zwischen Kontinuität und Wandel: Zur Kanonisierung seines erzählerischen Werkes in deutscher Sprache" (Ph. D. diss., Saarbrücken, 1993), p. 11. Brahms discovered the serialized German translation of Poe's tale in *Frankfurter Konversationsblatt* (October 14, 1846–October 21, 1846).

8. *Ausgewählte Werke von Edgar Allan Poe*, 3 vols., trans. W[ilhelm] E[dward] Drugulin (Leipzig: Kollmann, 1853–1854).

9. Anon., "Nord-Amerika: Henry Wadsworth Longfellow und die amerikanische Literatur," *Magazin für die Literatur des Auslandes* 49 (December 13, 1849): 593–594. Ludwig Herrig, "Die englische Sprache und Literatur in Nordamerika," *Archiv für das Studium der neueren Sprachen und Literaturen* 13 (1853): 241–245.

10. "Eine Hinabwirbelung in den Maalstrom. Aus dem Englischen von Adolf Strodtmann," *Deutsche Monatshefte* (New York) 6 (December 1855): 404–413.

11. Friedrich Spielhagen, "Edgar Allan Poe," *Europa* 15 (1860): 483–490.

12. Fritz Hippe, "Poes Lyrik in Deutschland," (Ph. D. diss., Münster, 1913).

13. Burton R. Pollin, "Thomas Mann and Poe: Two Houses Linked," in *Insights and Outlooks: Essays on Great Writers* (New York: Gordian, 1986), pp. 222–239.

14. Thomas Mann, *Buddenbrooks. Verfall einer Familie* (Berlin and Frankfurt/Main: Fischer, 1960), p. 636. My translation.

15. *E. A. Poes Werke*, 10 vols., Uebersetzt und Herausgegeben von Hedda und Arthur Moeller-Bruck (Minden: J.C.C. Bruns, 1901–1904). Louis P. Betz, *Studien zur vergleichenden Literaturgeschichte der neueren Zeit* (Frankfurt/Main: Rütten & Loening, 1902), pp. 16–82.

16. Marie Bonaparte, *Edgar Poe: Eine psychoanalytische Studie* (Wien: Internationaler psychoanalytischer Verlag, 1934).

17. Hanns Heinz Ewers, *Edgar Allan Poe* (Berlin and Leipzig: Schuster & Loeffler, 1906).

18. Foreword in *Das unheimliche Buch*, ed. Felix Schloemp (Munich: Georg Müller, 1904), pp. xi-xii. My translation.

19. Hoffmann, "Edgar Allan Poe and German Literature," pp. 70–80.

20. Günter Blöcker, *Die neuen Wirklichkeiten: Linien und Profile der modernen Literatur* (Berlin: Argon Verlag, 1957), pp. 124–132.

21. Rainer Maria Rilke, *Briefe an einen jungen Dichter* (Leipzig: Insel Bücherei, 1940), p. 47. My translation.

22. Hoffmann, "Edgar Allan Poe and German Literature," pp. 81–88.

23. Ernst Jünger, *Strahlungen* (Tübingen: Heliopolis-Verlag, 1949), p. 349. My translation. See also H. F. Peters, "Ernst Jünger's Concern with E. A. Poe," *Comparative Literature* 10 (1958): 144–149.

24. Thomas S. Hansen, "Arno Schmidt's Reception of Edgar Allan Poe: Or, the Domain of Arn(o)heim," *Review of Contemporary Fiction* 8.1 (Spring 1988): 166–181 (special issue on Arno Schmidt, ed. F. Peter Ott).

25. Franz H. Link, *Edgar Allan Poe: Ein Dichter zwischen Romantik und Moderne* (Frankfurt/Main: Athenäum Verlag, 1968).

26. Walter Benjamin, *Charles Baudelaire — Ein Lyriker im Zeitalter des Hochkapitalismus*, ed. Rolf Tiedemann (Frankfurt/Main: Suhrkamp, 1974), p. 41. My translation.

27. Hugo von Hofmannsthal, *Aufzeichnungen*, ed. Herbert Steiner (Frankfurt/Main: Fischer, 1959), p. 318.

# Poe in Belgium

J. P. VANDER MOTTEN

The nature and extent of Poe's reputation in Belgium begin with his reception in literary journals, which were a prominent feature of Belgian cultural life in the nineteenth century.[1] During the late 1870s and early 1880s, translations of Poe's poems and tales, brief accounts of his life, and scattered references to his work made his name known in literary and artistic circles. In a country with two languages and literary traditions, French and Flemish (Dutch), Poe became a widely read and influential author who is still enjoyed by many readers of both languages today.

Within a few years after his death in 1849, Poe was first introduced to the Belgian reading public in conjunction with Baudelaire, whose translations were the subject of an article appearing in *L'Indépendance Belge* on February 12, 1857. Emile Deschanel eulogized the stylistic qualities of Baudelaire's translations as well as the excitement aroused by Poe's breathtaking tales, which have the power, noted the critic, of taxing the reader's mind and nerves. Six months later in the same newspaper,[2] Deschanel praised Baudelaire's second volume of Poe tales while defending the French poet from attacks brought about by a lawsuit concerning the publication of *Les Fleurs du Mal* [*The Flowers of Evil*]. The reviewer's argument incorporated an abstract of Poe's ideas on the "heresy of the *Didactic*," the principle that was to make him a guide par excellence in aesthetic matters among the generation of La Jeune Belgique [Young Belgium] in the 1880s. Although the reputations of Baudelaire and Poe were often intertwined, the French poet's residence in Brussels from April 1864 to June 1866 did not enhance his own renown in Belgium or his fame as Poe's translator. Baudelaire's presentations on French artists and writers were not the success he had anticipated, and it is doubtful whether a planned lecture on Poe was ever given.

During the same period, Poe's reputation among the Flemish intelligentsia was growing, as suggested by an article published in 1877 by Gustaaf Segers (1848–1930), a Dutch and German teacher, Vondel scholar, and writer of realistic tales of country life.[3] His essay on the "greatest and most original of American poets" was designed to do justice to a writer all but unknown in Flanders and insufficiently appreciated in Belgium, according to the author. Although marred by factual errors, Segers's account had the virtue of pointing out the variety of Poe's accomplishments and submitting to his readers a condensed Dutch version (the first of its kind) of "Ligeia."

Segers's essay was the prelude to (though not the cause of) a surge of interest in Poe that coincided with an artistic revival in both French and Flemish literary circles during the period 1880 to 1900. The movement centered around the monthly journal *La Jeune Belgique*, which during its sixteen-year existence (December 1881 to December 1897) gave voice to a generation of young Belgian writers who vehemently reacted against the idea of an older, "national" literature that was believed to be academic, utilitarian, and didactic. Under the inspiring leadership of the journal's young founder, Max Waller [Maurice Warlomont] (1860–1889), collaborators never tired of confessing their adherence to the new creed of "art for art's sake." The international outlook of *La Jeune Belgique* is evident in the countless pages devoted to essays on foreign writers and translations of their works. This journal more than any other organ was instrumental in publicizing Poe's works as the repository of the tenets of "art for art's sake" and in doing so boosted his reputation among Belgian writers.

As early as May 1881 Waller had contributed a three-part essay on Poe that appeared in a short-lived publication that preceded *La Jeune Belgique*.[4] Generously quoting from Baudelaire's translations of the tales, Waller attempted a comprehensive characterization of Poe's genius: the sincerity of his pain, so well reflected in "The Raven"; the emotions of curiosity and fear underlying his works; his analytical and intuitive powers; and his untiring quest for an elusive, eternal beauty, personified in the characters of Ligeia, Lenore, and Morella. The numerous Poe translations, imitations, reviews, references, and critical assessments in the 1880s are evidence that Poe was riding the crest of an aesthetic wave and rapidly becoming a reference point in artistic circles. Contributors to *La Jeune Belgique* and other journals often prefixed Poe quotes as mottoes to their tales and prose poems. Images and characters from his verse were freely imitated. Poe himself was even the subject of an 1896 sonnet by Valère Gille.[5] Aspiring poets were ranked by how far they fell short of Poe's achievement, and established writers, such as Tennyson, were judged by the measure of Poe's respect for them.

The Flemish avant-garde periodical *Van Nu en Straks* [Of now and later], published from 1893 to 1901, was not as international in its literary orientation and less exclusively committed to the cause of "art for art's sake" than *La Jeune Belgique*. Nevertheless, Poe's works were a regular topic of conversation between two of the journal's founders, Emmanuel de Bom (1868–1953) and August Vermeylen (1872–1945).⁶ On one occasion Vermeylen confessed that he had been ruminating over Poe's dedication of *Eureka* to "those who put faith in dreams as in the only realities," an often-quoted line throughout the period. De Bom was equally impressed by Poe's work. In de Bom's story "Blonde gedachten" [Blond thoughts], the hero aspires to come of age artistically by ridding himself of the vicarious emotions gained from the reading of Baudelaire, Verlaine, and Poe, who had taught him "the poetry of the night, the fascination of horror, and the somber greatness of hallucinations."⁷

With the passing of the Aesthetic movement, the veneration of Poe as a poet of beauty seems to have gradually dwindled in favor of a growing preoccupation with Poe as the master of terror, surprise, and the fantastic. Interest in this aspect of his art can be seen in pre-1900 essays and translations by such diverse writers as Gustaaf Segers, Albert Giraud, Arnold Goffin, and Frans Van den Weghe, to cite only a few.⁸ From the 1920s on, Poe's name was almost exclusively identified with the tales of mystery and imagination, which became the basis of his twentieth-century reputation.

As Camille Mauclair observed in 1925, both the French- and Dutch-language literatures of Belgium have always shown a tendency toward the mystical and the fantastic, thus making it particularly difficult to disentangle with any degree of certainty works of purely "native" inspiration from those possibly or probably inspired by Poe's work.⁹ The fantastic strain in modern Belgian literature has as one of its sources the late-nineteenth-century Symbolist aesthetic, which in its allusive and speculative character bears a close affinity to the unreality of the fantastic. The Symbolist poet Charles Van Lerberghe (1861–1907) remarked in true Poesque fashion in 1897 that "there is no beauty without a certain strangeness, without a certain mystery," an idea that is applicable to works of several turn-of-the-century writers.¹⁰ Van Lerberghe's own poems and plays show a taste for the symbolic, the mysterious, and the terrifying, obviously derived from Poe. Together with Maurice Maeterlinck (1862–1949), also familiar with Poe's work, Van Lerberghe has been credited with introducing the "théâtre d'angoisse," well exemplified in Maeterlinck's *L'Intruse* [The intruder] (1890) and Van Lerberghe's *Les Flaireurs* [The scenters] (1889).¹¹ The creator of a world of haunting dreams and shadows, George Rodenbach (1855–1898) also underwent Poe's influence. The theme of his novel *Bruges-la-Morte* (1892), the revenge of the dead against the living, seems to have been inspired by "Ligeia"; various stories in *Le Rouet des Brumes* [The spinning wheel of mists] (1901) share thematic parallels, motifs, and aspects of atmosphere with "The Tell-Tale Heart," "The Imp of the Perverse," and other Poe tales.

Poe's influence on the theater in Belgium is particularly striking in the works of the playwright Michel de Ghelderode (1898–1962), who admitted to a lifelong interest in Poe. He was convinced that modern literature owed its sharpest perceptions to the American writer. As early as 1918 Ghelderode tried his hand at a one-act poetic piece, "La Mort regarde à la fenêtre" [Death looks in through the window], "something gloomy and very English" inspired by "The Masque of the Red Death." A few years later "Hop-Frog" provided the plot elements for *Escurial* (1927), in which the buffoon, Folial, the emblem of degraded humanity, meditates revenge against his unfeeling and cruel king. The overriding fear of death that pervades Ghelderode's theatrical art is also found in some of his tales, which are populated by half allegorical, eccentric, and specterlike characters who, against the background of somber Flemish medieval cities, confront the narrator (the author himself) with the metaphysical anxieties besetting his soul.

Greatly admired by Ghelderode, the bilingual Ghent author Jean Ray [Raymond De Kremer] (1887–1964) owed a double debt to Poe as the practitioner of two different genres: the detective story and the tale of horror. Ray's *Contes du Whisky* [Tales of whisky] (1925), which takes the reader into the realm of nightmares and terror, established his reputation abroad as the "Belgian Edgar Poe." Although Ray published some of his best work in the fantastic genre during the Second World War, it was not until 1961 with the publication of *Les 25 meilleures histoires noires et fantastiques* [The 25 best black and fantastic tales] that he earned long overdue recognition in Belgium.

Spellbound by Poe from his youth, Franz Hellens [Frédéric van Ermengem] (1881–1972) emerged after 1920 as the theorist and major practitioner of *le fantastique réel* [the real fantastic]. Rooted in the permanent elements of human nature and everyday reality, this mode of writing originated, according to Hellens, in such "prose poems" as "The Domain of Arnheim," "Ligeia," and "Morella" and has no other fantastic ingredients but the abstraction of a waking dream given poetical form.[12] The central character in many of Hellens's tales is the city of Ghent, itself a haunting specter among Flemish cities. Praised by Ghelderode for his Poe-like technical mastery of the short story in such collections as *Le dernier jour du monde* [The last day of the world] (1967), Hellens in his later work consciously inverted Poe's method of proceeding from the unknown to the known, from the fantastic to the real. Instead, he started from reality to end up in the fantastic, encountering the mysterious along the way without attempting to explain it.

On the Flemish side of the language border, the fantastic tradition was slower in coming. Not until the early 1950s do Dutch translations of Poe's tales, published simultaneously in Holland and Flanders, quite suddenly begin to reach an avid reading public. To cite one example, André Noorbeek's immensely popular *Fantastische Vertellingen* [Fantastic tales], first published in 1953 in Utrecht and Antwerp, went through five editions by 1957, and through fifteen by 1979. This renewed interest was perhaps aroused by the vogue of Magic Realism, initiated in Dutch literature during the 1940s by the Ghent novelist Johan Daisne [Herman Thiery] (1912–1978) in *De trap van steen en wolken* [The stairway of stone and clouds] (1942). Though not explicitly traced to Poe by Daisne himself, this mode of writing was in several respects closely related to Hellens's *fantastique réel*.

The major midcentury representative of the literature of mystery and terror was Roger d'Exsteyl [Roger Martens] (1929–1979), who was acclaimed as the initiator of the Flemish detective novel after the publication of his gruesome work *De Dames Verbrugge* [The ladies Verbrugge] (1953). The central theme of his tales is existential fear, the one motive underlying all fantastic literature, in his opinion. A friend of Jean Ray's, d'Exsteyl translated *The Narrative of Arthur Gordon Pym* into Dutch. His borrowings from Poe are most striking in some of the stories in the collection *Souper met vleermuizen* [Supper with bats] (1966), where the general atmosphere of gloom and doom, the sense of the hallucinatory and the macabre, and the search for a perfect beauty culminating in a confrontation with death are reminiscent of the American author.[13]

In the wake of Ray's and d'Exsteyl's examples, similar themes are being pursued with great enthusiasm by a generation of more recent Flemish writers, including Eddy C. Bertin (b. 1944), Julien Raasveld (b. 1944), and Guido Van Heulendonk [Guido Beelaert] (b. 1951), all of whose tales evince a marked interest in the horrific, macabre, and grotesque.[14] With their clever variations on such tales as "The Premature Burial" and "The Black Cat," Bertin and others seem to be primarily preoccupied with the convergence of the natural and the grotesque. Van Heulendonk's stories, collected under the significant title *De echo van de raaf* [The raven's echo] (1991), feed on the bizarre. The narrator's rewriting of "Usher" in "De val van het huis Usher (II)" [The fall of the house of Usher, II] is both an attempt to exorcise the fate toward which his ailing father is heading (in imitation of Roderick Usher) and a telling comment on the author's obsession with Poe.

In the century and a half since his death, the ebb and flow of Poe's reputation in Belgium has been closely connected with changing literary and artistic tastes. After a relatively slow discovery, Poe's fame as a high priest of the Aesthetic movement reached its zenith around the turn of the century in the context of a national culture as yet undivided by nonartistic issues. In the past six or seven decades, with the rediscovery of the fantastic and the growing taste for the detective story, other aspects of his art have moved to the forefront. On the eve of the twenty-first century, it is no exaggeration to claim that Poe's works continue to exert an attraction on novelists, playwrights, and short story writers in both French- and Flemish-speaking Belgium.

NOTES

1. The only study of Poe in Belgium that I have found is Emanuela Cristofari's unpublished thesis, "Influenza di Edgar Allan Poe sulle Lettere Belghe di Fine 1800 e Inizio 1900" (University of Rome, 1991). Her study is limited to Francophone literature of the late nineteenth century and focuses on only two authors, Georges Eekhoud and Georges Rodenbach. For some parallels between Poe and these authors, I am indebted to her work, which is useful as a reference tool on the reception of Poe in journals of the period.

2. *L'Indépendance Belge*, August 20, 1857.

3. Gustaaf Segers, "Een Amerikaansche Dichter — Edgar Poe," *De Toekomst. Tijdschrift voor Opvoeding en Onderwijs* 21 (1877): 212–222, 244–251.

4. Max Waller, "Les Etranges. Edgar Allan Poe," *La Jeune Revue Littéraire* 1 (1880–1881): 104–108, 123–126, 141–145. There was continuity between this literary journal and *La Jeune Belgique*; for example, Waller served on both editorial boards.

5. "Edgar Poë," *La Jeune Belgique* 15 (1896): 101.

6. *Het ontstaan van "Van Nu en Straks." Een Brieveneditie, 1890–1894. Teksten*, introduced and annotated by Leen Van Dijck, J. Paul Lissens, and Toon Saldien (Antwerp: Centrum voor de Studie van het Vlaamse Cultuurleven, 1988), p. 249.

7. Emmanuel de Bom, "Blonde gedachten," in *Van Nu en Straks, 1893–1901*, introduction and notes by A. M. Musschoot (The Hague: Martinus Nijhoff, 1982), p. 14.

8. Frans Van den Weghe, "Engelsche Letteren II: Edgar Allan Poe," *Nederlandsch Museum. Tijdschrift voor Letteren, Wetenschappen en Kunst* 4e Reeks 2 (1893): 346–357. The essay was reprinted in the author's *Vreemde Beelden en schetsen* (Ghent: Vanderpoorten, 1903), pp. 60–69, and supplemented with the original text of "Annabel Lee."

9. Camille Mauclair, "L'influence d'Edgar Poe en France," *La Revue Belge* 2 (1925): 29–48.

10. Herman Braet, *L'Accueil fait au symbolisme en Belgique, 1885–1900. Contribution à l'étude du mouvement et de la critique symbolistes* (Brussels: Académie Royale de Langue et de Littératures Françaises, 1967), pp. 136–137.

11. For an analysis of Poe's influence on Maeterlinck, see Célestin Pierre Cambiaire,

*The Influence of Edgar Allan Poe in France* (New York: Stechert, 1927, rpt. 1970), pp. 296–304.

12. Franz Hellens, *Le Fantastique réel* (Brussels: Sodi, 1966).

13. See Rik Lanckrock's introduction to d'Exsteyl's collection *Steekspel met schimmen* (Ghent: De Vlam, 1954); Eddy C. Bertin, "Roger d'Exsteyl. De Gentse demonenscheppper," in *Oostvlaamse Literaire Monografieen. Deel III* (Ghent: Provinciebestuur Oost-Vlaanderen, 1980), pp. 33–64.

14. For more information on this generation of writers, see the two anthologies edited by A. Van Hageland, *Land van de Griezel* (Zele: Reinaert, 1976, 1978). I am indebted to my colleague A. M. Musschoot of the Dutch Literature Department for her useful suggestions and for providing me with relevant materials.

# Poe in Great Britain

BENJAMIN F. FISHER

Poe's artistry seems initially to have attracted British notice when *The Narrative of Arthur Gordon Pym* was published and reviewed in England (1838), followed by pirated appearances in *Bentley's Miscellany* of two pieces from *Tales of the Grotesque and Arabesque* (1839), "The Fall of the House of Usher" and "The Visionary" (better known by its later title, "The Assignation"), in the issues for August and December 1840, respectively. With *Pym* first bringing Poe to British attention, we need not wonder that his reception thereafter continued to be checkered. Nevertheless, several reprintings indicate a continuing British interest in *Pym*, among them a pirated version using the title page from the first American edition, another in the low-cost *Novel Newspaper* in 1841, and a third in "The Shilling Library" in 1861. One reviewer's ideas characterize conceptions of Poe's work among many British readers in that period: "For those who possess a genuine love of the horrible, here is a rich and luxurious banquet," adding that there is in the novel much of "not only the *improbable* but the *impossible*." Several other reviewers compared Poe's methods in *Pym* with those of Defoe in *Robinson Crusoe* or *Captain Jack*, noting how both deftly created literary hoaxes and minimizing Defoe's oft-touted realism. Poe's book no doubt attracted readers who were enthusiastic for the sea fiction of Captain Frederick Marryat, as well as those whose zest for Gothic horrors it could have satisfied all too well. There seems to be no fiction in Great Britain from this early period, however, in which we might detect any influence of Poe's novel. Later in the century, after a spate of Antarctic exploration had occurred and after Jules Verne's takeoff, translated into English by Frances Sarah Hoey as *An Antarctic Mystery* (1898), had attracted admirers, *Pym* enjoyed a renaissance of critical attention from the British.[1]

Greater attention came Poe's way when his two volumes in Wiley and Putnam's "Library of American Books" began to circulate in the British Isles during 1845–1846. *Tales by Edgar A. Poe* (twelve stories which included the three Dupin titles), selected by Evert A. Duyckinck, whose choices Poe was subsequently to deplore to others, appeared in July 1845 and *The Raven and Other Poems* in January 1846. The *Tales* drew forth evaluations which, if often tacitly, placed them within the Gothic tradition. The *Spectator* critic (August 2, 1845) remarked that the tales were "mostly tinged with a spirit of diablerie or mystery, not always of a supernatural character, but such as caterers for news delight to head 'mysterious occurrences.' To unfold the wonderful, to show that what seems miraculous is amenable to almost mathematical reasoning, is a real delight of Mr. Poe . . . and in all cases he exhibits great analytical skill in seizing upon the points of circumstantial evidence and connecting them together." True to an inhabitant of the land where Dickens gave impetus to the Christmas story of supernatural parts, the critic added that Poe "also has the faculty essential to the story-teller by 'the winter's fire,' who would send the hearers trembling to their beds." We might also profitably recall that Tennyson's early attempt with Arthurian material, "The Epic" (1842), was framed as a tale of the supernatural, related over glasses of punch while the listeners gathered at the hearth. Such thoughts concerning Poe's fiction echoed in the London *Atlas* notice, which likewise labeled as Christmas-story fare these tales "of genteel *Terrific Register* description." [2]

Other voices in the British press sounded kindred notes; but despite the repeated censure directed at the subject matter in them, Poe's tales could not be wholly dismissed on grounds of their style. The writer for the London *Critic* (September 6, 1845), arguing that the black cat in Poe's tale "would have been a proper inmate for the 'Castle of Otranto,'" could not ignore possibilities (if admitting them grudgingly) that the cat might be "a figurative personification of the dark-brooding thoughts of a murderer" — thus confirming the dictum in Poe's own "How to Write a Blackwood Article" that "sensations are the great things after all," that is, that symbol and idea coalesce. Introducing a critique by Martin Farquhar Tupper, the editor of the London *Literary Gazette* for January 1846 concluded by dubbing Poe a "writer of original powers"; those "powers" to Tupper, however, evinced flaws, as seen in "The Black Cat," "Lionizing," "Mesmeric Revelation," and "The Fall of the House of Usher." Tupper did find a "marvellous train of analytical reasoning" in "The Murders in the Rue Morgue" and "The Mystery of Marie Rogêt" and paid respects to the "genius" in "A Descent into the Maelström" and to "The Conversation of Eiros and Charmion," the latter a tale filled with "terror and instruction," true to scripture and philosophical thought. A far briefer notice of the *Tales* in the *Literary Gazette* for August 1845 emphasized that Poe had not "disfigured [his style] by any gross Yankeeisms," notwithstanding his slipshod diction of more general sorts. Such British particularity concerning American usage was to persist in reviews of American books long afterward, as observations of G. W. Cable, Paul Laurence Dunbar, Mary Murfree, Stephen Crane, and Frank Norris at the turn of the century bear witness. In late 1849, after Poe's death, the poet-critic Coventry Patmore found Poe's tales worthwhile and Poe the best writer so far produced by America.[3]

*The Raven and Other Poems* carried a dedication to Elizabeth Barrett, and it was therefore bound to attract notice in her homeland. Poe had, of course, reviewed Barrett's *A Drama of Exile and Other Poems* in the *Broadway Journal* (January 11, 1845), giving the contents praise in general and particular acclaim to "Lady Geraldine's Courtship," from which he drew in composing "The Raven." Barrett in turn discerned insanity in the speaker in "The Raven" — a trait in that worthy's psychological makeup that still boggles some readers' minds — and functional artistry in the sound effects. Poe's intent in expressing admiration for Barrett's poetry, in both his published comments and correspondence, emanated from his hope of greater access to the British literary marketplace, just as his relationships with Dickens and Richard Henry Horne were calculated on his part. None of these efforts to cultivate a British acquaintance bore fruit, though, either in respect to Poe's securing entry to publishers or to the person's literary circles. Robert Browning, Elizabeth Barrett's husband, was later inspired in part by Poe's tale "Metzengerstein" as he created his renowned poem "Childe Roland to the Dark Tower Came."[4]

Tennyson and the pre-Raphaelite poets and painters also manifested no mean interest in Poe and his writings. The question of who influenced whom in the Poe-Tennyson literary relationship led to divergent commentary early on, and such responses continue; apparently Poe drew upon the English writer's verse on more than one occasion, for example, on "No More" (1831) while he composed "The Raven," elsewhere citing lines from Tennyson to bolster his own theories concerning versification. Tennyson himself disclaimed the authorship of "To One in Paradise," thus laying to rest the rumor that Poe had reprinted a poem by the Englishman under his own name. Another question of influence-plagiarism yoked Poe with the Irish poet James Clarence Mangan. That each worked independently of the other during the 1830s and 1840s, despite what one might have known of the other's accomplishments, has been well argued by Louise Imogen Guiney in her selective volume of Mangan's verse.[5]

Positive responses to Poe the poet came from D. G. Rossetti and his friend, the poet-critic A. C. Swinburne. Rossetti's own famous ballad, "The Blessed Damozel," grew out of "The Raven," Rossetti picking up where he thought Poe had left off. Rossetti also turned to Poe when he created several works in visual art, one of them, to be sure, "The Blessed Damozel," but also in pen-and-pencil or pen-and-ink sketches for "The Raven" (four of them), "The Sleeper," and "Ulalume." All contain themes common to Poe and Rossetti: lovers thwarted by death, eerie images and echoes of the past, and double(s)-characters. Rossetti found in Poe's work a kind of mysticism that appealed to him.[6] Swinburne's enthusiasm for Poe the man and Poe the writer courses through his correspondence over many years.

The publication of *Tales of Mystery, Imagination & Humour* in 1852 — which would continue to be a popular market item for decades, albeit under slightly variant titles — probably more than anything else during the next several decades brought Poe's work as a fiction writer before the British public, as is evidenced by the many allusions to that book during the later nineteenth century. Although the Dupin tales and "The Gold-Bug," or "The Gold Beetle" as it was re-entitled for British audiences, seemed to hold high popularity among Poe's fictional writings, they were by no means the sole objects of admiration from British readers, as numerous remarks from the later nineteenth century attest. Appearances of individual tales, for example, "The Purloined Letter" (abridged) in *Chambers's Edinburgh Journal* (November 1844), "The Facts in the Case of M. Valdemar" — which was reprinted several times in London newspapers during 1846 and as a separate volume in London the same year — or "The Gold-Bug," separately reprinted from the *Tales* in London (1846–1847), created another variety of currency for Poe's short fiction among the British reading public. No wonder that Elizabeth Barrett wrote to Poe concerning the veracity in "Valdemar," which had made the rounds of the British press to create a sensation. Editions of Poe's poems also continued to appear in Great Britain, possibly the most significant being *The Poetical Works of Edgar Allan Poe*, with a preface by James Hannay (1853), which maintained its popularity for decades, and *The Poems of Edgar Allan Poe*, edited by R. H. Stoddard (1874). As was the case with several of Poe's tales, "The Raven" was reprinted as a separate volume repeatedly in the British Isles, for its popularity did not flag as the century wore on.

Several other editions of Poe's writings also occasioned considerable comment in Great Britain, especially those by R. H. Stoddard (1884), reprinted as if the volumes were a new publication in 1894 — a ploy that did not escape exposure by British reviewers — and the more inclusive work of E. C. Stedman and George E. Woodberry, which was brought out in England by Laurence and Bullen in 1896. Many unquestioningly hailed the latter project as a definitive presentation of Poe's "complete" writings, although there is still no complete edition of his work a century later. Aubrey Beardsley, the notorious

Decadent artist in black-and-white graphics, was commissioned to illustrate the Stedman-Woodberry edition, although he never finished his assignment. His renderings of "The Masque of the Red Death," "The Murders in the Rue Morgue," "The Black Cat," and "The Fall of the House of Usher" suggest, for many, the essence of Poesque weirdness and fantasy.

Poe's life, too, provided a perennially interesting topic in Great Britain, where his literary reputation was at the mercy of the Griswold controversy. The infamous Rufus Wilmot Griswold (1815–1857) sent an obituary letter to the *New York Tribune*, published October 9, 1849, two days after Poe's death, in which he portrayed Poe as a drunk whose death would be mourned by only a few people. Since Poe had selected Griswold to be his literary executor, the obituary account of his life was given credence and had a great deal of influence on his reputation in the United States and abroad.

Just how effectively Griswold had done his work of vilifying Poe's character may be detected in many British accounts. For example, Horatio Mansfield's "Biography of Edgar Allan Poe" in *Tait's Edinburgh Magazine* (April 1852) praised "The Raven" but wondered how "so much intellectual power may co-exist with so much moral weakness." Another, "The Life and Writings of Edgar Allan Poe" in *Hogg's Instructor* (January 1854), lamented Poe's human deficiencies, paid scant respect to his poems, and commended structure and style features in the tales. George Gilfillan's "Edgar Allan Poe," originally in the London *Critic* (March 1854), then circulated widely in *A Third Gallery of Portraits* (1855), commenced with a decided bias: Poets have been, overall, "rather a worthless, wicked set of people [but] Poe was *the* most worthless and wicked of all his fraternity." A similar viewpoint informed "The Poets of America" in the *Irish Quarterly Review* (September 1855); Poe's abilities as a poet were lauded, but such commendation was offset by deploring his decadent life. Finally, "Edgar Allan Poe," B. R. Procter's review of Griswold's edition in the *Edinburgh Review* (April 1858), denigrated Poe's personal life but hoped that accounts of it would someday be subsumed by appreciation for such fine works as his critique of *Barnaby Rudge*, which had come to the fore among his writings. This article, the first about Poe in the influential Scottish journal since his death, would naturally have had a considerable readership in Great Britain.

As early as April 1857, however, W. Moy Thomas, in "Edgar Allan Poe" in the London *Train*, had challenged Griswold's accuracy, charging that the famous American anthologist-editor had allowed personal animosity to color his memoir of Poe and that those who unheedingly followed Griswold also merited censure. A far more prominent British champion of Poe appeared in

John Henry Ingram, whose work on Poe's behalf aroused as much controversy and animosity as it benefited its subject. Ingram's strictures against Griswold and his school were, to be sure, on the mark, but Ingram's own dealings with persons who had known Poe and who held important documents for a biographer were not above suspicion. He often "borrowed" materials permanently. The lengthy memoir to Poe's *Works* (1874–1875) constituted Ingram's first presentation of his subject's life, followed eventually in 1880 by a full-dress biography, the first of its kind. Subsequent investigations have pointed out errors in Ingram's work, but his biography must be credited as an attempt to rectify the slurs of Griswold and company and to supersede them with far greater factual accuracy.

British biographies of Poe in the wake of Ingram have not been legion. The most notable, David Sinclair's *Edgar Allan Poe* (1977), in no way surpasses the longstandingly reliable biography by the American academic Arthur H. Quinn, first published in 1941, although Sinclair's hypothesis that Poe's so-called alcoholism was the result of diabetes, which brought about his early death, is worth mulling. The popular detective novelist and chronicler of crime fiction Julian Symons contributed his offering to the shelf of Poe biographies in *The Tell-Tale Heart: The Life and Works of Edgar Allan Poe* (1978). Symons is on far more solid ground in his critique of Poe's works than he is in biographical matters. As an example of his weaknesses in depicting Poe's life, one may cite Symons's relying on Dr. John J. Moran's report of Poe's last days and death. Just because Moran was the attending physician does not make for reliability in his several increasingly romanticized-sensationalized versions of Poe's demise.[7] Ironically, then, the British biographical approach to Poe has come full circle from the earliest assays of such materials, with Ingram's determined effort, however successful, to revise the widespread colorful and sensational "legend" into factual, plausible proportions.

Perhaps because of Ingram's labors on Poe's behalf, and doubtless because the average reader's mind often found pleasing what the literary critic played down, Poe's work enjoyed a renaissance in Great Britain during the 1890s and on through 1909, the centenary of his birth. In the earlier period such interest was evident in the wealth of publications that either contained one or more pieces by Poe or included what an anthologist considered to be representative samples of his writings. The second type of book often spurred debate in the press. An additional impetus to Poe's popularity among the British at the time arose from admiration of his work by the cultural outlook that created ferment because it repeatedly fixed its attention on figures who had not enjoyed universal status as darlings of the critical establishment, and, as we have seen, Poe certainly was one of those figures. Beardsley was not the sole illustrator of Poe during this era, and British reviewers (as well as others) repeatedly mentioned the image of Poe or of his literary inclinations that was conjured by graphic arts accompaniments to his texts. The author who for many was the arch-Decadent poet of the 1890s, Ernest Dowson, claimed that the line from "The City in the Sea" — "The viol, the violet, and the vine" — was his favorite passage of poetry in English, and Dowson thus typified late Victorian lovers of Poe's "music." Other poets' works, and not only those who first published during the 1890s, also brought forth comparison with those of Poe.

The figure of Poe that had shadowed British mystery-detective fiction from the days of Dickens and Wilkie Collins resurfaced with verve at the close of the nineteenth century. The comparisons of the stories of Arthur Conan Doyle, for one — who soared to immense popularity on the wings of Sherlock Holmes — with Poe's Dupin tales mounted to legion numbers, and the earliest fiction of M. P. Shiel, *Prince Zaleski* (1895) and *Shapes in the Fire* (1896), invited repeated invocations of Poe as his inspiration, as did much of his subsequent fiction. The horrors that revolted many, but intrigued others, in Arthur Machen's *The Great God Pan* (1894) and *The Three Impostors* (1895) were often cast as examples of Poe redivivus. All of these books were titles in John Lane's well-known Keynotes Series of experimental fiction. Other stories of far more bleakly realistic dimensions in that series often contained allusions to the Poesque, for example, Caldwell Lipsett's "A Nightmare Climb" in *Where the Atlantic Meets the Land* (1896) and "Sir Julian Garve," a tale by Ella D'Arcy published in April 1897, in which snatches of "Annabel Lee" are quoted by a man strolling the beach just before he is murdered. The science-fantasy fiction of H. G. Wells and the adventure novels of H. Rider Haggard also called up remembrances of Poe's horrific adventure tales. Many detected a Poesque impact upon Bram Stoker's eerie novel of vampirism, *Dracula* (1897). William Butler Yeats knew, but did not particularly admire, Poe's works. There is no doubt, however, that Poe's outreach was great.

Poe's renown in Great Britain throughout the nineteenth century is epitomized in a remark by another writer who came into prominence during the 1890s, Vincent O'Sullivan, who wrote in the preface to *The Raven and The Pit and the Pendulum* (1899), one of those lavishly got-up editions of Poe's works that were thoroughly in the mainstream of the 1890s art of miniaturization: "But the truth is that he had a very real and even international fame for some years before his death: not a fame like that which is come to him since, a fame so great that if you mention writers of English in any country of Europe, the name certain to be recognized after Shakespeare's and perhaps

Byron's, is the name of Poe — no, not such a fame, but vivid and stirring for all that." The subsequent, authoritative, academic opinion from Clarence Gohdes that almost every later nineteenth-century writer of the macabre owed debts to Poe bolsters O'Sullivan's claim and should otherwise not be disregarded in matters of Poe's fame.[8]

In the twentieth century Poe's reputation and achievements have not been treated with the fanfare they received earlier in Great Britain. A flurry of interest in 1909 included critical appreciations by Walter De la Mare, whose later tale "A Revenant" features the shade of Poe as a character; Norman Douglas, whose several evaluations credited Poe with excellent artistic ability, which had often been overshadowed by ill-informed, prejudiced biographical emphases; and George Bernard Shaw, who praised Poe's art and noted that his very artistic bent occasioned low esteem for him among Americans but stimulated British championing of his causes. D. H. Lawrence's *English Review* (1919) critique, revised and reprinted in *Studies in Classic American Literature* (1923), placed Poe's tales as science rather than art because of their efficient dissectings of warped human minds. Nonetheless, Lawrence's study provoked renewed examinations of the Poe canon. Far less sympathetic readings of Poe came from Laura Riding and Aldous Huxley in the decade after Lawrence. In 1949 T. S. Eliot viewed Poe as a seemingly displaced European, thus, in Eliot's opinion, accounting for his vogue within French cultural circles.

More recent British work on Poe has taken the form of anthologizing and reception studies, although interesting allusions may be found in the detective fiction of such British mystery writers as Agatha Christie and P. D. James, not to mention many others of lesser renown. W. H. Auden's introduction to the Rinehart edition of Poe (1950) highlighted the importance of *Pym* and *Eureka* for serious study of Poe's thought and accomplishments. The several anthologies of Poe's writings and *Pym* brought out by Penguin, which have appeared since the mid-1970s, offer terse overviews of Poe's life and art, along with explanatory and textual notes of varying quality. J. R. Hammond's *An Edgar Allan Poe Companion* (1981) promises far more than is delivered in the way of assisting an understanding of its subject. Ian Walker's volume in the Critical Heritage Series published by Routledge (1986) brings together in handy form many contemporaneous reviews that would otherwise be difficult to find. Graham Clarke's four-volume gathering of similar materials in the Critical Assessments Series (1991), a spectrum of materials from early reviews through recent critical opinions, must be used cautiously because, unfortunately, it is riddled with errors.

Poe's writings have attracted increasingly serious and respectful attention from some of the greatest names in British literary culture — poets, fictionists, and critics alike. Choices for the earliest piratings from Poe, "The Fall of the House of Usher" and "The Visionary" ("The Assignation"), selected presumably because Harrison Ainsworth, editor of *Bentley's Miscellany* in 1840, found them Poe's most accomplished tales, may now be seen as indeed prophetic. The former quickly found perceptive interpreters who have proliferated exciting critiques of the tale and its author, and the latter has more recently been accorded an ever higher artistic status in the Poe canon. Issues of realism and hoax in *Pym*, raised when it was new, also continue to tease critics. Poe's work in all forms, we can readily see, elicited varied responses, and many British writers have honored him by adapting his productions to their own uses and by acclaiming his abilities as a critic; such honoring gained impetus during the 1890s on into the midpoint of the twentieth century. Poe's biography has also occupied many writers in Great Britain, where Ingram made the first extensive bid for being an objective biographer. Currently, revised selective editions of Poe's writings for Dent's Everyman Library indicate that his popularity may be on the upswing among the British.

NOTES

1. The quotation appears in the *Naval and Military Gazette and East India and Colonial Chronicle*, October 20, 1838, p. 677. Poe and Defoe are bracketed in reviews of *Pym* in the London *Torch*, October 13, 1838, pp. 383–385; *Spectator*, October 27, 1838, p. 1023; *New Monthly Magazine* (November 1838): 428. See also Dudley R. Hutcherson, "Poe's Reputation in England and America, 1850–1909," *American Literature* 14 (1942): 211–233; Francis B. Dedmond, "A Check-List of Edgar Allan Poe's Works in Book Form Published in the British Isles," *Bulletin of Bibliography* 21 (1953): 16–20; Benjamin F. Fisher, "Poe in the 1890s: Bibliographical Gleanings," *American Renaissance Literary Report: An Annual* 8 (1994): 142–168.

2. Materials on the Christmas story appear in Benjamin F. Fisher, *The Gothic's Gothic: Study Aids to the Tradition of the Tale of Terror* (New York and London: Garland, 1988); see especially p. 440.

3. *Memoirs and Correspondence of Coventry Patmore*, ed. Basil Champneys (London: Bell, 1900), vol. 1, p. 39.

4. See *Collected Works of Edgar Allan Poe*, ed. Thomas Ollive Mabbott (Cambridge: Harvard UP, 1968), vol. 1, pp. 356–357; Barbara Melchori, "The Tapestry Horse: 'Childe Roland' and 'Metzengerstein,'" *English Miscellany* 14 (1963): 185–193.

5. Poe-Tennyson links are cited (and sometimes discredited) in *Collected Works*, pp. 213, 314, 338, 356–357, 394, 420, 488; Gerhard J. Joseph, "Poe and Tennyson," *PMLA*

88 (1973): 418–428; Benjamin F. Fisher, "'Eleonora': Poe and Madness," in *Poe in His Times: The Artist and His Milieu* (Baltimore: Edgar Allan Poe Society, 1990), pp. 187–188. See also *James Clarence Mangan: His Selected Poems*, ed. Louise Imogen Guiney (New York: Lamson, Wolfe; London: John Lane, 1897), pp. 100–111.

6. Paull F. Baum, "Introduction," in *The Blessed Damozel: The Unpublished Manuscript Texts and Collation* (Chapel Hill: U of North Carolina P, 1937), pp. xxx–xxxi; Virginia Surtees, *The Paintings and Drawings of Dante Gabriel Rossetti: A Catalogue Raisonné* (Oxford: Oxford UP, 1971), vol. 1, pp. 4, 6; A. I. Grieve, "Rossetti's Illustrations to Poe," *Apollo* (February 1973): 142–145. Poe's impact on Rossetti's verse is also assessed by Thomas Ollive Mabbott, "Echoes of Poe in Rossetti's 'Beryl Song,'" *N & Q* 168 (1935): 77 ["Annabel Lee" and "To One in Paradise"]; J. P. Runden, "Rossetti and a Poe Image," *N & Q* 203 (1958): 257–258 ["To Helen" (1831) and Rossetti's "The Portrait"].

7. See W. T. Bandy's definitive study of Moran's untrustworthiness in "Dr. Moran and the Poe-Reynolds Myth," in *Myths and Realities: The Mysterious Mr. Poe*, ed. Benjamin F. Fisher (Baltimore: Edgar Allan Poe Society, 1987), pp. 26–36.

8. *The Raven and the Pit and the Pendulum. Seven Illustrations and a Cover Design by W. T. Horton and Some Account of the Author by Vincent O'Sullivan* (London: Leonard Smithers, 1899), p. xix; Clarence Gohdes, "The Reputation of Some Nineteenth Century American Authors in Europe," in *The American Writer and the European Literary Tradition*, ed. Margaret Denny and William H. Gilman (Minneapolis: U of Minnesota P, 1950), p. 120.

# Poe in Italy

MASSIMO BACIGALUPO

Edgar Allan Poe has had a remarkable influence on Italian literature, second to no other American writer. While Whitman, Melville, Hemingway, Pound, and Eliot have also had many followers, their influence is more limited in time and scope. Poe is just as present today as he was a hundred years ago.

Since Italian writers and critics have always been very interested in French literature, Baudelaire's and Mallarmé's admiration for Poe was readily picked up in Italy. As in France, Poe has always been defended by Italian writers against the strictures of American and British critics. Despite this original debt to France, major and minor Italian writers have made independent use of Poe's example, and the critical debate surrounding Poe's theories has been outstanding.

The first (anonymous) translation of Poe was *Storie orribili* [Tales of horror] (1858), followed by *Storie incredibili* [Tales of the incredible] (1863), equally anonymous, which included "The Murders in the Rue Morgue" and "The Oval Portrait." The first substantial collection (twelve stories) was *Storie incredibili* (1869), translated by Baccio Emanuele Manieri, who added an introductory essay citing Baudelaire's translation, from which he worked. Criticism began in 1870 with a ten-page "profile" of Poe by Eugenio Camerini in *Profili letterari* [Literary profiles]. On June 24, 1876, in Naples, Federico Persico gave a lecture on "Edgardo Poe" and his poetry, which, he said, was unjustly neglected in Italy. According to Ada Giaccari's indispensable survey in 1959, Persico, "the first known Italian critic of Poe, pointed out two essential characteristics of the American's work — anguish and hallucination."[1] "The Raven" was first published in Italian in 1881 in Scipione Salvotti's book *Da tenebra luce!* [From darkness light]. Unlike all subsequent translators, Salvotti was able to duplicate exactly the obsessive rhyme scheme of the original. An expanded and somewhat padded version of "The Raven" by Guido Menasci appeared in the periodical *Vita Nuova* [New life] in 1890 (using octaves for Poe's sextets). The first satisfactory translation of "The Raven" and other poems, by Ernesto

Ragazzoni, is found in the volume *Edgar Allan Poe: La vita e le opere* [Edgar Allan Poe: Life and works], edited by Ragazzoni and Federico Garrone (1896). This collection included "The Philosophy of Composition," "The Philosophy of Furniture," and a few unusual stories such as "A Tale of Jerusalem," "Mystification," "A Predicament," and "X-ing a Paragrab." Ragazzoni's translations of the poems, reprinted and expanded in *Poesie* (1927, 1956), have been widely admired. Gabriele Baldini, writing in the newspaper *Corriere della Sera* (February 22, 1968), calls Ragazzoni "the only admirable Italian translator" of the poems. By 1986 there were twenty-two translations of "The Raven." In a comparative study of these numerous renditions, Silvia Campanini finds that Mario Praz's version (1921) "best conveys the character of the original."[2]

Giaccari's research shows that the first translation of *The Narrative of Arthur Gordon Pym* appeared anonymously in 1900, followed in 1934 by an "unabridged translation" by Mario Benzi. *Eureka* was translated by Maria Pastore Mucchi in 1902. Leone Levi Bianchini's article on this work, "considered from the energetic point of view," appeared in a 1904 Festschrift. Publishing and critical interest in Poe were already high by the end of the century.

Poe himself appears to have confronted one of the chief monuments of Italian Romantic literature, Alessandro Manzoni's *I promessi sposi*, translated in 1834 by G. W. Featherstonhaugh as *The Betrothed Lovers* and reviewed anonymously in the *Southern Literary Messenger* for May 1835. Though attributed to Poe in J. A. Harrison's edition (*Complete Works* 8: 12), the review was re-attributed to Beverley Tucker by David K. Jackson (1936) and others.[3] After pronouncing Manzoni's novel "original" and criticizing the translation as "Italian, in English words," the reviewer praised the novel for Manzoni's depiction of the Milan plague and quoted a moving scene of a mother relinquishing the body of her dead daughter. It has been suggested that Poe was indebted to *The Betrothed Lovers* in his stories of the plague, "King Pest" and "The Masque of the Red Death." This connection between Poe and an Italian classic was noted in 1923 by one of Poe's most authoritative Italian champions, Emilio Cecchi, and has been debated at length by later scholars.[4]

Traces of Poe have been detected in Ippolito Nievo's massive novel *Confessioni di un Italiano* [Confessions of an Italian], posthumously published in 1867, which with *The Betrothed Lovers* is a contender for the title of the Great Italian Nineteenth-Century Novel. In Nievo, a notable humorous-dramatic writer, we find such Gothic elements as the obsession with the abyss, the cemetery, the maelstrom, life after burial — but it is not certain that he knew Poe. The American was well known, however, among writers in the group known as the Scapigliatura [disheveled], who were Bohemian poets and story-tellers active in Milan and Turin from 1860 to 1870. Iginio Tarchetti published a collection of *Racconti fantastici* [Fantastic tales] (1869), among many other books, taking his example from Poe. According to Roberto Cagliero, his story "Re per ventiquattrore" [King for twenty-four hours] in *Racconti umoristici* [Humorous tales] (1869) is Pym-derived.[5] Poet Emilio Praga, another Scapigliatura exponent, shows the influence of Poe in his best collection, *Penombre* [Penumbras] (1864).

Two of the best-known poets at the turn of the twentieth century have important affiliations with Poe. Giovanni Pascoli, a brilliant technician and Symbolist, did a brief imitation of "The Raven," probably in 1876 (four verses). It was first published posthumously in 1912 and reprinted in *Nuova Antologia* (October 1956). Pascoli's atmospheres and evocations of flowers opening at dusk and falling stars are often reminiscent of Poe. As early as 1899, the critic Corrado Zacchetti suggested that Pascoli's poem "Alba festiva" [Festive dawn] (1893) was indebted to "The Bells." Pascoli denied the influence, and Zacchetti returned to the subject in a 1921 article for *La Critica* (1921). "Alba festiva" is surely original, but the echo of Poe is still noted as a matter of course by commentators. The other major figure of this period, Gabriele D'Annunzio, was a confirmed borrower but got his Poe through Pater, Swinburne, Wilde, and, of course, Baudelaire. His novels *Il piacere* [*The Child of Pleasure*] (1889) and *L'innocente* [*The Intruder*] (1892) have lush interiors and Usher-like protagonists.

Poe is invariably present in the writers of the Decadent period of the fin de siècle. Arturo Graf, a minor but interesting poet, published a collection, *Medusa* (1890), with titles like "Pallida Mors," "Corvo" ["Raven"], "Teschio" ["Skull"], "Fantasmi" ["Ghosts"], and "Planctus Mundi." The Neapolitan poet Francesco Gaeta, author of *Sonetti voluttuosi* [Voluptuous sonnets] (1906), wrote in a review of 1905 that "the supreme reality of Edgar Poe is . . . his artistic genius" and that the concept of insanity was irrelevant.[6] An epigone of D'Annunzio, Enrico Annibale Butti, followed closely "The Fall of the House of Usher" in *Il castello del sogno* [The dream castle] (1910), a verse-play for reading rather than performance. Butti does not hesitate to provide Poe's catastrophic tale with a happy ending: Ebe (an art-nouveau Madeline) is resurrected permanently and escapes from her brother's haunted castle with the help of the gallant Guest.[7] Among novelists, Grazia Deledda from Sardinia took example from Poe in her early and more symbolic writing. Her Sicilian contemporary Luigi Capuana wrote *Un caso di sonnambulismo* [A case of sleepwalking] (1873) and "never abandoned his favorite writers — Stoker, Poe, Lombroso, Maupassant."[8] Cesare Lombroso, an influential criminal psychologist, studied Poe-related subjects in his book *Genio e follia* [Genius and madness] (1864). Finally, the Catholic novelist Antonio Fogazzaro was surely influenced by Poe in his first novel, *Malombra* (1881), one of his best. In his library he had copies of Poe's *Poems* (1875), given to him by a "Lady Ligeia" in 1880, and Baudelaire's translations, including *Eureka* (1871). In Fogazzaro's novel, Marina di Malombra believes that she is the reincarnation of an ancestress, Cecilia, whose last letter she has found in a drawer; she loses her mind and kills Corrado, a young writer who is supposed to reincarnate Cecilia's former lover. The critic Piero Nardi remarked that "tumultuous passions, mystical transports, fabulous atmosphere give this mediumistic novel its character."[9] The parallels with "Ligeia" are inescapable.

The beginning of the twentieth century did not bring to an end the influence of the American master of Decadence. Both revolutionaries and counter-revolutionaries, Fascists and Communists, delighted in Poe's work. The prime mover in Italian philosophy and criticism, Benedetto Croce, was a firm admirer, though not given to Decadent enthusiasms. He developed a definition of art as intuitive truth and counted Poe, along with such thinkers as Vico, Leibniz, Baumgarten, and De Sanctis, among his precursors. When his *Estetica* [Aesthetics] appeared in 1902 (English edition, 1909), he was pleased, he said, that English and American commentators compared it to Poe's philosophy, "because this comparison spoke to my mind and heart."[10] In a 1947 article, Croce discussed a translation of Poe's three principal essays on poetry, *Tre saggi* [Three essays] (1946), edited by Elio Chinol: "I have always considered Poe one of the rare minds who deeply understood the nature of poetry, even if today his logic exposition of his doctrine appears insufficient."[11] He goes on to defend and develop some of Poe's best-known dicta, like the one on the necessary brevity of a true poem, connecting this with his own distinction between "poetry" and "structure" (the plot and theology of *Paradise Lost* as against its poetic substance). This distinction, Croce claims, "has so little to do with material brevity or length that one can find it in a so-called epic or novel or tragedy or comedy, as well as in a canzone, sonnet or madrigal."[12] In his article Croce dismisses Yvor Winters's notorious attack on Poe: "Winters is still happy . . . with the 'content' of art as moral concept and with beauty as a 'manner' or 'form' that dresses the content, that is with the theory of rhetoric and literature, which is not the theory of poetry; and with this old and extraneous theory he attempts to defeat the genius of Poe, who with great inspiration was working in the new direction."[13] Winters's disregard of the merits of Poe's theory also makes him untrustworthy, Croce concludes, as a judge of Poe's tales and verses.

Croce was a dominant figure in Italian letters at the beginning of the twentieth century. Giuseppe Antonio Borgese, a Sicilian follower, important both as novelist and critic, compared Poe in 1913 to his near contemporary Giacomo Leopardi (1798–1837) and dwelled on Poe's musical technique.[14] Borgese's article reviews Federico Olivero's edition of Poe's *Le poesie*, published in 1912 by Laterza of Bari, Croce's own publisher. In 1932 Olivero brought out *Edgar Allan Poe*, the first Italian book wholly on Poe. A new edition in English was published in 1939 and reprinted in Italian by the same publishers in 1940. Croce was one of the mentors of the Florentine weekly *La Voce* [The voice] (1908–1916), which brought Poe and Whitman back to public notice. One of the early editors, cantankerous Giovanni Papini, wrote admiringly of Poe in *Testimonianze: saggi non critici* [Reports: Noncritical essays] (1918).

Another traditional writer who took his bearings from Croce was Emilio Cecchi, one of the century's most notable essayists. He developed a form of highly wrought vignette in prose, dealing with bizarre phenomena, notable people, travel scenes, and animals — a form partly indebted to Poe. In a polemic account of his travels in the United States, *America amara* [Bitter America] (1940), Cecchi recounts a visit to Poe's tomb in Baltimore, one of the few literary episodes of the book. The neglect of the grave and the fact that no one seemed to know where it was are presented as typical of the "bitterness" of America — a country that does not want to listen to Poe's prophecy of doom. "This terrible dead man," Cecchi writes, "has not yet finished dying."[15]

Cecchi continued to find inspiration in Poe and to come to his defense against his American detractors after the Second World War in four articles collected in *Scrittori inglesi e americani* [English and American writers]. In 1945 he noted happily that "despite these horrible times of ours, the centenary of 'The Raven' has not passed wholly unnoticed."[16] He spoke of a commemorative edition of the English text of "The Raven," with Mallarmé's translation, two drawings by Edouard Manet, and an "interpretation" by Ettore Serra (1945). Poe's most famous poem represented "a contribution by the creative faculty of America to the life of the mind of old and glorious Europe."[17]

One notices that with the dawning of the postwar era, Cecchi becomes a little more hopeful and considers Poe a forerunner of the Marshall Plan. In 1948 Cecchi reviewed Gabriele Baldini's guarded book, *Edgar A. Poe* (1947), the second full Italian study of Poe, and his annotated edition of Mallarmé's translations, with English and French text (1947). Assessing the younger critic's work, Cecchi complained that Baldini was unjust to Poe in the condescending tone of his biographical chapter and in dismissing *Pym* as a failure. He pointed out that Poe's "novel of adventure à la Jules Verne" has "a symphonic finale

worthy of the best of Wagner." [18] Cecchi defended Poe again in a 1950 centenary article, in which he speaks of another collection edited by Baldini, *Poe*
(1949), and records his disagreement with F. O. Matthiessen's statement (in
*American Renaissance*) that Poe is more important for his influence than for
his work. In 1954 Cecchi praised the first collected Italian edition of Poe, *Tutti
i racconti e le poesie* [Complete tales and poems] (1953), edited by Carlo Izzo.
Cecchi saw a problem in presenting Poe's minor pieces to a foreign audience
but compared these infelicities to Shakespeare's buffooneries. "In the modern
world," he concluded, "Poe is one of the truest literary heroes. In no place as
in his art can you find the first terrible intimations of what we are beginning
to call the Atomic Age." [19] Cecchi is the Italian writer who has been most
faithful to Poe. He was a conservative, which makes his disagreement with
Matthiessen's populist reading of American literature hardly surprising.

Poe looms nearly as large in the work of Cecchi's junior, Mario Praz, one
of the most influential literary scholars of the twentieth century. The work that
established his reputation, *La carne, la morte e il diavolo nella letteratura ro-
mantica* [The Romantic Agony] (1930; English edition, 1933), is an incursion
into Decadence in which Poe is often mentioned though not studied in detail.
In *Il patto col serpente* [The pact with the serpent], published in 1972 as a
postscript to the earlier volume, Praz included a long essay, "E. A. Poe, genio
d'esportazione" [E. A. Poe, genius for export]. Here he limited the importance
of Poe, a "minor artist" and an example of an international group of writers
who are viewed as geniuses abroad but deprecated at home. Praz was a better
interpreter of Poe when working creatively in Poe's own tradition, as in the
moving piece "Disse il Corvo: Mai Più" [Quoth the raven: Nevermore] (1945),
collected in *Lettrice notturna* [Woman reading at night] (1952). Praz says that
he refused a request from a newspaper to write on the centenary of "The
Raven," only to hear the word "nevermore" reverberate as he thought of all
the beautiful European things that the war had destroyed forever. In 1952 Praz
paid homage to Poe's grave in his essay "Red Baltimore," recalling Cecchi's
fearful illumination; the visit to the tomb of this "terrible dead man" is in the
process of becoming inevitable for Italian literary travelers, who are not particularly enthusiastic about American progress. Praz is also the author of the
excellent entry on Poe in *Enciclopedia Italiana* (1935). A collector and art historian, he pursued his Poesque interest in furniture and tapestries in *La filo-
sofia dell'arredamento* (1945), which takes its title from Poe's "Philosophy of
Furniture"; in *Mnemosyne: The Parallel between Literature and the Visual Arts*
(1970); and in his masterpiece, *La casa della vita* [*The House of Life*] (1958;
English edition, 1964), which is an autobiography in the form of a visit to his

private collection — an extraordinary, morbid, and humorous book true to Praz's (and Poe's) genius. Praz was personally surrounded by a sinister aura in which he delighted, in this again claiming descent from the original raven.

A wholly different account of Poe was offered in 1941 by Elio Vittorini, a young novelist from Sicily, in his famous anthology, *Americana*. He translated "Berenice" and the final chapters of *Pym* and commented enthusiastically on Poe, Hawthorne, and Melville as "masters of blood" who broke away from Europe and delighted in contradiction. Vittorini endorsed D. H. Lawrence's account of Poe's vampirism but was at pains to place it in a favorable light: "The man of the century, disappointed, weak, empty of life, full only of will-power, of perversity, cannot, in Poe's America, the new world, be anything but a vampire. He sucks life and is saved. Poe writes the song, the first or last verses, of his saving delirium. He is more American than we had ever suspected, and leads us by the roads of vampirism to gratuitous sea- and island-adventures, games of the mind that frees itself, to a new being."[20] Vittorini, a writer of the Left who never visited the United States, inaugurates a new reading of American literature as an antidote to the exhaustion of Europe, thus anticipating the postwar mood. But the Fascist censors found his enthusiasm suspect, and the first edition of *Americana* had to be scrapped, then reissued in 1942 minus most of Vittorini's prefaces and with a somber introduction by Cecchi. By then Italy was at war with the United States. Cecchi pointed out, however, that at the beginning of the "new war" everyone in Europe was reading American books, just as they had been reading Russian books in 1914.[21]

The continuing influence of Poe on writers of fiction at this critical juncture of Italian history and culture is also shown by his symbolic presence in a war story by Giorgio Bassani, "Una notte del '43" [A night of '43] (1954). The only witness to the execution of a group of anti-Fascists in Ferrara is an invalid whose window looks down on the square. The narrator imagines that on his bedside table there is a copy of *Pym* "in an edition that showed on the cover the great white phantom with a sickle, towering over the small skiff of the explorer," the volume being placed so that the cover is not visible. "It was enough to turn the book around: the white phantom, though still present, still there, didn't scare you any more!"[22] Poe's book becomes an element in a Poe-like setting, ironically commenting on the tragic events the story recounts.

Besides appealing to Anglophiles like Cecchi and to radical intellectuals like Vittorini, Poe played a decisive role in the genesis of Italian Modernist literature. Filippo Tommaso Marinetti, founder in 1909 and organizer of Futurism, cited him in a 1915 pamphlet, *Guerra sola igiene del mondo* [War — the world's only hygiene], as one of "our glorious intellectual fathers," first in line with

Baudelaire, Mallarmé, and Verlaine. He said that the Futurists now "hated" these "fathers" for their concern with the past, but he concluded with a celebration of the poetic intellect as "the most exalted of all — since those truths which to us were of the most enduring importance could only be reached by that analogy which speaks in proof-tones to the imagination alone" — a quotation from "The Colloquy of Monos and Una."[23] Poe is therefore a founder of Futurism, first among twentieth-century avant-garde movements. Surrealism, which also acknowledged Poe as a master, originated in 1919, and significant traces of Poe are to be found in the writings of Italian Surrealist author-painters, such as Giorgio De Chirico's *Hebdomeros* (1929) and his brother Alberto Savinio's extraordinary fiction *Hermaphrodito* (1918) and *La nostra anima* [Our soul] (1944).

While Marinetti quoted Poe in his 1915 manifesto, young Eugenio Montale wrote in his Genoese diary for March 1917: "The day before yesterday I chatted with Bonzi and we both glorified the great Poe. It is an undeniable truth that P. is the father, with Whitman, of modern poetry; which is to say, of all poetry. From him derive Baudelaire and Rimbaud, those other most notable colossi. Take these away and you don't have Verlaine, Laforgue, Mallarmé, etc. That is, you don't have anything. Poe is the father of *mystery* (right, Maeterlinck?). Without mentioning the aesthetic truths that he first perceived. And his profile as original *thinker*."[24] Montale was to become the most reputed Italian poet of the twentieth century. In 1956 he wrote an appreciation of Ragazzoni's versions of Poe's poems, and in 1957 he insisted that without referring to Poe and Whitman one could not understand "a whole section of Italian poetry, from the best followers of D'Annunzio (e.g., Adolfo De Bosis) to early Futurism and Dino Campana."[25] The latter was Poe-like in his destiny of a wanderer who died insane. His main collection, *Canti orfici* [Orphic chants] (1914), has many Poesque evocations in prose and poetry of cities, people, and landscapes.

Montale's poetry also presents several sinister interiors, evident in his poem "Gli orecchini" [ "The Earrings" ], and incorporeal dialogues, and it dwells on psychological oddities, as in the famous poetic "Motet" of the "two jackals on a leash."[26] Montale provided humorous explications of this poem and a few others in the tradition of Poe's "The Philosophy of Composition." He is indebted to Poe as a proponent of "pure poetry," an ideal he, too, attempted to follow. Montale also tried his hand successfully at small prose tales in which the bizarre and the uncanny are playfully evoked. These poet's tales, collected in *Farfalla di Dinard* [Butterfly of Dinard] (1960), are Poe-like in concentration and suggestiveness, though they present a much more amiable and relaxed account of human life. Another major poet of the first half of the twentieth century, Giuseppe Ungaretti, developed a Futuristic form of intense poems of only a few words to portray his experience of war and homelessness, thus picking up Poe's poetics and the less bourgeois elements of his persona.

Poe remained essential to the different versions of Modernism that flourished in Italy. In prose, Carlo Emilio Gadda's *Quer pasticciaccio brutto de Via Merulana* [*That Awful Mess of Via Merulana*] (1957), perhaps the most significant and dazzling novel of the century, centers on a sexual murder and an inspector's fruitless attempt to solve the case, thus recalling "The Murders in the Rue Morgue" even in its title. (Via Merulana is a long street in a popular Rome neighborhood.) A later novelist, Giorgio Manganelli, a follower of Gadda, wrote stories that are Poe-like fantasies. In "Un Re" [A king] from *Agli dei ulteriori* [To the ulterior gods] (1972), a mysterious being believes he controls everything but "is gradually defeated by a futile sound, harmonica or ocarina, whistle of reed, 'breath between perforated teeth.' . . . A tale à la Poe, with some elegant Kafkaism, becomes a diabolic and amusing transposition of our ritual daily fantasies." [27]

Manganelli also produced a fine translation of all of Poe's tales in 1983, doing for Italy what Baudelaire had done for France over a century earlier. With the two authoritative translations of *Pym* by Gabriele Baldini (1943, 1958) and Elio Vittorini (1941–1950), these are the best available attempts at giving us an Italian Poe. Manganelli followed Mabbott's 1978 Harvard edition; in his translator's afterword, he writes that "to live more than a year, daily, like man and wife, with Poe, is a wonderful and strenuous experience — a perfect honeymoon ending in uxoricide." Manganelli found Poe "much more varied than we usually think, now subtle, now aggressive, placid, or mercurial. His moving force is 'bad taste' mixed with abstraction and extravagance to produce unbelievable and unsurpassable results." [28]

Other sophisticated writers of fantasy influenced by Poe are Italo Calvino, who delighted in abstract "domains" (*Le città invisibili* [Invisible Cities], 1972) and psychological puzzles (*Palomar*, 1983). Umberto Eco's popular novels, *Il nome della rosa* [*The Name of the Rose*] (1981) and *Foucault's Pendulum* (1989), both refer to Poesque themes and genres (detection, mysticism, horror).[29] With Calvino, Poe's influence is partly mediated by Borges. In fact, Italian readers and writers are by this time equally sensitive to the original Poe and his American and English critics (Allen Tate's persnickety definition, "Our Cousin, Mr. Poe," is often quoted) and to his reputation abroad, as with Borges or Freud (whose theory of the uncanny has been enormously influential). French influence is also still strong, and "The Purloined Letter" became, after Lacan's and Derrida's commentaries, one of the more often quoted of Poe's stories. The handful of books on Poe that have appeared since Baldini's volume and the many essays in collections and journals also steer a course between American New Criticism, Formalism, Freudianism, Structuralism, and Deconstruction.

Besides such international best-sellers as Calvino and Eco, many other Italian writers can be linked to Poe. Italian fiction is often lyrical and surrealist, tragic and ironic — a picture of a mind revolving its thoughts rather than a social panorama. Thus Poe remains a constant inspiration. In Spagnoletti's history of twentieth-century literature, Poe is mentioned in connection with Anna Maria Ortese's strange novelette *L'Iguana* (1965); the early work of Dino Buzzati, a writer well worth exploring; and the poet Giorgio Caproni and his "Stanze della funicolare" [Stanzas of the funicular] (1952), where every stanza finishes with the obsessive refrain "alt."[30] One should also mention writers of serious fiction who constantly played with the thriller genre, like the Sicilian Leonardo Sciascia and the Turinese Mario Soldati. Soldati is masterful in "La giacca verde" [The green jacket] (1950), a story of a sort of doppelgänger, and "La finestra" [The window], a tale of the narrator's girlfriend's disappearance into the London cityscape. Another major writer of nocturnal semiautobiographical fiction is Tommaso Landolfi, who created a sort of raven-haunted existentialist persona in books like *Rien Va* [Nothing goes] (1963).

Among authors of fiction who established themselves in the 1980s is Francesca Duranti. Her *La casa sul lago della luna* [The House on Moon Lake] (1984) has an inescapably Poesque plot, with a magic portrait and a final surrender by the hero to a woman-vampire. Antonio Tabucchi, a follower of Borges, writes highly literate novelettes in which mysterious characters pursue mysterious traces in exotic settings, as can be seen in *Notturno indiano* [Indian Nocturne] (1984). A more youthful writer, Stefano Benni, places Poe among the patrons depicted on the cover of his *Il bar sotto il mare* [The bar under the sea] (1987) and has him narrate one of the tales in the book. Paola Capriolo, a practitioner of claustrophobic Gothic themes, proclaims herself a daughter of Poe in the title story of her collection *La grande Eulalia* [The great Eulalie] (1988).

More than a century after Luigi Capuana and Antonio Fogazzaro, Poe remains an essential ingredient in Italian fiction. In conclusion let me mention Giuseppe Tomasi di Lampedusa, a Sicilian prince and author of *Il gattopardo* [The Leopard] (1958). He speaks of Poe in passing in the lessons on English literature that he privately prepared for his friends, comparing *Pym* to Coleridge's "The Rime of the Ancient Mariner" for their common subject, their "extraordinary delicacy of tone and the transformation of the horrible adventures in a deep spiritual conflict." The relation of these works to other tales of fantasy, he says, "is like that of *The Brothers Karamazov* to a common thriller."[31] Tomasi is also the author of a lovely posthumously published story with the suggestive title "Lighea" — a tale of a young Sicilian classical scholar who is made love to by a siren, Lighea, and is finally claimed by her, many years later, in old age. Why Tomasi should have given his sensual siren a Poesque name is uncertain, but it is probably an homage to a master of fantasy who was both aristocratic and sensitive to the concerns of the majority, both intellectual and sensual, like his Sicilian admirer.

Poe's appeal has always been to readers of all classes and ages. If he made a conquest of Prince Tomasi (who confessed that he feared to read Poe in his lonely apartment), he was equally spellbinding for a barely literate Neapolitan schoolgirl. In her novel *Alonso e i visionari* [Alonso and the visionaries] (1996), Anna Maria Ortese writes suggestively of the remains of a character being returned "to Old America, to Boston, land of Exiles — I am chiefly thinking of one Poet, and of his fidelity to the invisible."[32] Asked about the allusion, she confirmed that the reference is to Poe and remarked: "Poe was the first great writer I read as a girl. I found a collection of his stories on a bookstall. I had no education but I immediately sensed the infinite power of this poet. He became a constant inspiration. To me, he encapsulates all the violence and elevation of the American myth."[33]

I wish to acknowledge the help of Michel David, formerly of the University of Grenoble, in the preparation of this chapter.

NOTES

1. Ada Giaccari, "La fortuna di E. A. Poe in Italia: Nota bibliografica," *Studi Americani* 5 (1959): 107. All translations of Italian quotations are mine.

2. Silvia Campanini, *La traduzione poetica dall'inglese in italiano: "Quoth the Raven: 'Nevermore,'"* Università degli Studi di Trieste: Traduzione, società e cultura, No. 1 (Udine: Campanotto, 1991), p. 80. Besides reprinting all previous translations, Campanini offers three new renderings of her own to illustrate different approaches to meter and rhyme.

3. See Robert D. Jacobs, *Poe: Journalist and Critic* (Baton Rouge: Louisiana State UP, 1969), p. 69, n. 14.

4. See Cortell King Holsapple, "'The Masque of the Red Death' and *I Promessi*

*Sposi*," *University of Texas Studies in English*, No. 18 (1938): 137–139; Giuseppe Lombardo, "Edgar Allan Poe e la prima traduzione americana dei *Promessi sposi*," *Nuovi Annali della Facoltà di Magistero dell'Università di Messina*, No. 3 (1985): 451–504; Fredi Chiappelli, *Poe legge Manzoni* (Milan: Coliseum, 1987).

5. Roberto Cagliero, "*Arthur Gordon Pym*'s Influence on Italian Literature," *PSA Newsletter* 15.2 (1987): 8. See also Sergio Rossi, "E. A. Poe e la Scapigliatura lombarda," *Studi Americani* 5 (1959): 119–139.

6. Francesco Gaeta, "Edgar Allan Poe," in *Prose*, ed. Benedetto Croce (Bari: Laterza, 1928), pp. 238–250. Quoted in Giaccari, "La fortuna," p. 109.

7. See Gigi Livio, "Poe e Butti," in *E. A. Poe dal gotico alla fantascienza*, ed. Ruggero Bianchi (Milan: Mursia, 1978), pp. 145–168.

8. Giacinto Spagnoletti, *Storia della letteratura italiana del Novecento* (Rome: Newton Compton, 1994), p. 68.

9. *Dizionario letterario Bompiani delle opere* (Milan: Bompiani, 1960), vol. 4, p. 517. See also Lucienne Portier, "La vaste culture étrangère d'Antonio Fogazzaro," *Atti e Memorie dell'Arcadia*, 3rd Series, 8.2–3 (1983–1985): 30–57.

10. Benedetto Croce, "Intorno ai saggi del Poe sulla poesia," in *Letture di poeti* (Bari: Laterza, 1966), p. 202.

11. Ibid., 197.

12. Ibid., 200.

13. Ibid., 202.

14. Giuseppe Antonio Borgese, "Le poesie di Edgardo Poe," rpt. in *Studi di letterature moderne* (Milan: Treves, 1915), pp. 167–174.

15. Emilio Cecchi, *America amara* (Florence: Sansoni, 1940), p. 221.

16. Emilio Cecchi, *Scrittori inglesi e americani* (Milan: Il Saggiatore, 1964), vol. 1, p. 81.

17. Ibid., p. 82.

18. Ibid., p. 84.

19. Ibid., p. 92.

20. Elio Vittorini, ed., *Americana: raccolta di narratori* (Milan: Bompiani, 1968), p. 44.

21. Elio Vittorini, ed., *Americana: raccolta di narratori dalle origini ai nostri giorni* (Milan: Bompiani, 1943), vol. 9; rpt. in Cecchi, *Scrittori inglesi e americani*, vol. 2, pp. 241–252.

22. Giorgio Bassani, "Una notte del '43," in *Le storie ferraresi* (Turin: Einaudi, 1960), p. 209.

23. Filippo Tommaso Marinetti, *Guerra sola igiene del mondo*; rpt. in *Teoria e invenzione futurista*, ed. Luciano De Maria (Milan: Mondadori, 1968), p. 306.

24. Eugenio Montale, *Quaderno genovese*, ed. Laura Barile (Milan: Mondadori, 1983), p. 35.

25. Eugenio Montale, "Emily," *Corriere della Sera*, May 4, 1957, rpt. in *Sulla poesia*, ed. Giorgio Zampa (Milan: Mondadori, 1976), pp. 494–495.

26. Eugenio Montale, "Due sciacalli al guinzaglio," *Corriere della Sera*, February 16, 1950; rpt. in *Sulla poesia*, pp. 84–87; cf. Eugenio Montale, "The Jackals at Modena," in *Selected Poems* (New York: New Directions, 1965), p. 55.

27. Spagnoletti, *Letteratura italiana*, p. 493.

28. *I racconti*, trans. Giorgio Manganelli (Turin: Einaudi, 1983), pp. 1035–1040.

29. Stefano Tani presents interesting perspectives on Poe, Calvino, and Eco in *The Doomed Detective: The Contribution of the Detective Novel to Postmodern American and Italian Fiction* (Carbondale: Southern Illinois UP, 1984).

30. Spagnoletti, *Letteratura italiana*, p. 493.

31. Giuseppe Tomasi di Lampedusa, *Letteratura inglese*, ed. Nicoletta Polo (Milan: Mondadori, 1991), vol. 2, p. 34.

32. Anna Maria Ortese, *Alonso e i visionari* (Milan: Adelphi, 1996), p. 232.

33. Anna Maria Ortese, Telephone conversation with author, August 13, 1996.

# Poe in Romania

THOMAS C. CARLSON

Because of Romania's Romance language tradition — unique in Eastern Europe — and its long-standing cultural ties with France, Poe came to this Balkan country almost immediately after the French translations of Borghers, Meunier, Baudelaire, and Mallarmé began appearing in the mid–nineteenth century. From the early 1860s, when the first Romanian translations were made, to the present, Poe's reputation has successfully adapted to the frequent and radical changes in the Romanian political and cultural climate. Today in Romania, Poe remains one of the most widely translated American writers of the nineteenth century.

Poe's initial reputation in Romania was based primarily on his work as a poet and theoretician. This emphasis was due in large measure to Titu Maiorescu (1840–1917), poet, teacher, and founder of modern Romanian literary criticism. It was, in fact, Maiorescu who published the first critical appraisal of Poe in Romanian: "O Cercetare Critica asupra Poezi Române de la 1867" [A critical examination of Romanian poetry] (1867).

In the course of praising the American writer as poet and theoretician, Maiorescu offered in detail his own aesthetic principles by means of which a great national literature might be written and evaluated. While in general much in Maiorescu's theories of creativity and aesthetic tenets can be traced to ideas then circulating in the European literary community, particularly from the German philosophers Schopenhauer and Hegel, specific emphases are clearly traceable to two of Poe's essays, "The Poetic Principle" and "The Philosophy of Composition," which Maiorescu knew through Baudelaire's translation, "La Genèse d'un poème" [The genesis of a poem].[1]

Like Poe, Maiorescu was appalled by the milk-and-water prettiness that passed for poetry in his day. Maiorescu insisted that poetry must be more ambitious, that the language of poetry must be purely affective, and that poetry must avoid imitation, sentiment, moralizing, and didacticism in general. Also like Poe, Maiorescu argued at length for unity of artistic effect, for brevity and compression, and even for the use of a carefully modulated refrain as essential ingredients of successful poetry. Poetry succeeds, he maintained, only when it transports the reader — and the poet — to the world of what he called "ideal fiction," a world of pure ideas divorced from temporal and spatial constraints. Such theorizing comes very close to Poe's concepts of "Ideality" and "Supernal Beauty" as defined in "The Poetic Principle."

Because Maiorescu enjoyed in Romanian literary circles a status equivalent to that of Emerson in nineteenth-century America, he was able to transmit quickly to his contemporaries his enthusiasm for the theories and the works of this strange new American poet. By the turn of the twentieth century many Romantic and Symbolist poets — among them the major figures Ion Luca Caragiale (1852–1912), Alexandru Macedonski (1854–1920), and Mihai Eminescu (1850–1889), the future poet laureate — had acknowledged Poe's genius and exhibited in their works traits and motifs tantalizingly similar to Poe's.

In addition to these poets' adoption of Poe's dark strain of lyricism in their own poetry and prose, Caragiale also translated "A Tale of Jerusalem" and "The System of Doctor Tarr and Professor Fether" in 1878 and "The Masque of the Red Death" and "The Cask of Amontillado" in 1898. Macedonski translated "Metzengerstein" in 1887 and supervised his students in the translation of a number of other tales; it is probable, too, that Eminescu translated "Morella" in 1876.

While this generation of Romanian Symbolist writers read and translated primarily from Baudelaire's versions of Poe, the influence of these French translations on their own work is difficult to determine. Like Poe, Eminescu, Caragiale, and Macedonski were well versed in German metaphysics as well as Romantic theory and the western European Gothic tradition. Yet in their poetry, fiction, and, in the case of Caragiale, plays, readers will readily recognize the melancholy tone and dark atmospherics that characterize so much of Poe's poetry and fiction. More specifically, readers will notice a familiar constellation of dramatic motifs and thematic concerns: a fascination with the macabre and the extinction of consciousness; the use of extreme psychological states and oneiric visions; an exploration of metempsychosis, the doppelgänger, and magnetism; claustrophobic enclosure frequently embellished with Gothic and/ or oriental elements; the journey as metaphor for spiritual quest; and the symbolic projection of psychological states onto architecture and landscape.

In Eminescu's oeuvre, the stories that exhibit the greatest affinities with Poe include "Avatarii Faraonului Tla" [The avatars of the Pharaoh Tla] and "Sărmanul Dionus" [Poor Dionus], both haunting, mythic tales of doomed love, doubling, and reincarnation reminiscent in particular of "Ligeia" and "Morella." Two other pieces of prose fiction, "Moartarea lui Ioan Vestimie" [The

death of Ioan Vestimie] and "Geniu Pustiu" [Barren genius], evidence catalepsy, hypnosis, and dream vision motifs similar to those found in "The Fall
of the House of Usher" and "Eleonora." [2]

A number of Caragiale's tales and plays — in particular, the grim two-act
play *Năpasta* [False witness] (1890) and the story "O Făclie de Paște" [An
Easter candle] (1889) — reveal many of these same Poesque motifs.[3] Both
plays are dramatic narrative studies in abnormal psychology, specifically of
horrible brutality committed by a seemingly peaceable figure. And both utilize
Poe's technique of offering plausible pathologies as possible counterweight explanations for behavior that otherwise might only be attributed to supernatural causes or visionary experiences. In the end, it is impossible to say whether
the similarities with Poe represent influences or more general affinities. The
fact remains, however, that both Eminescu and Caragiale knew Poe's work
intimately and translated him. Further, these two Romanian writers developed
a similar range of fictive techniques and themes so consistently and powerfully
that, as with Poe, the authors came to be identified with the myths and pathologies of the characters they had created.

The Romanian cult of Poe — for it amounted to that — was stifled tem-
porarily by World War I but rekindled itself in the turbulent yet culturally rich
interwar decades. A new generation of post-Symbolist poets hailed Poe as a
forerunner of literary Modernism. The poetry of the four major post-Symbolist
poets, Tudor Arghezi (1880–1967), Lucian Blaga (1895–1961), George Bacovia
(1881–1957), and Ion Barbu (1895–1961), shows the clear imprimatur of Poe.
The nature and extent of Poe's influence on this early Modernist experimen-
tation in Romania prompted critic Matei Călinescu to assert that "Poe contributed — to be precise, through the intermediate influence exercised by
Baudelaire, Mallarmé, and, in our century, Paul Valéry — to the crystallization
of a modern concept of poetry in Romanian literature." [4]

In 1931 another poet, Dan Botta (1907–1958), published a collection of
poems entitled *Eulalii* (the title echoing Poe's "Ulalume"), in which he paid
stylistic tribute to the master. The preface to this volume was written by
Ion Barbu, the post-Symbolist most influenced by Poe. Entitled "Veghea lui
Roderick Usher (Parafrază)" [Roderick Usher's vigil (a paraphrase)], the preface was an impressionistic encomium to Poe after the manner of his classic
tale. One critic has called this piece "the most vibrant homage ever given to
Edgar Poe by a Romanian writer." [5]

Poe's fiction also increased in popularity during the interwar period, primarily because of growing Romanian interest in Kafka, Dostoevsky, and Ex-
istentialism and, to a lesser extent, because of Poe's perceived anticipation of

Surrealism. The first two Romanian translations of *The Narrative of Arthur Gordon Pym* appeared in the 1920s, and in 1942 Dan Petraşincu, in the first book-length study of Poe in Romanian, *Edgar Poe, Illuminatul* [The illuminated Edgar Poe], summarized two decades of Poe criticism in his observation that in the American writer's work there exists "a vision and a feeling experienced by all. The American Edgar Poe, almost a hundred years ago in the midst of an age of ostentatious industrialization, sensed a crisis of human spirit which is only now reaching its full climax."[6]

For Romanians, World War II nearly confirmed the apocalyptic vision of Poe. After the war, with the Communist takeover, the arts in Romania were directed into the narrow, polemic channels of Socialist Realism and *Proletcultism*. The arts, that is, were expected to cleave faithfully to Socialist policy, which systematically rejected abstraction and private vision in favor of collective expression championing the new social order. As a result, a large number of Romanian artists were silenced, and many Western writers like Poe were exiled to a literary limbo. For more than ten years, few translations and fewer critical mentions of Poe appeared in the country.

Then, beginning in the late 1950s, Romania embarked on a dangerous but carefully calculated resistance to Soviet centralized planning for Eastern Europe. It was during this period of measured de-Stalinization, which would last almost ten years, that the country experienced the beginning of yet another rich period of literary activity. Tudor Arghezi, Lucian Blaga, and other prewar writers were "rediscovered," while a group of young, intensely personal lyrical poets — among them Nicolae Labiş (1935–1956), Nichita Stănescu (1933–1983), Cezar Baltag (b. 1939), and Grigore Hagiu (1933–1985) — began to enjoy wider currency.

Even some nineteenth-century writers previously disgraced for their aesthetic theories and political involvements found themselves rehabilitated. Chief among these was Titu Maiorescu. As Dennis Deletant has observed, Maiorescu "was an advocate of art for art's sake and a repudiator of the social role of art, and his readmittance into the public arena marked the abandonment by the Party of Socialist Realism as its aesthetic creed."[7]

Evidence that the cultural thaw extended to certain foreign writers came in two essays published in 1958 by eminent Romanian critics. Alexandru Philippide's "Introducere în Poezia lui Edgar Poe" [Introduction to the poetry of Edgar Poe] offered a review of French critical response and an eclectic reading of selected poems. Mihnea Gheorghiu's essay "Edgar Poe, Calomniatul" [Edgar Poe, maligned] reflects the lingering effects of the previous decade in its argument that Poe's was a literature of crisis corresponding to the nineteenth-century crisis caused by Western capitalist theory. But a start had been made.

Symbolically, Poe's full rehabilitation was signaled in 1963 with the publication of *Edgar Allan Poe: Scrieri Alese* [Selected writings], which included a large sampling of Poe's prose and poetry, much of it newly edited and translated. This collection was followed a year later by Mihu Dragomir's *Edgar Allan Poe: Poezii şi Poeme* [Poetry and poems] and, in its turn, by the two-volume *Proză* translated by Ion Vinea and Mircea Alexandrescu.

Also in 1965 a popular science fiction journal, *Povestiri Ştiintifico-Fantastice* [Tales of science fiction], dedicated an entire number as an "Homage to Edgar Allan Poe." It included new translations of "Mellonta Tauta," "A Descent into the Maelström," "Sonnet — To Science," "A Dream," and "Fairy-land," all preceded by a critical introduction by Ion Hobana. The publication of this volume is significant in that it reveals the nature of Poe's latest incarnation in Romania. Interest in Poe now was not primarily in his work as Romantic poet, theoretician, or Gothic artist but in his role as precursor, even founder, of contemporary science-fiction and fantasy literature, genres for which Romanians as well as writers and readers in Eastern Europe and the former Soviet Union continue to have an abiding passion.

In 1968, however, events in Eastern Europe, in particular in Czechoslovakia, put an end to this brief flowering of the arts. While Romania remained a maverick in its foreign policy — the government officially expressed its sympathies for the Czech people during the "Prague Spring" uprising — it also clamped down on free expression within its own borders. By 1971 President Nicolae Ceauşescu and the Romanian Communist Party reactivated its policy of regime-sponsored arts. Many writers once again suffered "internal exile," while many Western writers and artists, Poe included, languished yet again under a system whose stated policy was "to avoid publication of literary works which do not meet the demands of the political-educational activity of our Party, [of] books which promote ideas and conceptions harmful to the interests of socialist construction."[8]

Perhaps because of its perceived harmlessness vis-à-vis contemporary affairs of state, science-fiction and fantasy literature continued to be vehicles by means of which Poe remained in print after the clampdown. Neither did the new restrictions appear to affect the abiding Romanian fascination — even obsession — with "The Raven." The first Romanian translations of "The Raven" began appearing in the 1890s. Since World War I, eighteen major versions of the poem have appeared in print, twelve of these since 1958. New renditions were often accompanied by lively public debates concerning accuracy and translation strategy.[9] Fifteen of these "Raven" translations are included in a recently published (1987, 1990) two-volume edition of Poe's complete works in Romanian, skillfully edited by Liviu Cotrău, thus offering Romanian readers for the first time an assemblage of the best Poe translations.[10]

This latest edition, whose individual volumes appeared — with rich political and cultural symbolism — just before and then immediately after the 1989 revolution, clearly predict a continuing Romanian interest in Poe. The publication of these volumes would also seem to confirm an earlier observation made by Nicolae Iorga, Romania's most prominent twentieth-century historian, concerning certain long-standing cultural affinities between Romania and the West. Addressing a conference on Romanian- and English-language literatures in 1938, Iorga observed: "As our folk poetry clearly shows, we are people of mystery. A fundamental bond exists, therefore, between the mystery tradition of English literature and the foundation of our national literature, which itself is steeped in mystery."[11]

In the larger cultural sense, then, Poe's long and durable appeal to Romanian readers might be explained by what he would term "sympathies of a scarcely intelligible nature." Whatever the reasons, it seems clear that despite the vicissitudes of time and trend in the Balkans, and with the country's newly won cultural freedoms, Romania's romance with Poe will continue to thrive.

NOTES

1. Valentin F. Mihaescu, "Titu Maiorescu — Founder of Modern Romanian Literary Criticism," *Romanian Review* 44.2–3 (1990): 61–62.

2. To my knowledge, the aforementioned Eminescu tales are not available in English translation. For a standard Romanian edition of these tales, see *Mihai Eminescu: Opere Alese*, 8 vols., ed. Aurelia Ruşu (Bucharest: Editura Minerva, 1973–1986).

3. Complete English-language versions of *Năpasta* and "O Făclie de Paşte" are not available. Partial translations of these two works are included in Eric D. Tappe, *Ion Luca Caragiale* (New York: Twayne, 1974). For the definitive Romanian edition of Caragiale's works, see *I. L. Caragiale: Opere*, 8 vols., ed. Paul Zarifpol and Şerban Cioculescu (Bucharest: Cultural Natională; Fundaţia pentru Literatură şi Artă Regele Carol II, 1930–1942).

4. Matei Călinescu, "Eseurile despre Poezie ale lui Edgar Poe," in *Edgar Allan Poe: Principiul Poetic* (Bucharest: Editura Univers, 1971), p. xviii.

5. Călinescu, "Eseurile despre Poezie," p. xviii.

6. Dan Petrașincu, *Edgar Poe, Illuminatul* (Bucharest: Editura Culturală Românească, 1942), p. xvi.

7. Dennis Deletant, "Literature and Society in Romania since 1948," in *Perspectives on Literature and Society in Eastern and Western Europe*, ed. Geoffrey A. Hosking and George F. Cushing (New York: St. Martin's P, 1989), p. 128.

8. Quoted in Deletant, "Literature and Society," p. 140.

9. For a more complete history of Romanian translations of "The Raven," see Thomas C. Carlson, "Romanian Translations of 'The Raven,'" *Poe Studies* 18.2 (1985): 22–24.

10. *E. A. Poe: Annabel Lee și Alte Poeme: Versuri*, ed. Liviu Cotrău (Bucharest: Editura Univers, 1987); *E. A. Poe: Prăbușirea Casei Usher: Schițe, Nuvele, Povestiri, 1831–1842*, ed. Liviu Cotrău (Bucharest: Editura Univers, 1990).

11. Quoted in Monica Pillat-Săulescu, *Modernitatea Nuvelei Fantastice a lui E. A. Poe* (Bucharest: Universitatea din Bucharest, 1983), p. 191.

# Poe in Hungary

GYŐZŐ FERENCZ

The deep impression Edgar Allan Poe has made on Hungarian literature is well illustrated by a recent publishing error. The 1987 edition of the
collected short stories and plays of Mihály Babits (1883–1941), an outstanding
poet and essayist of the first half of the twentieth century, includes Poe's short
story "Hop-Frog" (under the Hungarian title "Ugri-béka") among Babits's
original works.[1] Although Babits published a selection of Poe's short stories in
1929, the Hungarian version of "Hop-Frog" included in the collection is not
even his own.[2] The tale had been translated by Piroska Reichard and published
in 1925.[3] It is difficult to figure out exactly how "Hop-Frog" managed to appear in the volume of short stories by Babits. What probably happened was
that Piroska Reichard for some reason had sent her translation to Babits, who
preserved the manuscript. The editor of the 1987 volume found it among the
poet's literary papers and, assuming it was by Babits, who had somehow failed
to publish it in his lifetime, posthumously added the tale to an ironically
more-than-complete edition of Babits's short stories. But to be fair to Babits,
it is important to add that only an enthusiastic editor, blinded by the excitement of an unexpected discovery, could have taken the story for Babits's own
work. A devoted Poe translator, Babits had thoroughly studied the great
American master and obviously learned from him. Nevertheless, he developed
his own idiosyncratic style that is quite distinct from Poe's. This incident, however, reveals a great deal about Poe's tremendous impact on Hungarian literature. All three aspects of Poe's presence are involved: his work appearing in
translation, his influence on Hungarian writers, and the scholarly task of re-
searching these two issues.

Poe's being mistaken for a Hungarian writer is preceded by a century-long
interest in his life and literary works. According to Béla Korponay, Poe made
his debut in Hungary in the journal *Hölgyfutár* [Ladies' messenger] in an 1856
article by Mór Kelemen that immediately provoked controversy.[4] While acknowledging the exceptional talent of the American author, Kelemen, prob-

ably hoping to heighten the curiosity of his readers, cast the moral aspect of Poe's character in an unfavorable light.[5] That same year *Hölgyfutár* included two short stories by Poe, "William Wilson" and "The Spectacles."

In the journal *Budapesti Szemle* [Budapest review], Károly Szász, a prolific poet-translator, echoed the moral charges in his article on a review of the Rufus W. Griswold edition of Poe's works that had been published in the *Edinburgh Review*.[6] In spite of his claim that Poe was "dishonest," Szász nonetheless translated "The Raven" for the very same issue in an effort to convince his readers that the poet was "immortal," thus offering in 1858 the first of several Hungarian versions of the poem.

While the first prose translations were made from German sources, Szász used the English versions. In his detailed analysis Korponay points out that Szász omitted three stanzas of the poem, the same ones that are missing from the text in the *Edinburgh Review*. Korponay comes to the conclusion that despite the widespread view of major French influence, Baudelaire had neither a mediating nor a motivating role in Poe's introduction to Hungarian readers and his rapidly growing popularity. Baudelaire's name appeared for the first time in Hungary in an article a decade later, in 1869, in the literary daily *Fővárosi Lapok* [Daily of the Capital] (K 45–46).

It is hard to tell whether the charges against Poe's personality arose from journalistic scoop-hunting or serious ethical considerations. But whatever motivations Kelemen and Szász had, one critic spoke up against their unjust moral judgments. Sámuel Brassai, in an essay published in 1858, reflected on the article by Szász and defended Poe, creating a debate that focused more on Poe's character than on his literary merits.[7]

It is not surprising to Hungarians that the attitude of the first articles on Poe took such moralistic approaches. These were the years of ruthless political oppression in Hungary after the suppression of the 1848–1849 revolution and the war of independence against Austria. While most of the country sank into disillusionment, the best minds were obsessed with facing the causes and consequences of the national tragedy. The intellectual atmosphere of the post-revolution years was saturated with moralizing. However, as Korponay notes, "the debate about the *Edinburgh Review* article in Hungary was beneficial rather than detrimental to Poe's reputation" (K 45). His popularity grew steadily during the following years. In 1867 a political compromise between Austria and Hungary was reached, an act that put Hungary on the road to accelerated industrial-urban development. The change in the political and social climate helped to promote Poe's influence. As a pioneer of modern magazine literature, Poe wrote short stories and essays that set an example for the new genre, which also became popular in Hungary.

The first collection of Poe's stories in Hungarian, published in 1862, was aimed at a broad readership. The titles of subsequent collections reflect the effort to entice general readers: *Poe Edgar érdekesebb novelláiból* [Some of Poe's more interesting tales], *Csodálatos történetek* [Wonderful stories], and *Rejtelmes történetek* [Tales of mystery].[8] Among the translators of these collections was the foremost writer of the period, Kálmán Mikszáth (1847–1910), who not only translated Poe but was also directly influenced by him. Korponay points out how Mikszáth adopted the famous shaving scene of the orangutan from "The Murders in the Rue Morgue" in his short story "A sipsirica" ["The Sipsirica"] and also how he borrowed certain elements of structure, style, and characterization in another tale entitled "Egy homályos történet" [A mysterious story] (K 45–46). Even much later Poe's works were often published to satisfy the appetites of readers of cheap best-seller literature; *Cudar gyönyörök* [Wicked pleasures] was the title of a collection in 1917.[9]

Poe's reputation in Hungary developed along two parallel lines. György Radó, in his essay "The Works by E. A. Poe in Hungary," states that "Poe's prose was popular in Hungary among the readers of cheap editions and at the same time among the connoisseurs of fine literature."[10] Indeed, Poe's works were translated by well-known writers and discussed by distinguished scholars in leading literary journals while at the same time appearing in numerous popular series, thus reaching the widest possible readership.

The turn of the twentieth century saw the sudden blossoming of the Hungarian short story, with a number of writers being influenced by Poe's prose in one way or another. Elek Gozsdu (1849–1919), Dániel Papp (1865–1900), Viktor Cholnoky (1868–1912), Károly Lovik (1874–1915), Gyula Szini (1876–1932), Gyula Krúdy (1878–1939), László Cholnoky (1879–1929), and Géza Csáth (1887–1919) are the most important prose writers who fell under the spell of the American writer. Poe's courage in testing the limits of endurance of the human psyche through strange experiences, his soaring imagination, his technique of describing in frightening detail events beyond human understanding, and his obsession with an esoteric view of death and love had a liberating effect on these writers.

Poe's poetry also became increasingly popular as prominent Hungarian poets tried their hand at translating favorite poems. In 1882 the aging József Lévay (1825–1918) made the second Hungarian translation of "The Raven." From the younger generation, Gyula Reviczky (1855–1889), whose short life shared certain similarities with Poe's, translated "To Helen" in 1880.[11] A poet of considerable talent, Reviczky became an acknowledged precursor of the twentieth-century Modernists, who admired Poe.

Although Poe's moral stand was questioned by certain critics, his name often emerged as a basis of comparison with the achievements of Hungarian poets. Korponay mentions that "as early as in the 1860 volume of the *Nővilág* we read that the mood of the epic poem [by János Vajda] recalls to mind the atmosphere of Poe's 'wonderful Raven'" (K 45). Vajda (1827–1897), a lonely figure in nineteenth-century Hungarian poetry much dismissed by the critics of his age, was considered by the twentieth-century Modernists to be their forerunner. Other poets of the period — József Kiss (1843–1921) and Jenő Komjáthy (1858–1895), for example — were seemingly well versed in Poe and revealed his influence in some of their poems. Kiss was not only a poet but also the editor of a popular literary journal at the turn of the century. *A Hét* [The week] regularly published translations from Poe, and Kiss's own poetry owes certain dreamy moods to the American poet. Komjáthy lived like an outcast in rural northeast Hungary, escaping into a wildly ecstatic dream-world.

Early in the twentieth century some of the best young Hungarian poets and writers gathered around the *Nyugat* [Occident], a biweekly progressive modernist literary magazine published between 1908 and 1941. André Karátson, author of an exhaustive study of Poe's influence on the *Nyugat* contributors, argues that Poe helped to liberate the minds and talents of Hungarian writers, inspiring them to develop their own ideas on art and life.[12] In Hungary, Modernism did not involve the avant-garde way of breaking the conventional codes of writing, although a good deal of experimenting with form, style, and language was going on. Karátson examines traces of Poe's influence on a number of Hungarian poets and prose writers.

Among the critical appreciations that came out of the *Nyugat* circle is a book by Artúr Elek (1896–1944), which played an important role in determining Poe's reputation in Hungary in the twentieth century.[13] Composed of two parts, the study analyzes the poet's personality and focuses on his poetry. Elek's positive evaluation once more generated a dispute, this time between the conservative "academic" and the new Modernist movements.

Endre Ady (1877–1919), Mihály Babits (1883–1941), and Dezső Kosztolányi (1885–1936) — three leading though substantially different voices of the *Nyugat* — were all conscious of the effect Poe had on their work. Poe's poetic imagery exerted an influence on some of Ady's love poems, although Ady uses less harmonious melodies and defective rhythmical forms, thus deliberately replacing the subtle musicality of metrical poetry with a more experimental polyphony. But his views on the poet's right to violate the moral codes of a hypocritical society, his drinking habits, his disorderly life, and his position as social outcast found an ancestor in Poe.

Babits and Kosztolányi, on the other hand, especially during their early years, were under the spell of the "art for art's sake" movement. They were both affected by the poetry of Baudelaire, Swinburne, Wilde, and Poe. Babits translated several of Poe's poems into Hungarian, including "The Haunted Palace," "Lenore," "Ulalume," "Annabel Lee," "The Conqueror Worm," and, of course, "The Raven." Later in his career he published *Grotesque and Arabesque*, which contained sixteen of Poe's short stories and the essay "The Philosophy of Composition."

Kosztolányi was not touched by the mysticism of Poe's works, though he admired the accomplished craftsman and the brave artist. He also translated some of Poe's poems, including "The Raven," affording greater freedom to his version than was traditional in translating poetry in Hungary. In a kind of a translators' contest, a third *Nyugat* poet, Árpád Tóth (1886–1928), great master of onomatopoeic effects, also prepared a translation of "The Raven" that is generally considered to be the best so far.

Poe found his most devoted Hungarian enthusiast in the person of Árpád Pásztor (1872–1940), who traveled to the United States three times to visit places associated with Poe. The result of his sustained effort was the publication of several articles and books, one of which is a strange miscellaneous volume entitled *Találkozásom Poe A. Edgarral* [Meeting Edgar A. Poe].[14] The book includes translations of some of Poe's poetry and prose, essays on Poe, and Pásztor's imaginary interviews with the poet, an incredible journal of a Poe devotee. In 1934 Pásztor published a selection from Poe's tales, *Túl életen és halálon* [Beyond life and death].[15] Although some of these translations are still included in various selections from Poe's prose, on the whole Pásztor played a greater role in spreading Poe's popularity in Hungary than in providing quality texts that meet the high standards of translation established by the *Nyugat* movement.

While publishers kept producing editions in cheap best-seller formats (an unknown translator published "Hop-Frog" under the bizarre title "The Revenge of the Dwarf"),[16] a distinguished scholar devoted significant energy to the translation of some of Poe's prose works.[17] György Király (1883–1944), a literary historian and critic who published an excellent academic book on ancient Hungarian poetry, was the first to translate *The Narrative of Arthur Gordon Pym*. *Pym* reached a young readership in 1943 when a translation especially adapted for children was published.[18]

After the Second World War Poe's complete poems came out in several different editions in 1949, 1959, 1974, and 1994.[19] The 1959 bilingual edition includes nine translations of "The Raven." Poe's short stories have appeared in various anthologies, and selections from his tales are regularly published in individual volumes.[20] The most complete Hungarian collection of Poe's works was published in 1981 in an annotated edition that contains the complete poems, thirty-one tales, *The Narrative of Arthur Gordon Pym*, and ten essays.[21] Several new translations were made exclusively for this edition, and each text, whether old or new, was carefully edited.

Poe's presence in Hungary goes back nearly 150 years, during which time some of the best writers fell under the spell of his unique art. It is ironic that Poe's influence on writers was strongest when his works appeared in poor, often flawed translations. Now that carefully edited, high-quality versions of his work are available, probably no contemporary writer claims to be the spiritual descendant of Poe. Even so, his works continue to fascinate general readers. He is ever present, not as a frozen classic but as a writer who is part of the intellectual climate of Hungary, a position he shares with only a few other authors from world literature.

NOTES

1. Mihály Babits, *Novellái és színjátékai* (Budapest: Szépirodalmi Könyvkiadó, 1987), pp. 464–473. The note in the text says that the manuscript is cataloged among Babits's literary papers kept in the Archive of the National Széchenyi Library, Budapest. No previous publication is indicated.

2. *Groteszk és arabeszk*, trans. Mihály Babits (Budapest: Atheneum, 1928).

3. *Ugri-béka*, trans. Piroska Reichard (Budapest: Lantos R.-T., 1925).

4. Béla Korponay, "Edgar Allan Poe in Hungary," *Hungarian Studies in English* 1 (December 1963): 43–62; hereafter cited as K. Information concerning Poe's first translations into Hungarian have been taken from this study.

5. Mór Kelemen, "Edgar A. Poe élete," *Hölgyfutár* 212 (1856).

6. Károly Szász, "The Works of the Late Edgar Allan Poe," *Budapesti Szemle* 4 (1858).

7. Sámual Brassai, "Adalékok Edgar Poe (amerikai költő) ismertetéséhez," *Szépirodalmi Közlöny* 5–8 (1858).

8. *Poe Edgar érdekesebb novelláiból*, trans. Ferenc Hang (Pest: Lauffer és Stolp Bizománya, 1862); *Csodálatos történetek*, trans. Ferenc Hang (Budapest: Zilahy Sámuel, 1878); *Rejtelmes történetek*, trans. Vilmos Tolnai (Budapest: Lampel Róbert, 1898).

9. *Cudar gyönyörök*, trans. Pál Dóczi (Békéscsaba, 1917).

10. György Radó, "The Works by E. A. Poe in Hungary," *Babel* 12 (1966): 21–22.

11. "A holló," trans. József Lévay, *Budapesti Szemle* 63 (1882); "Csak egyszer láttalak," trans. Gyula Reviczky, *Fővárosi Lapok* 256 (1880).

12. André Karátson, *Edgar Allan Poe et le groupe des écrivains du "Nyugat" en Hongrie* (Paris: Presses Universitaires de France, 1971).

13. Artúr Elek, *Poe Edgár — Két tanulmány* (Budapest: Nyugat, 1910).

14. Árpád Pásztor, *Találkozásom Poe A. Edgárral* (Budapest: Dick Manó, 1916).

15. *Túl életen és halálon*, trans. Árpád Pásztor (Budapest: Dick Manó, 1934).

16. *A törpe bosszúja* (Budapest: Tolnai, 1924).

17. *A vörös halál álarca*, trans. György Király (Budapest: Lantos, 1919); *A Morgue-utcai gyilkosság*, trans. György Király (Budapest: Révai Testvérek, 1921); *Arthur Gordon Pym csodálatos kalandjai*, trans. György Király (Budapest: Révai Testvérek, 1921).

18. *Arthur Gordon Pym, a tengerész*, trans. Andor Tiszay (Budapest: Forrás Kiadóvállalat R.-T., 1943; 2nd ed. Budapest: Bibliotheca Kiadó, 1957).

19. *Összes költeményei*, introduction and notes by László Kardos (Budapest: Franklin, 1949); *Összes versei*, introduction by Tibor Lutter, notes by György Radó (Budapest: Corvina Press, 1959); *Versei*, notes by Bálint Rozsnyai (Budapest: Európa Könyvkiadó, 1974; rpt. 1994).

20. *Az aranybogár* (Budapest: Szépirodalmi Könyvkiadó, 1959); *Rejtelmes történetek* (Budapest: Európa Könyvkiadó, 1967); *Az aranybogár — Nyolc rejtelmes történet* (Budapest: Magyar Helikon, 1972); *Az aranybogár és más elbeszélések* (Budapest: Európa Könyvkiadó, 1993); *Arthur Gordon Pym nantucketi tengerész elbeszélése* (Budapest: Európa Könyvkiadó, 1994).

21. *Válogatott művei*, notes by Győző Ferencz and Bálint Rozsnyai (Budapest: Európa Könyvkiadó, 1981).

# Poe in Croatia

SONJA BAŠIĆ

The earliest translation of Poe into Croatian was quite appropriately his most famous poem, "The Raven," which appeared in the leading cultural magazine *Vienac* (Zagreb) in 1875. Its translator was Aleksandar Tomić, a seminary teacher and later village parson who translated from a number of Slavic languages (Czech, Polish, Russian) and from French. We do not know from which language Tomić translated "The Raven," but we can be quite certain that it was not from English, a language known to very few Croats in the nineteenth century. Apart from a couple of versions of "The Raven" in the 1920s, no other translations of Poe's poems appeared in Croatia until the 1950s.

Tomić's rendition of Poe's masterpiece has some distinction, but it is inferior to Croatian translations of poetry that existed at that time. It treats the content of the original rather freely, both omitting and adding details. Part of this freedom was inherited from the previous generations of Croatian translators, who generally did not try to reproduce the atmosphere or style of the original and insisted only on creating a regular metric and rhyme pattern. Tomić's translation loses the suggestiveness and preciosity of Poe's poem. The death of Lenore is bluntly stated, and most of Poe's special touches are elided; for example, there is no mention of Aidenn, Gilead, nepenthe, and the Night's Plutonian shore. In addition, Poe's learned and elevated vocabulary is translated into colloquial speech and simplified, following the native Romantic traditions which, in an effort to produce a new modern national literature and reject the dominant German education and culture, followed closely the language and style of the folk literature of the country. In the hands of Tomić, Poe's lines became simplified versions with diminutives, colloquialisms, and local expressions typical of folk ballads.

Such simplifications, even distortions, also reflected a wish to satisfy the taste and intellectual level of the popular magazine audience to whom such translations were addressed and who would have found little use for the sophisticated virtuosity of Poe's style. The same translation style was applied to "The Tell-Tale Heart," published in a daily paper, *Narodne novine* (Zagreb) in

1883, and continued to be used until the mid–twentieth century, when Poe's works finally came into the hands of some of Croatia's best writers and most renowned translators of the English language. Until then, Poe's translations remained merely horror and mystery fare served to the average reader of the popular press. Translations of Poe's tales were more numerous than the poems; approximately forty stories were published between 1883 and 1914 and about the same number between the two world wars, some in several versions. Among the earliest were "The Black Cat" (1885), "The Oval Portrait" (1886), "The Gold-Bug" (1883), and "The Murders in the Rue Morgue" (1889). With few exceptions, these stories were translated by undistinguished translators and published in popular newspapers and magazines.

The tale of Poe's reception would certainly have followed the same pattern had it not been for one of Croatia's all-time literary greats, Antun Gustov Matoš (1873–1914), whose unbounded admiration brought Poe's literary achievement into the foreground of the modern Croatian literary consciousness. Fascinated by Poe after reading Baudelaire's account, Matoš made numerous references to the American writer in his essays and incorporated elements of Poe's work into his own poems and stories (see Part II, "Antun Gustav Matoš").

By the end of the nineteenth century a new generation of Croatian writers had matured, often loosely grouped together as Moderna [The Moderns]. Opposing foreign domination (Croatia remained part of Austria-Hungary until its defeat in the First World War), the previous generation had fiercely embraced the national tradition as a passionate, embattled, and finally successful attempt to re-establish a national language and literature. The Moderns took this achievement for granted and turned again toward Europe, only this time more deliberately toward French and English models. In 1909 Matoš wrote boldly: "There exists no national literature in Europe which has not been formed under the influence of another literature. The study of foreign cultures is therefore the best way to develop one's own, and the best nationalists are those who are good Europeans."[1] It therefore seems appropriate that Matoš should be the greatest admirer and follower of Poe in Croatian literature. The marginal American writer adopted by Europe was in turn adopted by a writer from the European margins in search of European forebears. Thanks to Matoš, Poe was finally established in Croatia as a great writer, a dark Romantic hero, and *poète maudit*, the spiritual brother of the French Symbolists and primarily of Baudelaire.

While Matoš's "love affair" with Poe's life and work became well known among the younger generation of aspiring writers, Poe's place on the Croatian literary map at the turn of the twentieth century was consolidated by the first propagator of Anglo-American literature in Croatia, the publicist and English teacher Vladoje Dukat (1861–1944). He wrote a long and very well informed survey of Poe's life and work in *Vienac* as early as 1900 and published another version in his *Slike iz povijesti engleske književnosti* [Images from the history of English literature] (1904), in which he assigned Poe one of the highest places in world literature. Several other tributes were paid to Poe's genius during this period. The brilliant young author Janko Polić-Kamov (1886–1910) described his impression of Poe in an essay: "My vision of Poe is that of a bird of ill omen flying across the silent sea of our secret self and disappearing some-where in space, leaving behind the shadow of its dark black wings. Or I imagine him like the memory of a cat's eyes in the dark; of a frightened dog on a deserted road; of a dolphin's back on the oily surface of the sea; of the shadow of ghosts who pull our legs at night. And this is why Poe is myste-rious; because of unfathomable fear, like all beauty and mysticism that live buried in the graves of our souls, where for the sake of their own absurdity they were born." [2]

Poe also inspired Janko's brother, Nikola Polić (1890–1960), to create the poem "Noćni gost, čitajući Poeovog Gavrana" [The nocturnal visitor: Read-ing Poe's "The Raven"]. Written during the First World War in an Austro-Hungarian barracks and published in *Novosti* in 1931, it evokes a fantastic ghoulish atmosphere suggesting the horror of war. The raven becomes a sym-bol of death and anxiety: "In such a night, in such a night / I'll peck your eyes with all my might."

After the First World War, Poe's popularity as one of the significant models for Croatian followers of fin de siècle aestheticism and "art for art's sake" came to an end. He had been an inspiration to those who opposed the overly na-tional, utilitarian, engaged attitudes of many of their predecessors and peers. Much later, in the 1970s, there was a minor resurgence of literary interest in Poe, a side effect of the great vogue of the Borgesian fantastic, shared for a while by a number of Croatian writers, including several leading contempo-rary fabulists such as Pavao Pavličić and Goran Tribuson.

More important for Poe's presence in Croatian culture, however, was the inspiration of two young men, hardly twenty years of age, to retranslate "The Raven" in 1951. The translators, Ivan Slamnig (b. 1930) and Antun Šoljan (1932–1993), soon became leading authors of their generation. Along with his own creative endeavors, Šoljan remained very active as a brilliant translator of fiction and poetry, including several plays by Shakespeare. In 1952 Slamnig and Šoljan published a small volume of their translations entitled *Američka*

*lirika* [American lyric poetry], which included "To Helen," "A Dream within
a Dream," "The Haunted Palace," "Annabel Lee," and "Eldorado." In 1961
they did another translation of "The Raven" that was almost completely different from the first. The two versions were published in a small separate volume along with Slamnig's translation of "The Philosophy of Composition"
and Šoljan's witty reminiscence, "How We Translated 'The Raven.'"[3] In this
essay, "The Raven" was used as a pretext for the authors to express their own
theories on translation and their defense of renditions that remain as close as
possible to the original.

The Slamnig/Šoljan translations were a landmark inaugurating a new era
in English-Croatian translations of modern poetry and fiction. Two older eminent Croatian poets had also tried their hand at translating "Annabel Lee."
Ivan Goran Kovačić (1913–1943), killed during the Second World War, created
a version that never went beyond a draft. Another rendition by the great poet
Tin Ujević (1891–1955) was published in 1950 but was not very successful.
Ujević also translated a small selection of Poe's tales (1952), which show the
stamp of a master but are stylistically uneven and contain translation errors.
*The Narrative of Arthur Gordon Pym*, translated by Leo Držić, was published
in 1955.

In the 1970s and 1980s two major projects produced new Croatian editions
of a large number of Poe's works. In 1974 I edited, annotated, and wrote the
introduction to a collection of new translations of ten Poe tales, *Crni mačak*
[The black cat].[4] In 1986 I was commissioned to edit a representative three-
volume, thousand-page edition of Poe's selected works, a comprehensive collection of mostly new translations by some of the best Croatian translators.[5]
The edition includes forty-three tales, *The Narrative of Arthur Gordon Pym*, a
selection of essays and poems, thirty-one letters I translated as part of a biographical narrative, and my concluding essay stressing Poe's relevance for contemporary readers both in Croatia and throughout the world.

Addressing Croatian readers, I concluded this major Poe edition by observing that in Poe we often find flashes of sensations and insights that turn this
disturbing and uncanny writer into our contemporary. Poe foreshadowed the
modern feeling of existential loneliness and void, both of which have obsessed
writers from Kafka and Camus to Butor and Pynchon. In Poe we recognize
some of our own literary and philosophical preoccupations, and this is why
we are ready to follow Borges and join hands with Poe across the abyss that
divides us. Poe has prefigured the cold uneasiness, the baroque play, and the
grotesque, even clownish attitudes of so many of our literary contemporaries,

bringing literature to the edge of reality, to the edge of reason, to the edge of meaning.

NOTES

1. A. G. Matoš. *Sabrana djela* 20 vols. (Zagreb: Jugoslavenska akademija znanosti i umjetnosti, Liber & Mladost, 1973), vol. 4, p. 268. All translations of quotations are mine.

2. Janko Polić-Kamov, *Članci i feljtoni, pisma* (Rijeka: Otokar Keršovani, 1958), p. 245.

3. *Gavran*, trans. Ivan Slamnig and Antun Šoljan (Zagreb: Biblioteka 'Književnik' No. 4, 1961).

4. *Crni mačak*, ed. Sonja Bašić (Zagreb: Školska knjiga, 1974).

5. *Priče. Knjiga prva, Priče. Knjiga druga, Doživljaji Arthura Gordona Pyma, pjesme, poetika, pisma. Knjiga treča*, ed. Sonja Bašić (Zagreb: Nakladni zavod Matice hrvatske, 1986).

# Poe in the Czech Republic

MARCEL ARBEIT

In 1869 the first Czech translation of "The Raven" appeared in the most popular Czech weekly of that time, *Květy* [Flowers]. During the next 125 years, sixteen more translations of the poem were published.[1] Sometimes it looked as if all translators of poetry thought they could not become real masters without coping with Poe's most famous poem. Perhaps the popularity of the piece was due to the frequency of "nevermore" in the minds and mouths of Czech people throughout history: The Austro-Hungarian monarchy? Nevermore! Another Munich Agreement and Nazi era? Nevermore! "Real" Socialism and Soviet troops in Czech lands again? Nevermore! Konstantin Biebl (1898–1951), in his Communist "Raven" (1950), even asks the bird to fly to the White House and say the famous refrain to Harry Truman. At any given time, Czech people, "weak and weary," were scared when somebody was tapping at their "chamber door" because it could have been the secret police, the inquisition from "The Pit and the Pendulum." Their "nevermore" was connected with a barely visible yet inconceivably huge and ominous bird, even if they were not familiar with Poe.

As in Russian, "The Raven" in Czech could have become a political poem, a metaphor of the murky life of social oppression, a parable for people used to reading between the lines. But translators decided otherwise. The better of them did not want to masquerade Poe as an antitotalitarian poet; the worse distorted the poem but for different reasons: they tried to adjust it to their own poetic individualities and fashionable "isms."

Alois Bejblík, author of a comprehensive study of translations of "The Raven," claims that the poem follows a mythical pattern using segments typical of ballads, common for Romantic poems in many European literatures (B 13–14). For this reason, Czech translators who had not yet read Baudelaire stressed the storyline and did not see Poe as "a predecessor of modern poetic alchemy" (B 23). This is the case for the author of the very first translation of "The Raven" into Czech, the journalist and minor poet Vratislav Kazimír

Šembera (1844–1891), as well as for Jaroslav Vrchlický (1853–1912), one of the most versatile nineteenth-century Czech poets.[2] The latter's translations of "The Raven" and thirty-two other poems by Poe, published between 1881 and 1890, were more poetic exercises than anything else. (The archaic, awkward language of his "Annabel Lee" is especially awful.) Nevertheless, his volume *Havran a jiné básně* ["The Raven" and other poems] (1891) was the first representative collection of Poe's poetry in Czech lands. The third translation of "The Raven," by Augustin Eugen Mužík (1859–1925), appeared in 1885, again in *Květy*. Mužík translated "nevermore" as *"nadarmo"* (in vain) and started the line of translators who deprived Poe's poem of all its qualities, then tried to have their approach vindicated (or to vindicate it themselves).[3]

The overwhelming majority of Czech people know Poe's poetry through Vítězslav Nezval (1900–1958). Nezval's case is rather paradoxical because, unlike most Czech translators, he was not competent in English. In order to translate Poe, Nezval had to have the word-for-word translations made by Albert Vyskočil, a Catholic essayist. Nezval presented Poe as one of the "cursed poets" together with Baudelaire, Rimbaud, and Mallarmé, thus becoming the first Czech translator of Poe to reflect Baudelaire's image of the American poet (B 37–45).

Nezval's goal was to make foreign poems sound like Czech originals, and he succeeded. His fourteen translations of Poe, published for the first time in 1928 and then numerous times in selected works and anthologies, read like masterpieces of Czech poetry.[4] Unfortunately, the real Poe is gone. The uncanny, unique atmosphere has evaporated; obsessions and nightmares are replaced by pleasant, noncommittal dreaming; and instead of the desperate metaphysical quest there is only a fairy-tale magic.[5] Rather than being sad, Nezval's narrator is continuously amused by the presence of the funny animal speaking in human tongue. Jiří Levý, one of the leading European theorists of translation, highlights the irony in the Czech text and points out an unintentional parody. In his opinion, "Nezval's version cannot stand the test as a translation which is supposed to grasp the meaning and mood of Poe's poem. But it has its charm and a touch of playfulness, if we are willing to take it as a slightly ironical paraphrase of motives which are to a great extent foreign to our contemporary thinking."[6]

The popularity of Nezval's translations of Poe had political causes as well: the majority of the pre–World War II artists and literary critics who had enormous influence on public opinion were on the Left and tended to reject everything depressing and pessimistic as "foreign" to the supposedly optimistic nature of the Czechs. Even when much better translations by Josef Hiršal (b. 1920) appeared in 1959, readers still preferred Nezval's versions. (Hiršal did not translate "The Raven," however.)

The very first Poe poem to appear in Czech was "Ulalume," published in 1856, together with translations of "The Bells," "Sonnet — To Zante," "Eldorado," "To F —— s S.O —— d," and "Hymn," in *Lumír*, another important literary magazine. Edmund Břetislav Kaizl introduced his translations with a biographical essay, "Edgar Allan Poe. Básník severo-americký" [Edgar Allan Poe: A North-American poet], which provided Czech readers with basic facts as well as rumors about Poe's life drawn almost exclusively from Griswold's account. For Kaizl, Poe ranks third among American poets after Longfellow (whose poems also appeared in *Lumír*) and William Cullen Bryant. In 1873 *Lumír* printed two other poems by "Edgar Allan Loe" (as spelled on the cover), "Lenore" and "Israfel," the translator hiding behind the name J. Ves . . . k.

The first scholarly study of Poe in Czech lands was by Jakub Arbes (1840–1914), a popular author of tales of mystery as well as social novels. In his 1870 fictionalized essay "Poe a jeho báseň 'Havran'" [Poe and his poem "The Raven"], published one year later in four installments in *Květy*, he describes the thirty-three-year-old Poe meeting his old Baltimore friends in a New York pub and telling them how "The Raven" came into existence. An adapted and abridged translation of "The Philosophy of Composition" is preceded by Arbes's statement that "at first sight, any reasonable reader can tell that [Poe's works] were written because they had to be written and became exactly what they are because they could not be different."[7] Arbes writes about true creation, immediacy, intuition, and even naïveté, thus undermining the belief in Poe's totally rational and almost mathematic approach toward the creative process as presented in his essays. He also compares Poe to Lord Byron and considers Poe's imaginary journey to Russia as fact.

In the last two parts of his study, Arbes criticizes Poe's later works as being aesthetically unsatisfying; points out his inability to describe passions like hatred, jealousy, and ambition; and draws attention to the fact that Poe never created female characters who were not "hysterical and pathological."[8] At the same time, though, he pays tribute to the poet whose work "reminds one of Medusa's face, from which unspeakable pain stares in petrified terror . . . , pain which arises in our chest as warm compassion and does not allow our eyes to be averted from the terribly beautiful cheek."[9] Although Arbes did not dwell on Poe's alcoholism, he reprinted his study in a volume of essays entitled *Nesmrtelní pijáci* [The immortal drunkards] (1884), where Poe found himself in the company of two famous heavy-drinking actors (Edmund Kean and František Krumlovský, a Czech tragedian) and a painter (Adrian Brouwer).

In the early twentieth century Poe had an influence on the Decadents and Symbolists grouped around *Moderní revue* [Modern review], which in 1919 published "The Conqueror Worm," "The Haunted Palace," and "To One in Paradise." Czech Decadents borrowed from Poe the images of decay, destruction, and death. Jiří Karásek of Lvovice (1871–1951), whose own poetry was influenced by Poe, was one of the fiercest critics of Vrchlický's translations and suggested that future translators should follow the French example by translating Poe's poetry into prose. Another important representative of Czech Decadence, Emanuel Lešehrad (1877–1955), considered "The Raven" to be an occult poem centered around the mystic numbers three, six, and nine (B 202–203).

Turning to Poe's fiction, we find that the quality of the translations is much better than for his poetry. The first Czech versions of "The Gold-Bug" and "Some Words with a ⁰Mummy" appeared in František Šebek's translations in 1853.[10] The beginning of the latter story was slightly "censored," however, when the second paragraph, mentioning the dish of Welsh rabbit and five bottles of Brown Stout, was unscrupulously omitted. Josef Schwarz's translation (1959), still definitive, revived the feast.

Jakub Arbes not only translated "The Oblong Box" but also created under Poe's influence a new genre in Czech literature, the "romanetto," a mystery and/or adventure novella with a rational, scientific denouement.[11] His first and enormously successful prose work of this type, *Svatý Xaverius* [St. Xaverius] (1873), combined the motive of the hunt for a hidden treasure from "The Gold-Bug" with the theme of a magic picture from "The Oval Portrait." The painter's cipher is decoded, but instead of gold the reward is a symbolic treasure of wisdom which, ironically, results in the protagonist's death.

Arbes never kept his affection for Poe a secret; he even named his only son Edgar. The American writer continued to influence Arbes's work, especially "Newtonův mozek" ["Newton's Brain"] (1877), in which he describes the dream journey of a deceased inventor and the narrator (his best friend) in their time machine to different points in the universe, from where it is possible to overlook the whole history of humankind, which appears to be exclusively the history of violence.[12] Knowing that some of his ideas were not original, Arbes has his protagonist mention Poe and Jules Verne, who had used them much earlier.[13]

The best-known Czech writer of the interwar period, Karel Čapek (1890–

1938), once said that he had never described his creative process because he was afraid of being accused of imitating Poe.[14] From his review of "The Unparalleled Adventure of One Hans Pfaall," in which he refers to Poe's soul as "midnight" and "owlish" and labels Poe as "no more a man, but a fragile psyche, no more a psyche, but a psychosis," it is evident that he knew Poe well and liked his works.[15] Josef Škvorecký (b. 1924), a Toronto-based contemporary Czech author, analyzed Čapek's famous short story "Šlépěj" ["The Imprint"] as a coded tribute to Poe.[16] Škvorecký published an insightful article on Poe as founder of the detective story genre in his collection of essays *Nápady čtenáře detektivek* [*Notions of the Reader of Detective Stories*] (1965). Twelve years later he included Poe themes in his autobiographical novel *Příběh inženýra lidských duší* [*The Engineer of Human Souls*].[17]

Two other Czech writers whose works are available in English translation show connections with Poe. Ladislav Fuks (1923–1994) rarely mentions Poe in his fiction, yet his powerful dark novels, which rank among the best ever produced in Czech lands, bear many similarities to Poe's short stories. In a scene from his novel *Spalovač mrtvol* [*The Cremator*] (1967), an employee of the Prague crematorium shows a new colleague the corpse of a young woman whose "skin is pink and her eyes cast down as though she were asleep" and who "looks as though she might wake and get up at any moment."[18] The woman is evidently in a state of catatonic sleep, known from "Berenice," "The Fall of the House of Usher," and "The Premature Burial," but the cremator says: "She has been pronounced dead. . . . To pronounce somebody dead is not only the most responsible, but also the most sublime official act carried out in the world. It is a decisive act, and we carry out our duties precisely."[19]

Ludvík Vaculík (b. 1926), one of the most controversial contemporary Czech authors, started his career as the editor of the Communist Party publishing house Rudé právo [Red right] and ended up as the author of "2,000 Words," a famous 1968 political manifesto against the Soviet invasion. In his second novel, *Morčata* [*The Guinea Pigs*] (1970), one of the central metaphors is taken from "A Descent into the Maelström." The main character, a Prague bank clerk, becomes gradually drawn to a mysterious engineer nicknamed Maelstrom, who forecasts the consequences of the vanishing of large numbers of banknotes from circulation. There is evidently a conspiracy, but it is difficult to figure out who are the conspirators and who are the victims. In Vaculík's book, the maelstrom serves as a metaphor for an economic crisis and as the symbol of "a vague feeling of anxiety," dating back to the protagonist's youth.[20]

Poe's tales continue to inspire contemporary Czech fiction writers who fill the general reader's imagination with familiar images long associated with Poe's poems and tales. For almost 150 years, Poe's works have been continuously translated and remain among the most popular by an American writer in the Czech lands.

NOTES

1. See *Havran. Šestnáct českých překladů*, ed. Alois Bejblík and Rudolf Havel (Prague: Odeon, 1985); hereafter cited as B.

2. "Havran," trans. Vratislav Kazimír Šembera, *Květy* 4 (1869): 366. A brief survey of the most important translations of Poe's works into Czech is in Milan Macháček, *Edgar Allan Poe, Bludná planeta* (Prague: Československý spisovatel, 1991), pp. 223–225.

3. "Havran," trans. Augustin Eugen Mužík, *Květy* 7 (1885): 57–61. The editor's explanatory note is on page 57. The self-justifying and sometimes apologetic essays of six other translators are published in B 104–107, 115–118, 122–124, 128–129, 135–136, and 157–158.

4. The complete publishing history of Nezval's translations of Poe is in Vítězslav Nezval, *Dílo XXV: Překlady I* (Prague: Československý spisovatel, 1982), pp. 544–546.

5. See Marcel Arbeit, "Každý svého Poea!," in Macháček, *Bludná planeta*, pp. 167–179.

6. Jiří Levý, *Umění překladu*, 2nd ed. (Prague: Panorama, 1983), p. 65. My translation. This insightful book is also available in German under the title *Die literarische Übersetzung. Theorie einer Kunstgattung* (Frankfurt on Main: Athenäum Verlag, 1969).

7. The best accessible translation of "The Philosophy of Composition" is by Aloys Skoumal in *Jak se dělá báseň*, ed. Jan Zábrana (Prague: Československý spisovatel, 1970), pp. 11–26. Jakub Arbes, "Poe a jeho báseň 'Havran,'" *Květy* 6 (1871): 53. My translation.

8. Arbes, "Poe a jeho báseň 'Havran,'" p. 78.

9. Ibid., p. 76.

10. "Zlatý chrobák," trans. František Šebek, *Lumír* 3 (1853): 721–725, 776–780, 802–806; "Několik slov s mumií," *Lumír* 3 (1853): 1019–1024, 1043–1046.

11. Features of the "romanetto" are discussed in more detail in *Dějiny české literatury*, ed. Miloš Pohorský (Prague: Nakladatelství ČSAV, 1961), vol. 3, pp. 345–349.

12. "Newton's Brain" was translated into English as early as 1896 and published in *Clever Tales*, ed. Charlotte E. Porter and Helen A. Clarke (Boston: Copeland and Day, 1897), pp. 120–204.

13. Rudolf Havel suggests also a parallel between Arbes's story "Ďábel na skřipci" and "The Raven" (B 169).

14. Jiří Langer, *Byli a bylo* (Prague: Československý spisovatel, 1963), pp. 96–97. Paraphrased in Jaroslav Peprník, *Angloamerické reálie v české literatuře* (Prague: SPN,

1988), pp. 145–146. This book is an invaluable source of information on the reception of British and American culture in Czech lands. It includes a list of references to fifty-nine American authors in the works of Czech writers from two centuries.

15. Karel Čapek, "Edgar Allan Poe: Bezpříkladné dobrodružství Hanse Pfalla," *Snaha* (September 5, 1908): 5. Published in English in Karel Čapek, "Edgar Allan Poe: The Unparalleled Adventure of One Hans Pfaall," *Studies in Weird Fiction* 14 (1994): 8–9.

16. See Josef Škvorecký, "A Discovery in Čapek," *Armchair Detective* 8 (1975): 183.

17. Josef Škvorecký, *The Engineer of Human Souls*, trans. Paul Wilson (London: Vintage, 1994), pp. 6–10.

18. Ladislav Fuks, *The Cremator*, trans. Eva M. Kandler (London: Marion Boyars, 1984), p. 49.

19. Ibid., pp. 49–50.

20. Ludvík Vaculík, *The Guinea Pigs*, trans. Káča Poláčková (London: London Magazine Editions, 1974), p. 38. See also Elizabeth Sabiston's review of *The Guinea Pigs* in *The International Fiction Review* 7 (1976): 153. It is easy to find political undertones in the novel; still it is not true that Vaculík "cleverly uses the stratagem of writing over bureaucratic heads by using an apparently safe American frame of reference." The book was not published in Czechoslovakia until 1991.

# Poe in Poland

F. LYRA

The earliest known public appearance of Poe's name in Poland dates from 1857, when he was mentioned in an anonymous survey of American literature published in the first edition of *Biblioteka Warszawska* (1811–1914), the foremost Polish periodical of the nineteenth century. The following year Adolf Hennel (1830–1869), a journalist, introduced Poe to the public at large with a biographical article indebted quite obviously to Charles Baudelaire. This article was followed by a translation from the French of "Morella" and "The Black Cat," the earliest Poe texts published in Polish.[1] Since Hennel was not a literary person, his contribution carried little consequence and was soon forgotten. In retrospect, however, he set the pattern of Poe's Polish reception for the next few decades: French (mostly Baudelaire's) and German renditions as textual sources for early Polish translations; Baudelaire's views of Poe's life and work as authoritative pronouncements against which early Polish critics interpreted their readings of Poe; and the Poles' preference for Poe's stories over his poetry, judging by the strikingly disproportionate number of collections in both categories. Still some critics, Artur Międzyrzecki for one, insist that Poe's greatness lies in his poetry, while Kazimierz Wyka ranks his tales higher because "they are more original and anticipate more."

Poe's status in Polish literary culture might be measured by attempts at undermining Baudelaire's priority in the recognition of his European career by assigning it to Felicjan Faleński (1825–1910). The attempts carried weight since they were offered by esteemed literary historians such as Tadeusz Grabowski, professor at the Jagiellonian and Poznań Universities and one-time visiting lecturer at the Sorbonne, and acclaimed writers, to mention only Adolf Nowaczyński, who enjoyed considerable popularity between the world wars. Grabowski stated authoritatively that Faleński knew and understood Poe before Baudelaire. Nowaczyński was less assertive though more sweeping when he suggested cautiously that Faleński's study of Poe might have been the first examination of Poe's work in the world. Juliusz Wiktor Gomulicki, one of Poland's foremost literary scholars, while discarding such opinions, nevertheless postulated that Faleński be placed next to Baudelaire and Barbey d'Aurevilly as one of the three earliest Europeans to recognize and appreciate Poe's genius.[2]

Faleński's 1861 essay, published in *Biblioteka Warszawska*, was until the appearance of my own comprehensive monograph in 1973 the longest and most penetrating piece on Poe in Poland, although it was limited to an analysis of his fiction.[3] A late Romantic among Positivists, however, Faleński was doomed to live as an even greater recluse than Poe, misunderstood and largely unappreciated by his contemporaries. Consequently, since he lacked the authority to command the Poles' attention, his contribution to the reception of Poe in Poland was "discovered" only during the high point of Modernism.

Unlike Baudelaire, who experienced a "shock of recognition" when he first read Poe, Faleński came to appreciate the American author gradually, and his observations tend to be inconsistent. In a letter to his future wife, Maria Trębicka, dated five years prior to the publication of the study, he deprecated Poe's tales, calling them "lifeless, paltry in invention, occasionally tasteless, mostly indifferent."[4] By the time he wrote the essay, he had reversed his opinion and confirmed its abrogation by translating five of Poe's stories, all published anonymously in *Biblioteka Warszawska* at various times in the 1860s. The reason for Faleński's change of attitude may never be known, though one possible explanation might be his decision to write short fiction himself, and thus at that point he developed a finer appreciation of Poe's art.

By and large few Polish writers openly admitted Poe's influence; even those who did were unable to specify the nature of their debt to him. For example, Bolesław Leśmian (1877/78–1937), probably Poland's greatest poet of the twentieth century, identified with Poe's tortured existence as well as with his work to such a degree that his translation of Poe's stories, published in two volumes in 1913, reads as if they were his own creation. In the history of Poe's reception in Poland, his collection stands out as a literary feat without precedent. In the introduction Leśmian projects Poe into his own life and raises him to the heights of sainthood, as if to compensate for the suffering Poe endured at the hands of his contemporaries (see Part II, "Bolesław Leśmian").

Without clues from authors, tracing Poe's effect on them turns into detective work, the results of which are not always unequivocal, even in cases where authors make direct reference to Poe in their own writings. For example, Karol Irzykowski (1873–1944), one of Poland's outstanding writers, mentions in his autobiographical notes, *Notatki z życia* [Notes from life], that he was not impressed when he first read "Hop-Frog" in German at the age of twenty. Gradually, however, as he became better acquainted with Poe, he modified his opinion. More important, the grotesque and psychological moments in Irzy-kowski's stories, and especially his famous innovative novel *Pałuba* (1903), strongly suggest Poe's presence.

In like manner traces of Poe have been found in Stefan Żeromski's master-piece *Popioły* [*Ashes*] (1904).[5] Whether Eliza Orzeszkowa (1841–1910), twice a candidate for the Nobel Prize in literature, benefited from Poe's *Extraordinary Stories*, which she ordered from her Warsaw publisher in late 1876, has yet to be ascertained.

No uncertainty exists about Poe's effect on Stefan Grabiński (1857–1936), author of, among others, six volumes of short stories acclaimed by contem-porary critics for their skillful construction which he admittedly learned from Poe.[6] The fantastic, psychopathological substance of his stories, his explora-tion of the irrational, and the bizarre and the grotesque, however, are not grounded in Poe but in his own life, that of a dreamer and loner beset with illness and indigence. Like his American master, Grabiński was exceedingly effective in creating moods of terror and mystery. His work appeals to sophis-ticated readers as it is reinforced by the use of Gustav Theodor Fechner's work in psychophysics, William James's writings on psychology and religious expe-riences, and Henri Bergson's metaphysics of life.

Unlike Grabiński, Roman Jaworski's (1883–1944) grotesque Modernist Ex-pressionism, infused with decadent catastrophism, was not appreciated by his contemporaries. His work, especially *Historie maniaków* [Stories of lunatics] (1909), conceals affinity with the darker side of Poe's imagination.

Grabiński's and Jaworski's contemporary Piotr Choynowski (1885–1935) likewise achieved his popular and critical recognition in short fiction as Poe's disciple in composition. Wilhelm Feldman first pointed out that the structure of Choynowski's tales exemplifies the theory of the short story that Poe out-lined in his review of Hawthorne's *Twice-Told Tales*.[7] Choynowski's affirmative attitude toward life and strong attachment to the best qualities of both the Polish gentry and the lower classes, however, bear no comparison with Poe. The incongruity of his Positivist and Sarmatian bent is as alien to Poe as it is close to Henryk Sienkiewicz who, in Julian Krzyżanowski's view, profited from Poe's detective fiction in his historical novels.[8]

Like Faleński, Zygmunt Niedźwiecki (1864–1915) directly availed himself of Poe's principles of storytelling through the translation of several of Poe's tales. His own short fictional works, published in nineteen volumes, are accom-plished realizations of Poe's theory, although in his preoccupation with social issues, Socialist ideology, and Realism he relates more to Guy de Maupassant than to Poe.

One of the reasons for Poe's deeply embedded presence in Poland lies in the spiritual and artistic affinity critics and scholars have discovered between Poe and some important writers, notably the Romantics, Modernists, and Neoromantics. Indications of affinity between Poe and Cyprian Norwid (1821–1883), first noticed by Faleński, may have been complemented by influence. Norwid certainly knew Poe's works in Baudelaire's translation and probably read them in English during his stay in New York (1853–1854), where he met an individual by the name of Griswold. Was this person Rufus Wilmot Griswold (1815–1857), Poe's infamous literary executor and author of a scurrilous memoir on Poe that was widely published? Norwid mentions Griswold in a letter to a friend written in London shortly after he returned from the United States, without providing Griswold's initials. In any case, the meeting between Norwid and Griswold did not include a discussion of Poe's works. Norwid remarked that he "talked to him only once for a quarter of an hour" on matters relating to Norwid's existential problems.[9]

In the last two decades of the nineteenth century the demise of Positivism, the onset of Modernism, with its overlapping and crisscrossing pan-European aesthetic currents, and the gradual emergence of the *Młoda Polska* movement, with its Neoromantic orientation, actuated circumstances conducive for the first time to a heightened interest in Poe, especially after the publication of Baudelaire's *Flowers of Evil* in Poland in 1894. Weighed against the influx of Parnassians, Symbolists, representatives of Young Germany, Young Belgium, and Young Scandinavia, and other foreign authors, Poe's presence in Poland during that period remained rather unobtrusive, despite a wave of interest among general readers. The first collection of his short stories (four tales) was published in 1897, followed by six other selections within the next fifteen years, all of them modest volumes, including only one of poetry. True, they belie quite extensive translation activity engaging numerous literati; published primarily in periodicals, however, most of the individual tales and poems were doomed to disappear in the archives. For instance, Antoni Lange (1861?–1929), the most prolific and competent translator of Poe's poetry, never published his translations in book form. Today's editors of new collections of Poe's poems, appreciating Lange's translations, include them in their volumes along with Barbara Beaupré's (?–1943) renditions. Her *Kruk. Wybór poezji* ["The Raven": Selected poetry], published in 1910, was the first and for exactly half a century the only collection of Poe's poems in Polish. Although a slim volume, it was nevertheless a remarkable achievement; it contains a translation of "Israfel," the only one in Polish. Apart from her translation accomplishment, corroborated by later reprints (her Neoromantic style notwithstanding), Beaupré was probably the first Polish translator to render Poe's poems from the original. Her source was J. A. Harrison's Virginia edition, whose introduction provided her with information concerning Poe's life and work, which she used in the introduction to her collection of Poe's stories published in 1909. Consequently, in her outline of Poe's biography, she managed to avoid Baudelaire's factual errors. Her translations of Poe's poems are reminiscent of Ola Hansson's renditions.

With due acknowledgment of the significant role the Modernists played in Poe's Polish reception in general, their contribution has been somewhat exaggerated; it is equivocal at best. True, the coryphaei of the movement, Zenon Przesmycki (1861–1944) (known also under the pseudonym Miriam) and Stanisław Przybyszewski (1868–1927), esteemed Poe highly. As a resourceful translator Przesmycki introduced Polish readers to more than a hundred foreign authors but translated only four of Poe's poems. Przybyszewski was greatly attracted to Poe on aesthetic grounds; several moments of his *Confiteor* resemble Poe's poetics, though his "satanism" and the idea of the "naked soul" can hardly be ascribed to Poe's inspiration. His fascination notwithstanding, Przybyszewski rendered only three of Poe's poems into Polish. As editor of the short-lived literary journal *Życie* (1897–1900), published in Cracow, he was more involved in promoting Poe in Poland. He accepted several translations of Poe's works and planned to publish *Eureka* which, in fact, has never appeared in Polish. Shortly before Przybyszewski took over as editor, *Życie* had published Ola Hansson's celebrated study of Poe. It compounded Poe's Polish image of victim, hero, decadent, exotic figure, psychopath, alcoholic, drug addict, mystic short of a saint, visionary, and outcast of the stereotypical view of the United States as a cultural wasteland.

By the middle of the first decades of the twentieth century Poe had infiltrated the Poles' collective consciousness as had perhaps no other foreign author. This penetration can be seen in the publication of a translation of "The Cask of Amontillado" in two issues of *Kaliope* (1906), a Warsaw high school literary paper, along with the student editors' appeal to readers for information on past Polish translations of Poe's works as part of a project on his reception in Poland. Poe served as a reference, and his texts generated names, sobriquets, and allusions. A Warsaw theater that opened in 1925 was named "The Red Mask"; Stanisław I. Witkiewicz jokingly used to call his anthropologist friend Bronisław Malinowski "Nevermore"; the poet Jerzy Żuławski entitled one of his poems "Nevermore," although its form and content bear no artistic debt to Poe.

The range of interpretations widened and included Marxist and psychoanalytical approaches. Among the latter was a brief discussion by Leon Blumenstok in his *Szkice psychiatryczne* [Psychiatric essays] (1891), which anticipated Marie Bonaparte's celebrated psychoanalytic study of Poe by four decades. Before the Neoromantics faded completely into history, one of their last representatives, Stanisław Wyrzykowski, avoided limbo by turning to Poe. No other Pole before or after him translated so many Poe tales. They were published in three collections between 1922 and 1924. Even more than Leśmian's, most of the translated stories constitute the core of the numerous re-editions of Poe's prose that, tantalizing Communist officialdom, became part of the Poe renaissance that began in 1956 with the two-volume edition of Poe's stories prepared by Władysław Kopaliński, which is still read today. It has been a renaissance indeed when we consider the fact that after 1924 Poe was close to oblivion in Poland. The leading literary groups of the interwar period — the Warsaw Skamander poets and the Cracow Avantgards — ignored him; Roman Zimny, the only Socialist critic permitted to commemorate the hundredth anniversary of Poe's death in 1949, "eulogized" him as "a poet of fear and defeat." The ideological thaw after 1956 generated a more favorable attitude toward the United States and allowed a closer look at its past and contemporary writers. Critics and poets such as Władysław Kopaliński, Leszek Elektorowicz, Artur Międzyrzecki, Gomulicki, and others, along with a new generation of translators, finally began to redraw the image of Poe that Baudelaire, Hansson, Przybyszewski, Leśmian, and their epigones had created.[10] It is no longer the image of a mystic, saint, victim to be pitied, philosopher, or madman; sophisticated readers no longer interpret his poems and tales biographically. It is an image more like one we have created of ourselves. But who is to judge whether it reflects the real Poe?

NOTES

1. A. H. [Adolf Hennel], "Edgar Poe, jego życie i pisma," *Gazeta Codzienna* 61 (1858): 3–4, 62: 3–4; the translations appeared in *Gazeta Codzienna* that same year, 64: 4, 68: 4, 73: 3–4, 82: 5, 89: 5–6, respectively.

2. Tadeusz Grabowski, *Polska poezja po roku 1863* (Cracow: Czas, 1903), p. 110; Adolf Nowaczyński, [no title], *Tylko dla kobiet* (1934): 32–33; Juliusz Wiktor Gomulicki, "Duch od pragnień (O Felicjanie Faleńskim)," *Ateneuum* 6 (1938): 783–821. Hypothetically, Grabowski's claim might be substantiated. Given Faleński's wide reading and exceptional literary erudition, he could have come across Poe's name as early as 1846 in connection with the literary scandal involving French renditions of "The Mur-

ders in the Rue Morgue." See Patrick F. Quinn, *The French Face of Edgar Poe* (Southern Illinois UP, 1957), p. 67 ff.

3. Felicjan Faleński, "Edgar Allan Poe i jego nowele," *Biblioteka Warszawska* 4.1 (1861): 1–44; F. Lyra, *Edgar Allan Poe* (Warsaw: Wiedza Powszechna, 1973). I have excluded Ola Hansson's long essay. A short summary of Faleński's views has been presented in Joan Delaney, "A Polemical Plagiarism: 'Two Early Critiques of Edgar Allan Poe in Polish and Russian,'" *Antemurale* 12 (1968): 315–320, in the context of her discussion of the strikingly close resemblance between Faleński's article and one published by E. Lopushinskij in the St. Petersburg periodical *Russkoe Slovo* only a month later. Delany offers a stimulating interpretation of the identical passages as well as those that are absent in the other author's article. She seems to be correct in asserting that Lopushinskij is a pseudonym, but her search did not produce his identity. In *Amerikanskaya literatura v russkikh perevodakh i kritike: Bibliografiya 1776–1975* (Moscow: Nauka, 1977), p. 206, Valentina Abramova Libman does not identify Lopushinskij either. Considering the extremely short time span between the appearance of both publications, and bearing in mind Faleński's and his father-in-law's active loyalty to the tsar, might not Lopushinskij be simply Faleński himself?

4. The letter, unpublished, is in the mauscript division of the Jagiellonian University Library, Cracow. Its existence was communicated to me by Juliusz W. Gomulicki.

5. Stanisław Zabierowski, "Statek potępiony. Z historii jednego z międzynarodowych motywów w *Popiołach* Żeromskiego," *Zeszyty Naukowe. Literatura Powszechna. Wyższa Szkoła Pedagogiczna w Katowicach* 1 (1963): 57–70. Of Poe's works, Żeromski valued most *The Narrative of Arthur Gordon Pym*.

6. Stefan Grabiński, "Książę fantastów," *Lwowskie Wiadomości Muzyczne i Literackie* 3 (1931): 1, 4: 1–2, 5: 2–3.

7. Wilhelm Feldman, *Współczesna literatura polska* (Cracow: Krakowska Spółka Wydawnicza, 1930), p. 569.

8. Julian Krzyżanowski, "Trylogia a powieść ludowa," in *Henryk Sienkiewicz. Twórczość i recepcja światowa*, ed. Aniela Piorunowa and Kazimierz Wyka (Cracow: Wydawnictwo Literackie, 1959), p. 385.

9. Cyprian Norwid, *Pisma wybrane*, ed. Juliusz W. Gomulicki (Warsaw: Państwowy Instytut Wydawniczy, 1968), vol. 5, p. 249.

10. A prime representative of the new generation of translators is Stanisław Barańczak, whose recent rendition of "The Raven" stands as a gem in the art of translation. See Stanisław Barańczak, *Ocalone w tłumaczeniu* (Poznań: Wydawnictwo, 1994), pp. 402–404. Barańczak's "Kruk" is the eleventh Polish version of Poe's poem.

# Poe in Spain

JOSÉ ANTONIO GURPEGUI

Certain historical events in Spain did not favor a strong interest in English-language writers on the Peninsula during the past century. The British grip on Gibraltar caused the Spanish government to discourage the study of English for political reasons, and Franco's forty-year dictatorship exalted the purely Hispanic to the detriment of any foreign cultural expression. Works by renowned Anglo-American writers were often read in French or in Spanish translation based on the French versions. This is the case of Edgar Allan Poe, whose influence on numerous Spanish writers since the latter part of the nineteenth century is unquestionable.

The most extensive study of Poe's influence on Spanish authors is John E. Englekirk's *Edgar Allan Poe in Hispanic Literature*, published more than sixty years ago.[1] According to Englekirk, Poe made his debut in Spain in 1857 when a revised version of "Three Sundays in a Week" appeared anonymously in a Madrid publication. The story was apparently translated directly from the English, since the tale had not been included in Baudelaire's 1856 collection. The Spanish version follows the original almost word for word, with the exception of the main characters, who were given Hispanic names (E 15–16).

The first mention of Poe in Spain is found in an essay by Pedro Antonio de Alarcón (1833–1891), published in *La Epoca* in September 1858, in which the author describes the enthusiasm of Spanish readers who managed to get their hands on a few copies of Baudelaire's translation of *Histoires extraordinaires*. Alarcón mentions that Poe was a popular author during the previous winter.[2] He gives a description of Poe's life that is largely based on Baudelaire's account but then adds his own embellishments when he mentions that Poe was born into a noble and very rich family and that his travels took him from Jerusalem to the land of the Eskimos. In Poe's stories Alarcón recognized an original, calculating intelligence capable of persuading the reader in the realm of the fantastic. Although Alarcón was strongly influenced by Baudelaire's essay on Poe, he nonetheless expressed his own enthusiasm for Poe's mathematical mind and psychological insights.

In the same year, 1858, the first collection of Poe's tales appeared in Spain, apparently based on Baudelaire's edition and bearing a similar title in Spanish, *Historias extraordinarias*. Nicasio Landa's prologue to the edition repeats many ideas from Baudelaire but also expresses admiration for Poe's ability to "exploit the marvelous in the field of science" and recognizes the psychological problems that come from the instinct of perversity.[3] From 1858 on, short articles and reviews started to appear in various newspapers and magazines, such as the article by Juan Prieto in *Revista Hispano-Americana* on January 15, 1867. Prieto praises Poe's vast erudition and was the first in Spain to appreciate the beauty of Poe's cosmological poem *Eureka*.

In 1871 Manuel Cano Cueto, a Sevillan poet, wrote an article on Poe that was later used as a preface to a translation of Poe tales published in Seville. Writing at the age of twenty-two, Cano Cueto was very moved by what he perceived to be Poe's sad life in the United States, which, he remarks, "is not the right country to produce poets" (F 72). He considered Poe a sort of redeemer of the materialistic American people, one of Baudelaire's favorite themes. After an emotional description of Poe's personal life, Cano Cueto expresses keen insights into Poe's literary importance: "Edgar Poe is undoubtedly the founder of a new genre. His imagination is strange; there is in it something of the scalpel, something mathematical . . . there is no writer of modern times who has so great a faculty for making stories out of the inmost sensations of the soul" (F 73). Such laudatory descriptions must have made Spanish readers all the more eager to read the American writer.

Another preface to a Poe translation played an important role in forming Spanish opinion. Alfonso Hernández Catá wrote an introduction to two collections of Poe's tales which were in circulation for many years around the turn of the twentieth century. In a rather exaggerated fashion he remarks: "Never since Shakespeare has the English language been handled with such art" (F 75). Catá's study is remarkable in the sense that he understood the importance of Poe's influence on other writers, mentioning specifically Verne, Gautier, and Maeterlinck.

As in other European countries, the 1909 centenary of Poe's birth was celebrated in Spain with tributes to the American author. One of the most comprehensive studies on Poe in Spanish was written for the occasion by the critic Ángel Guerra, who published his article in *La España moderna* in April 1909. His tribute opens with a description of the neglect and contempt Poe suffered in his native land, then moves on to praising Poe's unusual character and originality. "Edgar Poe has nothing of the American," remarked Guerra. "He is something apart, completely exotic if you will, in Yankee intellect and literature" (F 78–79). Echoing the theme of the poet rising from his ashes, an image found in Mallarmé's poem "The Tomb of Edgar Poe," also written for the centenary, Guerra remarks that when Poe was buried in America, "the Yankees thought that they had also buried in oblivion the talent of their greatest poet" (F 83). Then Guerra credits Europeans, specifically Baudelaire, with having the intellectual and literary sensitivity that rehabilitated the American poet and made him renowned abroad.

Between 1858 and the centenary in 1909 Poe was highly praised by Spanish critics as a writer of tales and as a poet. When we look for Poe's influence on Spanish authors, we return to the first author of a critical study on Poe, Pedro Antonio de Alarcón, who left clear evidence of his admiration for Poe in his *Narraciones inverosímiles* [Implausible stories] (1883), a volume of fantastic tales written in a style that is unique to this particular work. In "El año de Spitzberg" ["The Year of Spitzberg"], the protagonist is banished to the North Pole, a plot reminiscent of "A Descent into the Maelström." In "La mujer alta" ["The Tall Woman"], the narrator sees a woman in an alley, and from that point on he starts a mental idealization like the one in "Berenice." "El amigo de la muerte" ["The Friend of Death"] finds a parallel in "The Masque of the Red Death"; in Alarcón's story the protagonist has a fixation with being immortal, and death meets him at the end of the tale to send him to the North Pole.

Another Spanish writer of tales and novels, Pio Baroja (1872–1956), openly admitted his admiration for Poe as well as the influence the American writer had on his work. Poe's legacy to Baroja is considerable from both thematic and stylistic perspectives. Thematically, one can see a pessimistic attitude toward society, although in Baroja's case — unlike Poe's — the existential bitterness is related to religion and politics, and life appears as a depressing chaos leading to apathy and personal paralysis in most instances. Stylistically, Poe's influence is more evident, especially in the importance given to action and in what Baroja specialists call his "visionary element." Baroja's *Las inquietudes de Shanti Andia* [The worries of Shanti Andia] (1911) recounts the adventures of a Basque sailor who returns home after sailing around the world. The treatment of intrigue, adventure, and characterization suggests the strong influence of Poe's *The Narrative of Arthur Gordon Pym*.

Poe's direct influence on a Spanish poet is most evident in the works of Emilio Carrere (1881–1947), whose poem "El bardo maldito" [The cursed bard] depicts the solitary poet alone with his friend the raven (E 422–423). Carrere's Bohemian lifestyle and drinking habits led to his becoming known as "the Spanish Poe," although the title had little to do with the artistic quality of his writing. A number of poems in Carrere's collection *El caballero de la muerte* [The knight of death] show imitations of Poe's themes and poetic techniques. In this volume Carrere translated Baudelaire's 1856 preface to the *Histoires extraordinaires*. Englekirk remarks that "in both choice of theme and verse technique [Carrere] fairly overwhelms one with reminiscences of, and resemblances to, [Poe]" (E 421). Englekirk then offers convincing examples from Carrere's poems and tales. Carrere could also be considered the Spanish Baudelaire in the sense that he translated Poe's work, wrote essays about him, and identified with his personal life.

During the two years he spent in France, Francisco Villaespesa (1866–1936) became acquainted with Poe's work through Baudelaire's translations. The author of more than twenty books of poetry and several plays, Villaespesa died in extreme poverty. The death of his beloved Elisa is the theme of a number of poems that seem to be inspired directly from Poe, especially from "Ulalume" and "Ligeia." In two of Villaespesa's collections of poems, *In Memoriam* and *El libro del amor y de la muerte* [Book of love and death], the death of a beautiful woman, which Poe considered the most poetical of all themes, is expressed in Poesque images and language (E 443–450).

Like Villaespesa, Juan Ramón Jiménez (1881–1958; Nobel Prize winner in 1956) became familiar with Poe's poetry during a stay in Paris, where he was immersed in the poetic creations of Verlaine, Mallarmé, and the French Symbolists.[4] Jiménez understood that the psychic contents of any verbal creation must be everlasting and independent from the original intention of the poetical creation as an empirical reality. He admired Poe's ideas set forth in "The Poetic Principle," especially the definition of poetry as "the Rhythmical creation of Beauty." In his poem "Nocturno," Jiménez expresses the subtleties of this concept of poetry. Although most of the traces of Poe's influence on Jiménez are vague, there are a couple of cases in which a direct connection is evident. For example, the Spanish poet entitled a small collection of poems "Nevermore" and quoted lines from "The Raven" to introduce them. On a visit to the United States, Jiménez made a pilgrimage to Poe's cottage, which he recalls in his *Diario de un poeta recién casado* [Diary of a recently married poet] (1916).

Eugene Del Vecchio's article on Antonio Machado (1875–1939) traces the affinities between Poe and the Spanish poet that were pointed out by other scholars. An earlier study by Gutiérrez focused on the parallels between the two authors' poetics, their notions of time, dream, forgetfulness, love, and poetic intuition. Olivia Areti studied the use of the refrain in Machado's poetry, which follows Poe's recommendation in "The Philosophy of Composition" that the refrain suggest rather than describe. Del Vecchio then examines an "undetected affinity," which he defines as "an important aspect of Poe's and Machado's poetics [that] focuses on the relationship between vigil (duermevela) and sleep, day-dreams and dreams."[5] Antonio Machado had lived in Paris, where he was in touch with French Symbolist poetry. In his early volume *Soledades* [Solitudes] (1903), there are many images reminiscent of Poe. Antonio's brother, Manuel Machado (1874–1947), was also influenced by Poe, whom he probably came to know during his two-year stay in Paris. His collection of poetry, *Alma* [Soul] (1904), reflects that influence and seeks the very essence of the human being to explore a person's inner world and deepest yearnings.

The connection between Miguel de Unamuno (1864–1936) and Poe has been explored by Thomas R. Franz, who traces points of influence through Baudelaire, Mallarmé, and Valéry.[6] Unamuno read Poe as early as 1907 and published an article in 1923 in which he encouraged readers to judge Poe on his work instead of on the negative aspects of his life. Franz discusses the detective format Unamuno uses in *La novela de don Sandalio, jugador de ajedrez* [Novella of Don Sandalio, chess player] (1930), which is recounted by a narrator similar to Poe's in "The Murders in the Rue Morgue" and Valéry's in *Monsieur Teste*.

Gregorio Martínez Sierra (1881–1948) openly admitted Poe's influence along with that of Verlaine. He tried to portray the mysterious atmosphere in some of Poe's stories. At the age of nineteen he wrote the tale "Almas ausentes" [Absent souls] (1900), which follows closely Poe's tale "The System of Doctor Tarr and Professor Fether." This latter tale held a particular fascination for Adolfo Llanos y Alcaraz (1834–1894), who created a musical-dramatic adaptation of it called "Quién es el loco?" [Who is the crazy one?] (1867). Alice Pollin gives a detailed analysis of the humorous points of comparison between "Tarr" and "Loco" along with Llanos's comic allusion to Poe's "Ligeia."[7]

Ramón Pérez de Ayala (1881–1962) was one of the most important literary figures of his time. At the beginning of his first book of poems, *La paz del sendero* [The peace of the track] (1903), he quotes a paragraph from "The Poetic Principle," which suggests that he found an affinity in Poe's poetics. Three more twentieth-century writers can be closely connected with Poe. Eduardo Marquina (1879–1946) sought temporal as well as spatial detachment in his lyrical plays, similar to some of Poe's poems and tales. His poem "Vendimión" [Harvest] (1909) seems to be directly influenced by Poe, and his tale "La dueña del mundo" [The woman of the world] bears a close resemblance to "Ligeia" in terms of physical setting and the study of passion.

Wenceslao Fernández Flores (1885–1964) was first of all an author with a great sense of humor and irony, but, like Poe, his works showed an overwhelmingly pessimistic and bitter view of society. Ramón Gómez de la Serna (1891–1963) was interested in Poe from a critical point of view, as can be seen in his biography *Edgar Poe: el genio de América* [Edgar Poe: The American genius] (1953). Artistically, Poe's influence shows up in a collection of compositions Gómez calls "greguerías," which he describes as spontaneous thoughts that come from the unconscious mind and from things.

Poe's influence on contemporary authors is scarce, except for the possible effect on Juan Madrid in his detective stories and on Cristina Fernández Cubas, on whom Poe's influence is suggested by Enrique Murillo in his introduction to her novels *Mi hermana Elba* [My sister Elba] and *El año de Gracia* [The year of grace] (1992). Some excellent critical work on Poe has been done in Spain during the last decade, especially the studies by Francisco Javier Castillo, author of *Aspectos estilísticos en la obra narrativa de E. A. Poe* [Stylistic aspects of Poe's narrative work] (1991). Poe's detective stories have been analyzed by María José Alvarez Maurín and Manuel Broncano, while Fernando Savater has done a critical study of Poe's tales in *La infancia recuperada* [Childhood recovered] (1979), which is an interesting study from a Freudian point of view, although not a piece of literary criticism.

It was not until 1970 that Poe's works received in Spain the editorial attention they deserve. Alianza Editorial brought out an edition of Poe's tales that had been translated and introduced by Julio Cortázar, published by the University of Puerto Rico in 1956. These two volumes were followed by the translation of *The Narrative of Arthur Gordon Pym* (1971), *Eureka* (1972), and Poe's essays and criticism (1973). As we approach the end of the twentieth century, Poe continues to be a widely read author in Spain, and his work draws the attention of critics and doctoral students who pursue the connections between Poe and Spanish writers.

NOTES

1. John E. Englekirk Jr., *Edgar Allan Poe in Hispanic Literature* (New York: Instituto de las Españas, 1934; rpt. New York: Russell and Russell, 1972); hereafter cited as E.

2. The article was later reprinted in Pedro Antonio de Alarcón, "Edgar Poe," in *Juicios literarios y artísticos* (Madrid: Sucesores de Rivas de Neyra, 1883), pp. 101–119.

3. A detailed description of Landa's prologue is given by John De Lancey Ferguson in his chapter on Poe in *American Literature in Spain* (New York: Columbia UP, 1916),

pp. 55–86; hereafter cited as F. Englekirk acknowledged Ferguson as his source for Landa.

4. For a detailed study of Poe's influence on Jiménez, see Carmen Pérez, "Raíces Norteamericanas en la Obra de Juan Ramón Jiménez: E. A. Poe y la Poesía Juanramoniana," *Anuario de Estudios Filologicos* No. 2 (1979): 212–229.

5. Eugene Del Vecchio, "E. A. Poe and Antonio Machado: An Undetected Affinity," *Discurso Literario* 5.2 (1988): 395–400; T. Labrador Gutiérrez, "Presencia de Edgar Allan Poe in Antonio Machado," *Archivo Hispalense* 57.175 (1974): 87–119; Olivia Areti, "Antonio Machado e la poetica di E. A. Poe," *Studi Ispanici* (1979): p. 131–140.

6. Thomas R. Franz, "Unamuno and the Poe/Valéry Legacy," *Revista Hispánica Moderna* 50 (1997): 48–56. See also M. Thomas Inge and Gloria Downing, "Unamuno and Poe," *Poe Newsletter* 3 (1970): 35–36.

7. Alice M. Pollin, "Edgar Allan Poe in the Works of Llanos y Alcaraz," *Hispanofila* 79 (September 1983): 21–37.

# Poe in Portugal

MARIA LEONOR MACHADO DE SOUSA

Poe's reception in Portugal is best understood when placed in the un-usual political and historical context that prevailed in the country in the nine-teenth century. The invasion by Napoleon's armies in 1807 caused the flight of the royal family to Brazil, allowing the establishment of an unwanted British rule, and the civil war for the cause of liberalism created an atmosphere that was not favorable to the flowering of the arts. Portuguese literature, which by the end of the eighteenth century had already declined because of the Inqui-sition and censorship, was practically nonexistent. The works that did appear were weak and generally estranged from the new ideas and movements that had inspired writers abroad.

Out of this negative situation came a positive development in the mid–nineteenth century: many of the Portuguese intellectuals and writers who had chosen exile returned from France and England eager to share new aesthetic ideas and authors with others in their country. Romanticism developed much later in Portugal than in other countries; while Portuguese authors were still producing historical novels or drama and creating overly sentimental poetry, the rest of Europe was already following new trends. Translations — some anonymous and often second-rate — were frequently published in periodicals that flourished during the latter half of the nineteenth century.

The first documented work by Poe in Portuguese appeared in 1857 when an unknown journalist by the name of António Carrilho published a translation of "The Unparalleled Adventure of One Hans Pfaall" in the newspaper *A Opi-nião*. The first chapter is headed by the words "Edgar Poe" and "historias extraordinarias," indicating that the translation was probably based on Baude-laire's version of the tale, which was included in his 1856 collection *Histoires extraordinaires*. The choice of this story, which was not translated into Portu-guese again until 1971 in Poe's complete tales, shows how randomly translators picked their texts. "Hans Pfaall" is not typical of Poe's style and certainly not one of his most popular stories. Appearing in the same newspaper a year later was a story "O fantasma" [The ghost], which was called "an American tale," suggesting that it was Poe's. The subject seems to be a variation of Dickens's *A Christmas Carol*. The Portuguese translators were quite casual in their selection and modification of borrowed material. In 1858 "The Conversation of Eiros and Charmion" was also published in a serial, again most likely having been translated from Baudelaire.[1]

Around 1865 new winds were blowing in Portugal, and a lively group of young men, most of whom had studied at the University of Coimbra, rebelled against the dominant literature, which had reached excesses that would later be called Ultra-Romanticism. Members of this group, later known as A Geração de 70 [Generation of the Seventies], still used bombastic Romantic wording but were open to new trends, especially those coming from France. Through Baudelaire, they discovered Poe. Antero de Quental (1842–1891), the greatest poet of this generation, translated "The Assignation," which appeared as an anonymous piece in a country newspaper under the heading "Contos (inéditos) d'Edgar Poe" [Unpublished stories by Edgar Poe].[2] Since Baudelaire did not translate this tale, the source was probably William Hughes's *Contes inédits d'Edgar Poe traduits de l'anglais* [The unpublished stories of Edgar Poe translated from the English] (1862), or it was translated directly from English, which Antero knew from his childhood. "The Assignation" is the first typical Poe tale to appear in Portugal, typical in the sense that it combines mystery with the decadence that would mark literature at the end of the nineteenth century. Antero's translation of the poem included in the tale — later printed as a separate poem, "To One in Paradise" (with some modifications) — shows a variation from the original version, which was not included among Baudelaire's translations. Instead of addressing a dead woman, Antero refers to a married woman whose love he had lost, suggesting an episode from his own youth. In addition to this change, he was quite free in rendering the text while keeping some images connected with the sea and Poe's repetition of "no more." This poem, untitled but with the heading "From the English of Edgar Poe," appeared again in Antero's volume of poetry *Primaveras românticas* [Romantic springtimes] in 1872.

One of the earliest critical assessments of Poe in Portugal dates to 1865 when Teófilo Braga, the first systematic historian of Portuguese literature, wrote in a letter to a friend that "the tales of Edgar Poe, the most extraordinary imagination in America, have the fantastic of the insolubility of the philosophical problems that make the action; they sometimes reach high metaphysics. . . . Edgar Poe has the force of imagination and ideal surpassed by the positivism of a manufacturing society proud of its industrial character; in his tales there is the hallucination of madness."[3] Although Braga was critical of the negative aspects of Poe's personal life, caused by alcoholism in his opinion, he nevertheless fell under the influence of the American writer's tales. Three of Braga's stories published in 1865 reveal numerous parallels with Poe: "Aquela máscara" [That mask], "Lava de um crâneo" [Lava from a skull], and "A ogiva sombria" [The gloomy ogive].

The greatest novelist of the Generation of the Seventies, Eça de Queirós (1845–1900), also expressed his opinion about Poe. Referring to Baudelaire's translations he remarked: "Through those pages there passes the demon of perversity, now immobile and grayish-blue like cypresses, then merry, cheerful, falling head over heels, displaying his ripped clothes, laughing while showing his rotten teeth, dreadful and dissolute as a clown in the streets. . . . Poe does not have the vague illuminism of Hoffmann nor the cold imagination of Darwin. Poe tells the truth about fears and visions, reality. His book is the delirious epic of the nervous system." [4] Although Eça's words do not exactly praise Poe, he reveals a fascination with certain aspects of Poe's work that influenced his own early tales, such as "O Defunto" [The deceased] and "A Ama" [The nurse].

During the twenty-five-year period after the first translation in 1857, Poe's tales were published randomly in numerous periodicals and seemed to attract readers by their morbidity, mystery, and strangeness. The first collection of his tales was published in 1889 by Mécia Mousinho de Albuquerque, who edited another volume the following year. [5] Her collection remained the most extensive in Portuguese until a complete two-volume edition came out in 1971 and 1972, unfortunately in a poor translation. [6]

Álvaro do Carvalhal (1844–1868) had apparently read some of the early translations and fell under Poe's spell for several of the six short "delirious" stories he wrote in 1866 and 1867. The collection was published by a friend in 1868 after Caravalhal's death at the age of twenty-four. His tales were written in what has been considered the baroque style, strongly emotional and artificial, characteristic of the Ultra-Romantic period in Portugal. Caravalhal drew from Poe the sarcastic tone with which he described the most gruesome details. By mentioning Poe, he acknowledged his debt to him in "O punhal de Rosaura" [Rosaura's dagger] and "Os canibais" [The cannibals]. The death of Rosaura and her apparent return to life show a direct influence of "The Fall of the House of Usher." Poe's influence is also apparent in Carvalhal's "A febre do jogo" [The fever of gambling]. Although Carvalhal was not a great writer, his tales are an important example of the atmosphere that enveloped the literary interests of the time. Renewed interest in his work inspired a new publication of his tales in 1978. [7]

Poe was also admired in Portugal as a poet. "The Raven" appeared for the first time in 1887, published in a regional newspaper by an unknown Paulo de Magalhães, whose source was admittedly Baudelaire's version.[8] The poem became more widely known in Portuguese when Mécia Mousinho de Albuquerque included it along with "The Philosophy of Composition" in her 1890 volume of the collected tales.

The generation of Portuguese poets who wrote from the last years of the nineteenth century through the first decades of the twentieth all fell under the spell of Symbolism and Decadence, where Poe's influence was generally felt. This influence can be seen clearly in the works of José Duro (1875–1899) and Roberto de Mesquita (1871–1923). Duro wrote a sonnet entitled "O Corvo" [The raven], which is included in his only book, *Fel* [Gall], dedicated to "Antero and Poe."[9] In his poem the raven is presented as a herald of his lover's approaching death in the setting of a dark night. For Duro, the raven symbolizes his own destiny; he refers to "my raven, wavering and sick." In other poems by Duro, the general atmosphere and mood are strikingly similar to Poe's. Roberto de Mesquita also left only one book of poems, most of which had first been published in periodicals.[10] Again, Poe's influence is evident in the pessimistic view of life, the choice of dark and mysterious atmosphere, and the insistence on a past that could suggest only misfortune and decay.

The twentieth century began under the sway of Modernism in Portugal. Two of Modernism's greatest names, Fernando Pessoa and Mário de Sá-Carneiro, were both familiar with Poe, especially his tales. Pessoa translated his own favorite poems, "The Raven" in 1925 and "Annabel Lee" and "Ulalume" in 1926, for the literary magazine *Athena*. Fascinated by Poe's life and work, Pessoa created a Poesque tale, "A Very Original Dinner," at age nineteen and a long fragmentary one, "The Door," both written in English and ascribed to the heteronym Alexander Search.[11] Pessoa was captivated by Poe's poems and tales throughout his life, as can be seen in the notes and fragments of creative endeavors he left behind (see Part II, "Fernando Pessoa"). Sá-Carneiro also wrote poems and tales that reveal Poe's influence. Pessoa was aware of the effect of Poe on the work of his fellow author. Speaking of Sá-Carneiro, he observed: "His imagination was one of the very finest in modern literature, for he outdid Poe in the reasoning tale, in 'The Strange Death of Professor Antena.'"[12] Pessoa could also have mentioned mystery, which is the starting point of all the tales by Sá-Carneiro.

Other Portuguese poets tested their talents by translating "The Raven." In 1929 Máximo das Dores, an unknown poet at the time, published a collection of his own poems that concluded with a rhymed translation of "The Raven."[13]

Since the poet knew no English, as he indicates in a note, his version was based on Mallarmé's translation. With the French text presented along with the Portuguese, it is evident that Dores misunderstood specific lines. For example, Poe's "many a quaint and curious volume of forgotten lore" (translated correctly by Mallarmé as "*maint curieux et bizarre volume de savoir oublié*") becomes the Portuguese equivalent of "quaint books in which we forget everything." The translation of Poe's poetry was tried again in 1957 with a volume included in a minisize paperback collection. Entitled *O verme vencedor e outros poemas* [The conqueror worm and other poems], the eighteen poems were all new to Portuguese readers, except for "The Raven" and "To One in Paradise." [14] Some of the poems may have been printed earlier in periodicals, but there does not seem to be any trace of them. The volume was a novelty because it was part of a new series for the general reader; unfortunately, the quality of the translations is very weak.

Poe's tales have continued to be published as single texts, largely because of the growing interest in mystery fiction. A new collection of nine tales came out in 1978, followed by another volume of nine in 1984.[15] Perhaps due to the more recent influence of visual effects, four of Poe's tales have been published in a cartoon series. Under the heading "classics in cartoon," the volume of illustrated Poe stories includes "The Pit and the Pendulum," "The Fall of the House of Usher," "The Cask of Amontillado," and "The Murders in the Rue Morgue." [16]

The daunting task of translating Poe's complete tales was attempted in 1944, but only one volume was produced. The 1971–1972 edition includes the tales plus some of Poe's poems in verse translations. Through these volumes and the cheaper paperback editions that appear every few years, Poe continues to be a popular writer among general readers in Portugal.

NOTES

1. *Diário de Lisboa*, September 30, 1858.

2. *O Século XIX* (Penafiel), December 1864.

3. Teófilo Braga, "Carta a José Fontana," in *Contos fantásticos* (Lisbon: Tipografia Universal, 1865).

4. Eça de Queirós, "Poetas do Mal," in *Gazeta de Portugal* (1866); later included in Eça de Queirós, *Prosas bárbaras* (Porto: Lello e Irmãos, 1903).

5. Mécia Mousinho de Albuquerque, tales in *Biblioteca Universal Antiga e Moderna* (Lisbon: Companhia Nacional Editora, 1889, 1890).

6. *Histórias completas*, ed. João Costa (Lisbon: Editora Arcádia, 1971–1972).

7. Álvaro do Carvalhal, *Contos* (Coimbra: Imprensa da Universidade, 1868; rpt. Lisbon: Editora Arcádia, 1978). "The Cannibals" was made into a film by the well-known Portuguese director Manoel de Oliveira.

8. *A Aurora do Cávado* (1877).

9. José Duro, *Fel* (Lisbon: Empresa Literária Lisbonense, 1898).

10. Roberto de Mesquita, *Almas cativas* (1898; Famalicão: Tipografia Minerva, 1931).

11. Both texts are dated 1907 but were first published by Maria Leonor Machado de Sousa in *Fernando Pessoa e a literatura de ficção* (Lisbon: Novaera, 1979) and together, only in translation, in *"Um jantar muito original" sequido de "A Porta"* (Lisbon: Relógio de Água Editores, 1985).

12. This statement is part of a text that Pessoa wrote in English in 1916 and is now included in Fernando Pessoa, *Páginas íntimas e de auto-interpretação* (Lisbon: Edições Ática), p. 141.

13. Máximo das Dores, *Engano d'alma* (Lisbon: Imprensa Libânio da Silva, 1929).

14. *O verme vencedor e outros poemas* (Lisbon: Organizações, 1957?).

15. *Histórias extraordinárias* (Lisbon: Edição Amigos do Livro, 1978); *Histórias extraordinárias* (Lisbon: Publicações Europa-América, 1984).

16. Edgar Allan Poe, *Histórias extraordinárias*, Biblioteca RTP, Clássicos em Banda Desenhada (Lisbon: Editorial Pública, 1986).

# Poe in Spanish America

SUSAN F. LEVINE AND STUART LEVINE

Poe is both highly respected and extremely influential in Spanish America. Prominent members of significant literary movements — Modernism in the late nineteenth century, innovative groups in the 1920s, the "boom" of the 1960s — such as Rubén Darío, Horacio Quiroga, Jorge Luis Borges, Julio Cortázar, and Carlos Fuentes, along with numerous lesser known figures, have made Poe a major literary force.

There are striking similarities among these major writers who have responded strongly to Poe. Familiar with French literary interests in Poe, they tended to identify Baudelaire, and at times themselves, with him. They were, or considered themselves to be, in some way psychologically different from most people. They tended, moreover, to have unusual family backgrounds. Highly educated, they were also interested in altered states of consciousness, dreams, mysticism, archetype, and the collective unconscious and connected Poe to those interests. The same is true of some of the lesser known Spanish American admirers of Poe.

Since the late nineteenth century, when the Spanish American Modernists brought Poe's life and works into the Spanish American literary consciousness, Poe has been a popular figure; only the nature of his popularity has changed, following literary currents. Modernists responded principally to Poe's poetry and to his image as alienated artist. Since early in the twentieth century, Poe's psychological fiction, detective stories, and theory of short story composition have received more attention. While the aura of decadence and alienation in Poe's life still has a powerful effect, most authors he affects today know that Poe was a highly skilled, artistically controlled writer. Commentators now look at ambiguity in Poe's writings, finding "multiple intentions" in works in which comedy undercuts an apparent seriousness as the rational and the irrational interpenetrate. Recent critical tendencies have altered the complex way contemporary critics interpret Poe's Spanish American connections. Generalizations, of course, oversimplify, especially when one speaks of such a diverse and enormous area as Spanish America, but Poe's popularity there remains unquestionable.

The Modernists were the first Spanish American writers to celebrate Poe and to reflect on his influence. The critic and novelist Arqueles Vela (Mexico, 1899–1972) remarks that Poe's literary theory, which is evinced in his poetry and which influenced Baudelaire and the French Symbolists, contains the Modernist poetic.[1] Poe's poems appeal to the Modernists, he writes, because of their musicality, their coloristic and symbolic language, and their evocation of unusual states of mind. Specific connections between Poe's work and Spanish American Modernist composition can be traced, as Vela has done, to "The Philosophy of Composition." Modernists responded strongly to Poe's idea of creating a melancholic tone and to his rationale for using the theme of the death of a beautiful woman, specific sounds to create specific effects, interior rhymes and new variations of meters, repetitions, and onomatopoeia. They adopted Poe's dictum that the poet is the creator of beauty.

Critics agree that the initial bonds in the Modernists' relationship to Poe are Antonio Pérez Bonalde's (Costa Rica) translation of "The Raven" in 1887 and Rubén Darío's (Nicaragua) interest in Poe. Max Henríquez Ureña, in one of the most complete studies of Modernism, stresses the importance of Pérez Bonalde as well as that of Colombian poet José Asunción Silva, whose "Día de difuntos" [Day of the dead] (1892) and "Nocturno" (1894) are technically and thematically similar to some of Poe's poems.[2] In the first attempt to provide a comprehensive study of Poe's place in Hispanic literature, John Englekirk reported a flood of Spanish translations of Poe's poetry at the end of the nineteenth century.[3] The well-known 1894 translation of "The Bells" by Guatemalan Domingo Estrada, for example, is only one of many translations of the same poem. Englekirk mentions several Modernist journals that published translations and essays dedicated to Poe, a trend that has continued in Spanish American journals over the years.[4] Like other scholars, he acknowledges the importance of the Pérez Bonalde translation but believes that "Poe does not assume universal importance in Spanish America . . . until he is proclaimed one of 'los raros' [exceptional ones] by Rubén Darío" (E 89–90). Englekirk's work has been a touchstone, still most helpful when read in conjunction with other studies.

*Los raros* shows that Rubén Darío (1867–1916), leader and genius of Modernism, was familiar with both Poe's poetry and tales.[5] Darío's essay on Poe in *Los raros* expresses unqualified esteem. Using the often unreliable Ingram biography, he provides a Baudelarian portrait of Poe as an alienated writer in the materialistic environment of the United States. Like Baudelaire, Darío felt a kinship to Poe. His Poe is a prototypical suffering artist, handsome, and a constant dreamer — the image adopted by the Modernists. Darío, who suffered severely from nightmares, sleep disorder, and, likely related, alcoholism, identified with what he took to be Poe's creative process: the muse awakened during altered states of consciousness. While Darío's poetry and tales show traces of Poe's influence, his essays reveal an abiding interest in Poe's personality (see Part II, "Rubén Darío").

Among the Modernists frequently said to be reminiscent of Poe are José Asunción Silva (1865–1896); Julio Herrera y Reissig (Uruguay, 1875–1910), who came to Poe through his admiration of the French Symbolists; and Leopoldo Lugones (Argentina, 1874–1938), poet and writer of short fiction. The same year that Darío published *Azul* (1888), which brought him major recognition, Leopoldo Díaz (Argentina, 1862–1947), a poet about whom Darío wrote a poem in 1897, published a sonnet to Poe. Díaz translated some of Poe's poetry, which had a significant influence on his own (E 153).

Poe's influence in Spanish America was felt next in the short story, both in his theory — the creation of a single effect within a preestablished design — and his topics: inexplicable perversity or evil; the double; reincarnation; the death of a beautiful woman; visionary beauty expressed through ornate, complex, grotesque patterns; and mystical, organic universal oneness. These recurring motifs have inspired numerous Spanish American writers.

One of the most notable writers inspired by Poe is Horacio Quiroga (Uruguay, 1878–1937), who first produced Modernist prose but became best known for evoking psychological horror in a more direct style. Quiroga's obvious tie to Poe is in the title story from his second collection of tales, *El crimen del otro* [The crime of the other] (1904), a story about the sort of murderous perverseness found in Poe, which is at the same time a Poe-like wild parody. Quiroga, like Darío, is a major author who can be characterized as having an afflicted personality and who was strongly attracted to Poe.[6] Roberto Ibáñez sees a reflection of Quiroga's interest in the Decadents and Poe in the macabre nature of his early stories, but the bond extends beyond theme.[7] In his critical discussions of what makes a good story, Quiroga includes Poe's ideas on intensity, brevity, and unity of effect. In his own tales Quiroga is a master of the singular and total effect prescribed by Poe (see Part II, "Horacio Quiroga").

Poe was certainly important for the Argentine writer Jorge Luis Borges (1899–1986). That Borges, who wrote a sonnet about Poe, had a good critical sense of Poe's work is evident in numerous essays and in his discussion of Poe in *Introducción a la literatura norteamericana*.[8] Borges recalls that his first readings were in English, Poe's stories among them.[9] Elsewhere Borges offers a definition of the genre of detective fiction and a brilliant defense of Poe's place as its creator. It is a genre in which Borges himself has written very successfully. Poe's influence on Borges's detective stories was creatively studied in the 1980s by John Irwin and Maurice Bennett (see Part II, "Jorge Luis Borges").

Borges's observation about the compelling force of Poe's persona might provide an explanation for the connection Macedonio Fernández (1874–1952) finds between himself and Poe. Fernández was a flamboyant Argentine author influential on Spanish American authors since the early decades of the twentieth century. Although older than Borges, he had participated with Borges and other young writers in the avant-garde movement Ultraísmo in the 1920s. Jo Anne Engelbert observes that while Borges championed an idealist creative theory, Fernández was the writer who wrote according to it, creating works completely open in structure and without specific conclusion.[10] He did not, like Borges, follow Poe's theory of writing with the end in mind. Nevertheless, Fernández mentions Poe in his chaotic novel *Museo de la novela de la Eterna* [*Museum of the Novel of Eterna*] (1967). Referring to Eterna's "previous existences as a romantic heroine," he states, "behold Eterna, who was called Leonora in Poe, and Rebecca in *Ivanhoe*, and who can also be discerned in Lady Rowena" (JAE 166). Engelbert notes that "apparently speaking as himself" earlier in the book, Fernández writes: "I think I resemble Poe very strongly, although recently I have begun to imitate him a little; I believe that I am another Poe. . . . It is not a resemblance; it is — who knows? — a reappearance. As I wrote the poem 'Elena Bellamuerte' I felt I was Poe in sentiment, and nevertheless the text does not show any literary similarity" (JAE 166). The reference to "Elena Bellamuerte" is to a poem written shortly after the death of Fernández's beloved wife, Elena de Obieta. Although written in 1920, the poem was first published in 1941. The statement of identity with Poe — of being Poe — is made within the context of a "text-in-the-making," with deliberate confusion of "the principles of identity, congruence, and rational development" (JAE 135). Fernández sees the possibility for having more than one identity, a theme Poe treats in several tales.

Among the late-twentieth-century Spanish American writers who knew Poe's work well, Julio Cortázar (1914–1984) has shown the greatest interest; he translated all of Poe's fiction. He includes direct and indirect references to Poe in several of his works, acknowledges Poe's influence when discussing his own literary development, and incorporates Poe's ideas into his own theory of the short story (see Part II, "Julio Cortázar"). Although Cortázar identified Poe with Baudelaire and at times with certain Poe narrators, he saw that Poe was a professional, controlled writer with the ability to convert obsessions into literature. Cortázar, too, had that ability, as well as Poe's fondness for combining the serious with the comic, the transcendent with the absurd.

Carlos Fuentes, a Mexican novelist who, along with Cortázar, gained international fame during the "boom" of the 1960s, also acknowledges Poe's early influence. Like Borges and Cortázar, Fuentes acquired from Poe a desire to explore beyond apparent reality.[11] Parallel realities in the fiction of Fuentes are like those found in Poe's stories, but often they have different social and aesthetic implications. In *Aura* (1962), as in Poe's stories "Ligeia" and "Morella," Fuentes deals with reincarnation in a story that is Gothic in manner and setting. In *Cambio de piel* [*A Change of Skin*] (1967), Poe becomes an integral part of a complex pattern, as Fuentes weaves a series of references to "Ligeia" into the story. In *Terra Nostra* (1975), his references to Poe are even more complex and innovative. Structured as a subterranean voyage, the book incorporates references to Poe's sea narratives (see Part II, "Carlos Fuentes"). Fuentes suggests the power of words to change society and appears to write in order to change the world through literature. His ambiguous, open works require reader participation; they thus give readers the freedom to create their own fictions to alter reality. His references to Poe are one thread in a complex fabric of words used in new contexts so that readers can themselves be creative — as Macedonio Fernández wanted.

Poe's Spanish American literary influence extends well beyond the major authors discussed so far. Spanish American literary historians attest to his effect on writers of lesser fame. The critic Kessel Schwartz, for example, sees in *La cuidad muerta* [The dead city] (1911) by Abraham Valdelomar (Peru, 1888– 1919) a "mood of brooding horror, in imitation of Edgar Allan Poe."[12] He refers to Poe as one of the "remote ancestors" of Magic Realism and mentions that Rafael Arévalo Martínez (Guatemala, 1884–1975), another writer of short fiction, "inherited much from Poe, Lautréamont, and Nerval" (S 105, 112). Schwartz calls Carlos Droguett (Chile, b. 1912) "an author who accepts Poe and Proust as his primary guides" and finds two of Héctor Albert Alvarez Murena's works "obviously influenced by Kafka, Poe, and Horacio Quiroga" (S 156, 250).

Arturo Torres-Ríoseco and Enrique Anderson Imbert discuss Poe's connection to most of the same authors noted by Schwartz.[13] Torres-Ríoseco mentions an essay on Poe by Cuban essayist and poet José Enrique Varona (1849–1933) in *Desde mi belvedere* [From my Belvedere] (1917) and cites Poe's influence on the well-known Argentine novelist Ernesto Sábato (b. 1911) (TR 265,

312). Anderson Imbert notes possible influence on Argentine author Atilio Chiappori (1880–1947) and finds the titles *Annabel Lee* and *El Vampiro* for novels by the Honduran Froilán Turcios (1875–1943) evocative of Poe (AI 415, 403). In a study of prose fiction of the Cuban revolution, Seymour Menton shows how the story "Un 'bum'" (1965) by Lino Novas Calvo is "clearly inspired" by "The Cask of Amontillado."[14]

Mexican critic Emmanuel Carballo, in his analysis of twentieth-century Mexican writers, mentions the indebtedness of José Vasconcelos, Rafael Muñoz, and Carlos Fuentes to Poe.[15] A major intellectual force in Mexico in the early decades of the twentieth century, Vasconcelos (1882–1959), when asked about early influences on his work, told Carballo that he read Shakespeare and Poe as a boy in Eagle Pass (C 34). Muñoz (1899–1972), novelist of the Mexican revolution, once remarked, "I know each of Poe's tales" (C 271). As the case of Muñoz might suggest, references to Poe appear in surprising places.

Over the years there have been numerous critical studies of Poe in Spanish America, some as introductions to translations. Englekirk calls Santiago Pérez Triana's introductory article to Antonio Pérez Bonalde's translation of "The Raven" the "first serious study of Poe by a Spanish American" (E 86). Although Pérez Triana expressed a preference for Poe's poetry, he also discussed the fame Poe attained abroad as a writer of fiction, largely through Baudelaire's translations. Pérez Triana knew Baudelaire's translations and generally followed his interpretation of Poe's life. His essay discusses the construction of Poe's verse and the difficulty of translating it. Englekirk concludes that Pérez Triana's article, accepting "the errors and failings of Poe with characteristic generosity and admiring deference to the American's genius," sets the "general tone" for subsequent studies (E 89). His judgment seems to hold true.

Later essayists discuss Poe in a variety of contexts. H. A. Murena (Argentina, 1923–1975) examines Poe's role as catalyst for the nihilism of certain late-nineteenth- and early-twentieth-century European writers whose sense of alienation made them feel like exiles within their own countries.[16] He accords Poe an important position in a lineage of disaffected authors from the "malditos" through the Surrealists. Murena sees disenchantment with American society in both Poe's biography and his tales. As he reads some stories, they show a pattern: the decline of past glory leads to an opportunity for a new start unencumbered by heritage. His interest in Poe likely has more to do with his own view of history than Poe's, but his interpretation retains the familiar theme that Poe's works symbolically refer to his alienation from American society.

Octavio Paz (1914–1998), renowned Mexican poet and essayist, also discusses Poe in historical terms: "Poe is the first literary myth of the Europeans, by which I mean that he is the first American writer converted into a myth. . . . More than an invention, Poe is Baudelaire's translation. . . . Poe is the myth of the brother lost not in a strange and hostile land but in modern history. For all these poets the United States is not a country; it is the modern age." [17]

In 1960 Venezuelan critic Armando Rojas published "Edgard Allan Poe en la América Hispana," an article valuable, despite a few factual errors, both as an affirmation of Poe's importance in Spanish America and for its bibliographical references. [18] Although his assessment of Poe harkens back to Baudelaire, Darío, and Pérez Triana, his discussion of the publication of a number of articles on Poe in the literary journal *El cojo ilustrado* [The illustrated cripple] is useful. [19]

The fact that translations of Poe's fiction have appeared more often in Mexico, Argentina, and Chile than elsewhere in Spanish America is likely a key to Poe's notable popularity in those countries. Darío is believed first to have read Poe when working in Chile; Quiroga lived in Uruguay and Argentina; Borges read Poe in English at an early age in Argentina; Cortázar, also Argentine, and Carlos Fuentes, who grew up in Mexico, Chile, and the United States, read Poe as youths. Donald Yates observes that "only in the chief cultural centers of South America is detective fiction of any type published." [20] He mentions that Buenos Aires is the principal location of "native production" but that there is also activity in Mexico, Chile, and Uruguay. Besides the appeal of innovation in Poe's poetry and the similarities that Spanish American authors thought they perceived between themselves and Poe (or Poe as Baudelaire reinvented him), there is the fact that Poe wrote in — indeed, largely invented — certain genres that were popular in major publishing centers of Spanish America. As bibliographical studies show, Poe had an impact all over the region; perhaps we read more about his influence in Mexico and the southern cone simply because those are the largest publishing centers.

It is safe to assume, given the longevity and extent of Poe's popularity in Spanish America, that authors from all parts of that area of the world will continue to look to his works for inspiration. Poe's presence as archetypal author, one who sees beyond the ordinary at any given time, is lasting. The influence of both this mythic Poe and of his somewhat less appealing, though no less talented, "other" whom Poe scholars continue to piece together — the "real" Poe — seems bound to endure.

NOTES

1. Arqueles Vela, *El modernismo: Su filosofía, su estética, su técnica* (Mexico: Editorial Porrúa, 1949; rpt. 1972), p. 22.

2. Max Henríquez Ureña, *Breve historia del modernismo* (Mexico: Fondo de Cultura Económica, 1954).

3. John E. Englekirk Jr., *Edgar Allan Poe in Hispanic Literature* (New York: Instituto de las Españas, 1934; rpt. New York: Russell and Russell, 1972); hereafter cited as E.

4. See Hensley Woodbridge, "Poe in Spanish America: A Bibliographical Supplement," *Poe Studies* 2 (1969): 18–19, and "Addenda and Corrigenda," *Poe Studies* 4 (1971): 46; Boyd G. Carter, *Las revistas literarias de Hispanoamérica: Breve historia y contenido* (Mexico: Ediciones de Andrea, 1959).

5. Rubén Darío, "Edgar Allan Poe," in *Los raros,* in *Obras completas* (Madrid: Afrodisio Aguado, 1950), vol. 2, pp. 255–270. Englekirk reports that Darío's essay on Poe first appeared in *La Nación* of Buenos Aires in 1893 (E 90). *Los raros* was first published in 1896.

6. Margo Glantz, "Poe en Quiroga," in *Aproximaciones a Horacio Quiroga,* ed. Angel Flores (Caracas: Monte Avila Editores, 1976), pp. 93–118, cites several major critics who have discussed this relationship.

7. Roberto Ibáñez, "Prólogo" to Horacio Quiroga, *Obras inéditas y desconocidas,* vol. 7, in *Sobre literatura,* ed. Angel Rama (Montevideo: Arca Editorial, 1970).

8. Jorge Luis Borges, "Edgar Allan Poe," in *El otro, el mismo, Obra poética* (Madrid: Alianza Editorial, 1975), p. 225. See *Poe Studies* 6 (1973): 29–30 for Robert Lima's translation.

9. Roberto Alifano, *Twenty-four Conversations with Borges: Including a Selection of Poems,* trans. Nicomedes Suárez Arauz, Willis Barnstone, and Noemi Escandell (Housatonic, Mass.: Lascaux, 1984), pp. 1–2.

10. Jo Anne Engelbert, *Macedonio Fernández and the Spanish American Novel* (New York: New York UP, 1978); hereafter cited as JAE.

11. See Emmanuel Carballo, *Diecinueve protagonistas de la literatura mexicana del siglo XX* (Mexico: Empresas Editoriales, 1965), pp. 427–428.

12. Kessel Schwartz, *A New History of Spanish American Fiction* (Coral Gables: University of Miami, 1971), vol. 2, p. 47; hereafter cited as S.

13. Arturo Torres-Ríoseco, *Nueva historia de la gran literatura iberoamericana* (Buenos Aires: Emecé Editores, 1945; 1960); hereafter cited as TR. Enrique Anderson Imbert, *Historia de la literatura hispanoamericana,* vol. 1 (Mexico: Fondo de Cultura Económica, 1961); hereafter cited as AI.

14. Seymour Menton, *Prose Fiction of the Cuban Revolution* (Austin: U of Texas P, 1975), pp. 238–239.

15. Carballo, *Diecinueve protagonistas*; hereafter cited as C.

16. H. A. Murena, "Los parricidas: Edgar Allan Poe," *Realidad* 6 (September–December 1949): 129–153.

17. Octavio Paz, *Children of the Mire*, trans. Rachel Phillips (Cambridge: Harvard UP, 1974), pp. 116–117; translation of *Los hijos del limo* (Barcelona: Seix Barral, 1974), pp. 160–161.

18. Armando Rojas, "Edgard Allan Poe in la America Hispana," *Revista Nacional de Cultura* 23 (September–December 1960): 152–161.

19. In 1909 a centenary volume was dedicated to Poe. The odd title of the publication is explained in Guillermo Korn, *Obra y gracia de El Cojo Ilustrado* (Caracas: Instituto de Investigaciones de Prensa, Universidad Central de Venezuela, 1967).

20. Donald Yates, "The Spanish American Detective Story," *Modern Language Journal* 40 (May 1956): 228.

# Poe in Brazil

CARLOS DAGHLIAN

Lúcia Santaella remarked in her introduction to a 1984 translation of Poe's tales that "it is impossible to think of the fantastic literature boom in Brazil or in other parts of Latin America without thinking of Poe." [1] In Brazil, the only Portuguese-speaking country in Latin America, Poe's early reception developed independently from the American author's renown in the Spanish-language countries of the continent.

Poe had the good fortune of being discovered by Brazil's most outstanding writer, Joaquim Maria Machado de Assis (1839–1908), novelist, short story writer (ten volumes), essayist, and poet. Born into a poor family of Negro blood, Machado was endowed with a keen intelligence able to grasp the subtleties of his own language plus English, French, Spanish, and Latin. Alberto I. Bagby suggests that Machado read Poe in English as well as in Baudelaire's translation. [2] Among the books found in Machado's extensive personal library after his death were early editions of Poe in English. Whether by reading from English or French sources, Machado was captivated by the American author and played a major role in making Poe known in Brazil in the 1880s.

Machado made the first translation of "The Raven" into Portuguese in 1883, long before Fernando Pessoa presented his version in Portugal in 1925. For the average Brazilian reader, Poe is most famous as the author of "The Raven," largely due to the interest aroused by the various translations of the poem and the debate dealing with which one is the best. The poem was translated again by Gondin da Fonseca in 1926, by Milton Amado in 1944, and by Benedicto Lopes in 1956, who rendered it in the form of twenty-two sonnets. The poet Emílio de Menezes (1866–1918) had earlier paraphrased Machado's translation in a sequence of eighteen sonnets. In 1958 the Brazilian philologist and linguist J. Mattoso Câmara Jr. (1904–1970) compared Machado's translation to Pessoa's and argued for the superiority of the Brazilian poet's version. Câmara states that in spite of some possible defects, Machado's translation "magnificently preserves the qualities which seduce us in the English text." [3] He points out that the sixteen-syllable line was never spontaneously attempted in Portuguese, therefore he considers Machado's use of eight-, ten-, and twelve-syllable lines as the right choice. In 1976 the Brazilian poet, translator, and semiotician Haroldo de Campos took a different approach, defending Pessoa's translation as the best. Sérgio Bellei continued the debate in his 1988 article in which he discusses Machado's translation as an "appropriation" by a writer who felt the need to show himself and the literature of his country as belonging to Western culture, whereas Pessoa "really" tried to translate the poem.[4] In 1994 Ivo Barroso, a prize-winning poetry translator, made a case for Milton Amado's rendition of "The Raven," pointing out that it "is a great oral poem" and that "its author earned notoriety by reciting it in public."[5] Barroso concludes his essay by saying that Amado was faithful to Poe's intention of writing a poem that could be enjoyed by anyone. Like Poe, Amado was suffocated by the narrow-minded provincial atmosphere in which he lived. For Amado, to translate Poe was a kind of identification with the poet. Thus "The Raven" is not only a popular poem in Brazil, it is also the subject of lively debates concerning poetics, translation, and linguistics.

Evidence of Poe's influence on Machado is the subject of Sônia Brayner's 1976 study, "Edgar Allan Poe e Machado de Assis." She points out that in chapter thirty-seven of Machado's novel *Quincas Borba*, in an installment first published in a newspaper in 1886, the author wrote: "D. Tonica felt the croak of the old raven of hopelessness. 'Quoth the Raven: Never More [*sic*].'"[6] A study by Augusto Meyer mentions the presence of "The Man of the Crowd" in *Quincas Borba*.[7] More extensive clues to Poe's presence in Machado's literary endeavors are the similarities between Poe's "The System of Doctor Tarr and Professor Fether" and Machado's "O Alienista" ["The Psychiatrist"], both of which treat an absurd situation in a "private Mad House," as Poe calls it. The stories deal with doctors specializing in mental problems (Dr. Maillard and Dr. Simco Bacamarte) who, in a humorous situation, find the lunatics sane in their own exotic way and the "normal" people (including themselves) disturbed to the point of exchanging places with the patients. The similarities between the two narratives derive from the common location and thematic procedure: the "madhouse," the director's system, and lunacy as a nonsystem, that is, the unlimited perspective of human reason. Both stories deal with madness, ambiguity, and inversion, aspects dear to both writers. The paradigm of inversion is the fundamental element of the influence of Poe's story on Machado's. The authors convey a satire: a license and a scientific dogma would suffice to classify any person as mad. Poe's influence on Machado's "O Alienista" is especially significant when we consider that the Brazilian writer's tale is one of his most popular short works and is regarded as one of his best.

Suggestions of Poe's influence on other Brazilian writers provide fertile ground for further research. Oscar Mendes notes that Poe's influence can be found in some of Monteiro Lobato's (1882–1948) short stories.[8] The six-volume *A Literatura no Brasil* [Literature in Brazil] edited by Afrânio Coutinho contains a series of references to Brazilian authors who were supposedly inspired by Poe's works. For example, like Poe, the Romantic poet Álvares de Azevedo (1831–1852) looked for the ideal or the idealized woman. Hugo de Carvalho Ramos's (1895–1921) short stories reflect his readings of Hoffmann and Poe "through the psychological atmosphere of his stories" and, as critics have pointed out, through his stylistic accomplishment. In the discussion of the Symbolist movement, Poe is regarded as an important precursor who through the French had an influence on Cruz e Sousa (1861–1898), the greatest Brazilian Symbolist poet.

Mário Faustino (1930–1962), a young and promising modern Brazilian poet killed in a airplane crash who wrote about several American poets, admired Poe's craft and concern with artistic techniques. Antonio Manoel dos Santos Silva studied Faustino's artistic development, concluding that for Faustino, Poe was a competent craftsman, an example to follow because of his perfect versification, precise and sober diction, ability to adapt new forms, and clarity and exactness.[9] In short, Poe had a perfect command of the poetic tools and enjoyed freedom while dealing with fantasy.

The recognition and dissemination of Poe's work in Brazil can be fairly assessed by considering the translations of his poetry, fiction, and criticism into Portuguese as well as by the number of books, articles, academic theses, and papers presented at scholarly meetings dealing with his life and work. Although too numerous to describe here in detail, a few examples are worthy of mention.

A catalog entitled *Livros Norte-Americanos* [American books], intended to include all the translations of American authors into Portuguese published prior to 1987, listed only six Poe items, which is by no means complete. It missed, for example, Paulo Vizioli's translations of poems and José Paulo Paes's translations of short stories. Poe's works have been translated into Portuguese since the nineteenth century and have been included in all kinds of anthologies. They have also been the object of a number of artistic experiments.

Most of the relevant criticism produced in Brazil appeared after the publication of Poe's complete works in Portuguese by an outstanding Brazilian publishing house in 1944. Oscar Mendes (1902–1982) translated Poe's prose and edited the volume, and Milton Amado (1913–1974) rendered his poetry. Working from the original English, Mendes pointed out that earlier Brazilian translations were made from Baudelaire and therefore contained errors and omissions. In 1965 a new edition of this translation was published in a beautifully presented volume, which has been regarded as a kind of definitive edition of Poe's works. Biographical and critical studies by Harvey Allen, Charles Baudelaire, and Oscar Mendes, who commented on Poe's influence abroad, were added to the volume, which also contains illustrations, a bibliography, and a chronology. But, of course, nothing can be definitive about Poe, and new translations and adaptations of his work continue to appear. Even special editions seem to find a market that satisfies the publisher's expectations. Clarice Lispector (1925–1977), a well-known Brazilian fiction writer, rewrote eleven of Poe's short stories for young people. In 1993 a publisher in Porto Alegre brought out a trilingual edition of "The Man of the Crowd" with the original English, Baudelaire's translation, and Dorothée de Bruchard's Portuguese rendition juxtaposed on facing pages decorated with Manet's sketches.

Poe inspires a great deal of scholarly attention in Brazil. Doctoral dissertations, articles, and book chapters explore his work from many different perspectives. For example, anthropologist Roberto da Matta dealt with "The Black Cat" and "The Devil in the Belfry" in an article and a book chapter, respectively, by following the guidelines of Lévi-Strauss's structural anthropology.[10] A major study of *The Narrative of Arthur Gordon Pym* by José Alcides Ribeiro is included in a 1996 monograph dealing with the press and fiction in the nineteenth century.[11] Other studies too numerous to mention here examine Poe's tales, essays, and poetry. While remaining a popular author among general readers, Poe continues to be an important writer in academic circles in Brazil.

NOTES

1. Lúcia Santaella, "Estudo Crítico: Edgar Allan Poe (O que em mim sonhou está pensando)," in *Os Melhores Contos de Edgar Allan Poe*, trans. José Paulo Paes (São Paulo: Círculo do Livro, 1984), pp. 150–151.

2. Alberto I. Bagby Jr., "Machado de Assis and Foreign Languages," *Luso-Brazilian Review* 12 (1975): 225–233.

3. *Edgar A. Poe: Ficção Completa, Poesia & Ensaios*, ed. and trans. Oscar Mendes and Milton Amado (Rio de Janeiro: Aguilar, 1965), p. 103.

4. Sérgio Luiz Prado Bellei, "'The Raven,' by Machado de Assis," *Luso-Brazilian Review* 25.2 (Winter 1988): 1–13.

5. *Edgar A. Poe: Ficção Completa*, p. 252. See also *"O Corvo" e Suas Traduções*, organized, with an introduction, by Ivo Barroso; preface by Heitor Cony (Rio de Janeiro: Lacerda Editores, 1998).

6. Sônia Brayner, "Edgar Allan Poe e Machado de Assis," *Suplemento Literário de Minas Gerais*, June 19, 1976, pp. 1–2.

7. Augusto Meyer, *A Forma Secreta* (Rio de Janeiro: Lidador, 1965), p. 170.

8. Oscar Mendes, "Influência de Poe no Estrangeiro," in *Edgar A. Poe: Ficção Completa*, pp. 53–56.

9. Antonio Manoel dos Santos Silva, "Mário Faustino's Critical Testimony," in "Poesia e Poética de Mário Faustino" (Ph. D. diss., Universidade Estadual Paulista, São José do Rio Preto, 1979).

10. Roberto da Matta, "Edgar Allan Poe, o 'Bricoleur': Um Exercício em Análise Simbólica," in *Arte e Linguagem* (Petrópolis: Vozes, 1973), pp. 9–28; "Poe e Lévi-Strauss no Companário: ou, A Obra Literária como Etnografia," in *Ensaios de Antropologia Estrutural* (Petrópolis: Vozes, 1973), pp. 93–120.

11. José Alcides Ribeiro, *Imprensa e Ficção no século XIX: Edgar Allan Poe e A Narrativa de Arthur Gordon Pym* (São Paolo: Editora Unesp, 1996).

# Poe in Japan

NORIKO MIZUTA LIPPIT

Walt Whitman and Edgar Allan Poe were the two most widely read and loved American writers in the Meiji (1868–1912) and Taisho (1912–1926) periods in Japan. While Whitman inspired fervor for nationalism and democracy with his references to Japan in *Leaves of Grass*, the affinity of modern Japanese writers with Poe was purely literary. By the end of the Taisho period, it became obvious that Poe, rather than Whitman, secured the central place among Western writers as the most vital source of inspiration for their Japanese counterparts as Aestheticism became the dominant trend in Japanese Modernism and the grotesque and fantastic permeated popular culture.

In the era when an atmosphere of freedom and Modernism was colored with the silently spreading anxiety about the impending war and panic, Japan produced a high culture of Decadence and Aestheticism under the influence of French literature of the fin de siècle, as well as a popular culture of the grotesque and eroticism in entertainment, films, detective stories, and thrillers. What is significant in respect to Poe's influence in Japan is that Poe continued to be a source of inspiration long after the Taisho period of Aestheticism and Modernism passed, through the nationalistic era during the Second World War and the decades of democracy and Marxism in the postwar period. Poe has continued to be popular even today, not only among writers of different literary ideologies, styles, and tastes, with scholarship on Poe established in criticism, but also among the young generation of lovers of popular culture, science fiction, thrillers, and horror movies.[1] Moreover, Poe was the object of a new fervor in the Japanese post-Modernist era of the 1970s and 1980s in manga and computer games.

Even before the first translations of Poe's stories were published in 1888, his works were known among students of English language and literature through textbooks used for instruction, making Poe one of the earliest foreign writers to be introduced into Japan. Yet it was Aeba Koson's rough translation of "The Black Cat" in the daily newspaper *Yomiuri Shimbun* on November 3 and 9, 1888, and his translation of "The Murders in the Rue Morgue" in the same publication on December 10, 23, 27, and 30, 1888, that made Poe known to a general readership, thus securing his popularity in Japan.

"The Raven" followed the tales to Japan when Motoki Tadao's translation and biography of Poe appeared in 1891.[2] From this point on, "The Black Cat," "The Raven," and the Dupin stories continued to generate a steady interest and appreciation during the Meiji era; there are at least ten known Meiji translations of "The Black Cat." Morita Shiken's translation of "The Purloined Letter" in 1886, highly praised for its precision and faithfulness to the original, appeared with his special mention of Dupin. "The Murders in the Rue Morgue" and "The Mystery of Marie Rogêt" aroused the interest of writers and the reading public in both the genre of detective stories and in the character of the aesthete detective.[3]

Morita Shiken, a journalist and the chief editor of the newspaper *Hochi Shimbun*, evidently came to know of Poe through Jules Verne (the translation of *Around the World in Eighty Days* appeared in the same newspaper) and translated "The Pit and the Pendulum" immediately following "The Purloined Letter," a translation praised by Ueda Bin as the best Japanese translation of Poe.[4] The detective stories advertised in the original version of Verne's works were translated into Japanese one after another. By the end of the Meiji period, the two routes of Poe's introduction were evident: one through scholars and students of English literature and the other through journalists whose interest was in promoting the reading public's taste for Western popular culture, including detective stories and thrillers.

It was Lafcadio Hearn, however, who was most influential in introducing Poe to Japan and who played the decisive role in laying the foundation for the acceptance and understanding of Poe's writings. Hearn began teaching literature at Tokyo University in 1886 and delivered a special lecture series entitled "Notes on American Literature," which turned out to be the first systematic presentation and interpretation of American literature and literary history in Japan. Not only did Hearn treat Poe's works — mainly his tales — extensively and with enthusiasm in those lectures, but he also delivered a separate lecture entirely on Poe's poems.[5]

With Hearn began the second phase of Poe's introduction to Japan, giving rise to the emergence of new writers and poets inspired by Poe. Ueda Bin, a student of Hearn's and the translator and editor of the most influential collection of Western poems, *Kaichoon*, continued to emphasize Poe's influence on Baudelaire, Mallarmé, and such English Romantic poets as Rossetti, Swinburne, and Thompson.[6] Ueda Bin's emphasis on Poe's French connection and the Symbolist elements of his poems set the direction for modern Japanese poetry, which was searching for a way to emerge from the tradition of the regulated short poems of tanka and haiku.

The introductions by both Lafcadio Hearn and Ueda Bin determined the way Poe would be understood in the future by Japanese writers. Poe's works are most typically opposed to Didacticism and Naturalism in literature, whereas Japanese literature in the Meiji period was dominated particularly by Naturalism. Tanizaki Junichiro once remarked that "if you do not write a naturalistic novel, you are not a writer."[7] Hearn's emphasis on Poe's exploration of the psychic realm and on the elements of mystery and grotesque fantasy in his works, together with Ueda Bin's association of Poe with the French Symbolist poets, provided new insights and opened a new literary realm for writers discontented with Naturalism. The influence Japanese poets received from Baudelaire, the Symbolist poets, and the English writers of the Aesthetic school cannot be overemphasized. It is in this context that Poe was typically understood and admired by Japanese writers.

Yet the study of Poe in the Meiji period was limited largely to introductory remarks, and the translation and understanding of his works remained generally superficial. It was in the Taisho period that the writers who were influenced by Poe began to reflect in their own works the insights and inspiration received from the American author. Poe's influence can be seen mainly in the five areas of Japanese literary development and movements. The first is the influence vital in the development of modern Japanese poetry of the Taisho and early Showa periods, culminating in Hagiwara Sakutaro's Symbolic and Surrealistic poems, free verse written in colloquial modern Japanese. The second is the influence on the development of Aesthetic literature, with the emergence of such major writers as Tanizaki Junichiro and Sato Haruo. The third area where Poe's influence was indispensable was in short fiction as a genre, with Akutagawa Ryunosuke, the most pronounced spokesperson both for short fiction and for Poe, admitting openly his indebtedness to Poe in creating his own short fiction. The fourth area is the development of popular literature, especially of the grotesque and the detective story. Edogawa Rampo, taking his literary name from Edgar Allan Poe, stands out as the first Japanese mystery and detective story writer who, learning deeply from Poe, developed the genre of placing the mystery and madness of existence as its raison d'être. The fifth area where inspiration from Poe is evident is in Japanese literature of the city. Tokyo, a fast-growing metropolis of the early twentieth century, produced a new urban social and cultural environment of uprootedness and alienation where aspiring artists and intellectuals, including women, and working-class people emigrated from the countryside. It is quite fascinating to detect Poe's influence on literary women who left their families to come to Tokyo in search of a new independence, gathering around new literary media for women. *Seito*, the first and most radical feminist journal, published the translations of twelve of Poe's tales consecutively in almost every issue throughout its short life. Ozaki Midori, among others, stands out as a writer whose works reflect the insight she developed through her reading of Poe, especially the insight into the inner hysteria and the psychic wandering in the urban environment of alienation, namelessness, and loneliness. Edogawa Rampo, too, was a writer of the city, as was Akutagawa Ryunosuke, both of whom acknowledged as the source of their sensibility the anxiety and fear stemming from urban life. These five areas in which Poe's influence is clearly evident produced major writers and artists of modern literature and of popular literature and culture in prewar Japan.

Among the writers of Aestheticism who reflect the influence of Poe as interpreted by Hearn and Ueda Bin, Hagiwara Sakutaro and Tanizaki Junichiro are unquestionably the two most significant and representative Japanese authors.[8] However, Japanese writers of Aestheticism did not necessarily start as Romantic writers. The "diabolism" of early Tanizaki Junichiro, for example, was initially a part of his Naturalistic endeavor to unveil the irrational, instinctive side of existence, while early on Hagiwara Sakutaro was concerned mainly with exploring sadistically the depths of his personal wounded psyche. In the process of their literary investigation of the alienated, often criminal, psyche, the realm of the unconscious and the grotesque, they turned increasingly to the search for a myth (a vision of a self-sufficient world of dream) that would justify their exploration of the grotesque and evil. It is in regard to the Romantic quest for a vision of destructive transcendence, toward which these writers' aspirations and endeavors led, that their learning from Poe and Western dark Romanticism bears deepest significance.

Since Baudelaire and Poe had already been introduced to Japan in the nineteenth century and were greatly admired, the foundation was laid for the Japanese reception of European Aestheticism. For writers such as Tanizaki Junichiro and Hagiwara Sakutaro, the rejection of Meiji culture and the discovery of Gothic themes in both Western dark Romanticism and Edo culture forced them to pursue further their search for the origin of their aesthetic sensibilities and their cultural home. Kafu's return to Edo, Natsume Soseki's return to Zen Buddhism and Taoism, Tanizaki Junichiro's return to Heian culture, Hagiwara Sakutaro's return of the wanderer to a mythical home called Japan, Kawabata Yasunari's return to Kojiki, and Mishima Yukio's metempsychosis all represent an attempt to return to the source and to establish a myth that would re-create a self-sufficient world of the senses. Each of these writers tried to restore the "original unity" by exploring the psychic realm of fear, the world of sensuous beauty and eroticism, and the world of the grotesque.

Hagiwara Sakutaro (1886–1942), Japan's leading modern poet and one of the first to use free verse, started his poetic career under the strong influence of such Japanese Symbolist poets as Kitahara Hakushu and Kambara Ariake, in addition to Poe, Baudelaire, Nietzche, and Dostoevsky.[9] He admired Poe in particular, and his world of poetry is highly reminiscent of Poe's. Sakutaro begins with a definition of himself as a diseased man, and his world is perceived through nerves shaped to abnormality by his sickness. It is a world in decay, and in its center a great void opens its mouth, evoking a sense of fear of life. In confronting nothingness, the poet confronts his own diseased face, his own double. The lonely poet wanders in the universe of "flowing time, darkness and the silent moment" ("The Penitent," 1916), driven by a fear of the unknown and led by the light and shadows that flicker in his subconscious, following the footsteps of fate toward a final vision that awaits him beyond reality.

In Sakutaro's later period, his sense of fear, loneliness, and the sterility of life became systematized as his sense of the loss of the original home, and recovery through the destruction of his body became his return journey. This systematization into the loss of the original home and its recovery is the process of his return to his Japanese cultural origins and is indeed the process of his mythmaking.[10] Finally, he reached the idea of eternal return through a spiral descent into the depths of the poet's soul. Poe's poet in *Eureka*, whose grotesque and arabesque imagination brings the entire universe to its primordial unity through his suicidal and centripetal concentration on himself, is fundamentally akin to the poet Sakutaro.

Sakutaro, like Poe, tried to express his vision of transcendence and the process of attaining it through the music of words. His poem "The Rooster" illustrates the depths of his empathy with Poe's world. Sakutaro explained that in writing this poem he was inspired by "The Raven" and that he tried to practice the principles of poetry writing that Poe describes in "The Philosophy of Composition."[11] The use of a mysterious animal, of the refrain, and of melancholy as a theme and the evocation of mental scenery by the use of sound and its repetition are all reminiscent of "The Raven."

Tanizaki Junichiro (1886–1965) started his literary career under the strong influence of Poe, Baudelaire, and Wilde. Tanizaki's attempt to separate art from life, placing art above life, and his characters' antimoralistic and antisocial pursuit of sensuous pleasure can be considered as constituting the basis

of the literature of "diabolism." Tanizaki's heroes' sadomasochistic desire for
sensuous pleasure proves to be a distorted effort to attain a sense of life
through seeking unattainable feminine beauty, the pursuit of the absolute.
Tanizaki's heroes feel a deep sense of alienation that spurs them to perverted
efforts to recover from it, and his grotesque expresses these efforts to overcome alienation (see Part II, "Tanizaki Junichiro").

In the post–World War II period we can see further evidence of the significance of Poe and dark Romanticism and the deep-rootedness of their influence on Japanese literature in the writings of Mishima Yukio. The Japanese
writers of Aestheticism, who form the mainstream of modern Japanese literature, reveal the links between traditional Japanese literature and the ideas and
aesthetics of Poe and dark Romanticism. In each case their introduction to
and learning from Poe played an important role in their rediscovery of the
Japanese literary tradition.

Modern Japanese detective stories and the genre of grotesque tales emerged
as a by-product, albeit a legitimate one, of the movement of Aesthetic art and
literature. Although Poe's detective stories were known to the general public
in the late Meiji period through Morita Shiken's translations in *Hochi Shimbun*, it was undoubtedly Edogawa Rampo who established a Japanese genre of
detective and grotesque stories and who, through his own admiration of Poe,
made the American author known to the general public as the father of the
Japanese detective story. Poe's influence in arousing the readers' interest in the
genre and in tales of the grotesque and terror through Rampo cannot be overemphasized. Not only were writers and artists inspired to explore the realm of
crime and "the terror of the soul," but the general readers of popular literature
welcomed Poesque characters and the aesthete outsider, equipped with the
insight and perception into the dark realm of the mind. A journal of mystery
and detective stories called *Shin Seinen* [New Generation], published with
Beardsley-inspired drawings, was responsible for creating the era of "the grotesque, eroticism and nonsense" in the 1920s.[12]

Edogawa Rampo (Hirai Taro, 1894–1965), an enthusiastic follower of Poe
since he read "The Murders in the Rue Morgue" at the age of twenty-one,
adopted the pen name with the publication of the "Nisen doka" [Two-sen
copper coin] and "Ichimai no kippu" [A ticket] in 1914, works that reflect obvious influences from "The Gold-Bug" and "The Purloined Letter." Rampo
founded the Association of the Lovers of Detectives in 1925, the forerunner of
the Association of Japanese Writers of Detective Stories formed after the Second World War, and set fire to a boom in detective stories. "Panorama to

Kitan" [A strange story of Panorama Island] (1927) is obviously based on an idea taken from "The Domain of Arnheim" and "Landor's Cottage." Rampo was so prolific that his collected works were published in 1931, the thirteenth volume of which contains his own translations of six of Poe's tales. He wrote only a few essays on Poe's detective stories but believed that for the detective story to survive as a literary genre, it should succeed in the line of Poe's detective stories in which mystery and ratiocination create the center of attraction and enjoyment.

Although the Akechi Kogoro series was very popular and Rampo was loved immensely by readers, he was a unique and strange personality. A hermit aesthete and a wanderer in the city, he was obsessed with and indulged in dreams, fantasy, and the psychic realm of fear and death, often crossing the boundary of the rational, social, and moral into the grotesque and bizarre. His early stories reflect his fetishism of dark rooms, dolls, colorful costumes, eyes and lenses, small things, lies, and precision. Rampo himself could be a character in one of Poe's tales.

In 1949, the centennial of Poe's death, Japanese newspapers and magazines published many articles, including several by Rampo, on Poe's literary contributions. Three separate special lectures to commemorate Poe were organized simultaneously, one sponsored by the Yomiuri Shimbun and the Association of Japanese Writers of Detective Stories and the others organized at Waseda and Rikkyo Universities, which indicates the wide range of Poe's reception in Japan. The Association of Japanese Writers of Detective Stories used the image of Poe's face carved on a silver ring as the badge for its members, and the prize they gave to the best work of the year came with a plaque that had Poe's torso on a green copper plate, thus commemorating Poe's unshakable place in the field of Japanese detective stories.[13]

Poe's influence was decisive in the development of short fiction in Japan, with Akutagawa Ryunosuke (1892–1927), who stands close to the Aesthetic group, playing the most vital role. Delving into the grotesque and terror as a writer, he showed great interest in Poe as a person, finding in him "the devil" of self-consciousness, the anxiety-stricken urban man who, dependent on drugs, sped steadily to his own mental and physical destruction. In "Jigoku-hen" [The hell screen] (1918), Akutagawa depicts an insane artist who is so obsessed with his pursuit of the painful, the ugly, and the sinful that he not only loses humanity but also life as his art absorbs it with the completion of the work.

Poe's influence is most evident and significant in Akutagawa's discussion of the short story. Akutagawa built his world of short fiction on old legends and folktales of Japan and Asia, such as those contained in *Konjaku Monogatari* (twelfth-century Buddhist tales), and on stories by modern Western writers. In a sense, Akutagawa's short fictions are twice-told tales; he built his own modern world of fiction by retelling the old tales, creating a self-sufficient cosmos in fictional literary space by connecting the past and present, the native and foreign, and the real and imaginary. Akutagawa was strongly attracted to Poe's art of storytelling and to his method of constructing a self-sufficient world of fiction with the clear calculation of its effect on his readers.[14] In "Tampensakka toshiteno Poe" [Poe as a short fiction writer] (1922), Akutagawa praises Poe's technique of "combining harmoniously the realistic and the romantic," the technique used in *The Narrative of Arthur Gordon Pym*.

It was Natsume Soseki, Akutagawa's mentor, who first introduced Poe to Japanese readers as the father of short fiction. Soseki's assessment of Poe's skill in storytelling and his method of constructing fiction, a method that Soseki calls "meticulous, accurate and scientific," is articulate and to the point.[15] Soseki's praise of Poe as a unique, imaginative writer with a scientific precision for detail no doubt had a great impact on other writers. In his article entitled "Poe no sozo" [Poe's imagination], Soseki emphasizes Poe's scientific imagination, comparing Poe to Jonathan Swift, a writer Soseki greatly admired.

A fascinating aspect of the Poe connection in modern literature is the publication of his translated stories in Japan's first feminist journal, *Seito*, not just once but in eleven successive issues. *Seito* was founded in 1911 by Hiratsuka Raicho, Japan's first ideologue of feminism and a writer and philosopher. Her manifesto for the journal, "in the beginning the woman was the sun," inspired young women to form a feminist movement around Raicho and the journal. *Seito* initially was mainly a literary journal, a forum for literary and artistic expression for women, and in that context the publication of Poe's tales did not appear unnatural. Poe continued to be translated even after the journal moved on to become a forum for political issues concerning women's rights and other ideological issues of feminism. It is not clear how Poe caught the fancy of the feminists, for it was obvious that Poe had little relevance to Japanese women's condition and little to offer to promote feminism itself. Poe may have been brought to *Seito* by Iwano Kiyoko, an active member of *Seito* from its inception and the wife of Iwano Homei, a critic and writer who wrote much about Poe's "diabolism" in connection with his own works. It is clear, however, that Poe was read and appreciated by the feminists of *Seito* enough to be repeatedly published, often translated by Raicho. Although Raicho was a committed feminist, her interest in and connection with Poe opened among women writers and artists new areas of sensitivity for the mysterious and fantastic, for the grotesque and arabesque of Modernism. It is certain that Poe's connection with Japanese feminist writers is a special case in Poe studies. This can be seen in the undeniable influence Poe left on Ozaki Midori, a Modernist and Expressionist writer whose early connections were with the radical Modernist and feminist literary and artistic activities surrounding *Seito*.[16]

Ozaki Midori (1896–1979), whose only volume of collected works includes fewer than twenty short stories, several poems, essays, fragments, review essays on movies, letters, and a translation of Poe's "Morella," became addicted to a painkilling drug during her stay in Tokyo as a young writer from the countryside. Although she was recognized as a unique literary talent, she could not recover from the damage caused by the drug and abandoned writing for good after she was forcibly taken back to her native town by her brother in 1932. From that point on she was almost completely forgotten in the literary world and was believed to have been dead until 1958, when a critic, Iwaya Daishi, compared Ozaki with Oe Kenzaburo, who had just made a brilliant debut as a young writer of the new generation. In 1968 Hanada Kiyoteru, an important figure for Poe enthusiasts in the postwar period, in his essay on Abe Kobo, a major writer in the 1950s and 1960s and another Poe fan, talked about his unforgettable experience of reading Ozaki Midori's works in his youth. What connects Abe Kobo, Hanada Kiyoteru, and Ozaki Midori is their shared interest in the American writer. Ozaki's collected works were published posthumously in 1979.

In the post–World War II literary scene, which started with the criticism of the writers' support of the war and with the strong fervor for Marxist revolution, Poe strangely enough aroused new enthusiasm in literary criticism and writing. Two influential figures in the post–World War II literary era, Hanada Kiyoteru (1909–1974), a literary critic, and Haniya Yutaka (1910–1996), a writer-philosopher-critic, developed their literary and philosophic stance by placing at its core Poe's view of the universe in *Eureka*.

Haniya Yutaka's *Shirei* [The dead spirit] (1946–1997), the unfinished novel of more than nine thousand pages on which he continued to work until his death in 1997, explores the relationship between being and consciousness, delving into the realm beyond perception, nothingness, as the origin of all existence. His consistent references in his exploration have been to Dostoevsky and Poe, particularly Poe's *Eureka*.[17] In his endeavor to question the original nothingness of being and the consciousness of being, in the question of how to determine one's own existence or nonexistence, Haniya delved into me-tempsychosis, referring to Poe's "Original Oneness" and life's cyclical return to it, which was close to his idea of metempsychosis. His idea of origin, to and from which existence repeats itself cyclically, was developed with Poe's *Eureka* in mind.

In contrast to Haniya, who chose, like Poe, the infinite space of the universe as his metaphysical and literary space, Hanada Kiyoteru learned from Poe the grotesque imagination and ironic perspective on life and society needed to survive the chaos of the transitional period. Hanada adopted Poe's destructive transcendence as an intellectual weapon against the military government dur-ing the war and, after the war, against both dogmatic Marxism and naive hu-manism, the two dominant ideologies in the immediate postwar era.[18] Poe's grotesque imagination, which considers himself both serious and mad, tragic as well as comic, together with Poe's paradoxical thinking, which finds death in life and life in death, obviously inspired Hanada by providing a perspective for his rebirth, the restoration and revitalization of his dead spirit and intellect crushed during the war through a forced conversion from Marxism.[19]

Poe's influence is evident also on two young writers who emerged in the 1950s, Mishima Yukio (1925–1970) and Abe Kobo (1924–1993), who achieved international recognition as representative writers of the mid–twentieth cen-tury. As part of the first generation of the postwar writers, they reflect Poe's apocalyptic sensibilities, his sense of ending in an absurd existence. Both can be called writers of the lost generation who spent their youth during the war believing in their imminent death. Abe Kobo's works deal with a protagonist who is placed in the extreme predicament of life and death, where he is de-prived of any identity as an individual and even as a human being. The pro-tagonist in "Suna no onna" [The woman in the dunes] (1962), trapped in a sand dune while searching for a rare species of insect, must strive for his sur-vival, his dignity and meaning of life against nature and the universe, without the mediation of society.

Mishima's entire corpus is based on his central theme of betrayed death; in "Kamen no kokuhaku" [Confessions of a mask] (1949), a protagonist whose confession of his homosexuality forms the center of the story declares that he was expecting to die for the emperor during the war and that he is merely passing the rest of life after the war. A sharp critic, Mishima talks of Poe with admiration and with a perceptive understanding of Poe's works, which he di-vides into two categories: "the elegant stories with the smell of death which remind us of the ghost stories of the Noh plays" and the farces with the "obsessive laughter and the bored intellect." Several of Mishima's short stories can clearly be seen as his attempt at Poesque farce. In his essay referring to Poe's farce, Mishima writes that Poe displayed his taste for intellectual nonsense and that the intellect that has hidden itself completely in nonsensical tall tales becomes paradoxically most beautiful and artistic.[20] Mishima also refers to Poe frequently in his novels, letting his characters talk about Poe's stories and characters. In his famous essay on Kawabata Yasunari, the recipient of the Nobel Prize and the writer whom Mishima considered as his mentor, he compares Kawabata's lonely face to that of Poe's "man of the crowd."

Japanese interest in Poe did not wane through the 1970s and 1980s, and even in the 1990s Poe has continued to be one of the most beloved foreign writers, with his works continuing to be widely read and appreciated. With the increasing popularity of science fiction and manga in the last three decades, Japan experienced a new emergence of young writers drawing inspiration from Poe. A work of manga, *Poe no ichizoku* [A family of Poe] (1972), by Hagio Moto, in which variations of almost all of Poe's themes are found, had sold three million copies by the 1980s, and with it Poe secured what seems to be an unshakable position in manga, thus widening the contemporary readership of Poe to the younger generation.

What is most remarkable, however, in the contemporary development in Japan's interest in Poe is the depth and breadth of scholarship which, succeeding the bloom of literary criticism on Poe in the first half of the twentieth century, continues to produce books and critical essays in the fields of comparative literature, American studies, theory of criticism, and cultural studies. With such perceptive scholarly studies of Poe's poetry, novels, and criticism as the works by Tanizaki Seiji, Shimada Kinji, Yagi Toshio, and Satoya Shigenobu, among many others;[21] such unique and thorough studies as Nakamura Tohru's on Poe in Japan; such studies as Tatsumi Takayuki's on Poe and science fiction, Motoyama Chitose's on Poe and the grotesque, and Takemura Naoyuki's on Poe's view of the universe;[22] and other works by younger scholars and critics equipped with recent critical theories, Poe continues to be in the latter half of the twentieth century one of the most studied and written about foreign writers in Japan.

NOTES

1. Shimada Kinji, "Nihon ni okeru Poe," *English & American Literature* 15 (December 1954): 121–141; Shimada Kinji and Miyanaga Takashi, "Nihon ni okeru Edgar

Allan Poe no unmei," *Bulletin of the College of General Education* 27–46 (1954–1984); Kimura Takeshi, "Poe to Meiji-Taisho bundan," in *Nichibeibungaku koryushi no kenkyu* (Tokyo: Obunsha, 1958); Shinagawa Chikara, "Nihon ni okeru Poe," *Nihon hikakubungakukai kaiho* Nos. 4–21 (1959–1960); Ota Saburo, "Poe shokai no ato," *Geppo* 1–3; *Poe zenshu*, ed. Saeki Shoichi (Tokyo: Sogensha, 1970); Nakamura Tohru, "Nihon de no Poe," *Bulletin of the College of General Education* 9–25 (1977–1986); Satoya Shigenobu, "Nihon kindaibungaku ni okeru Poe no eikyo," in *Poe no meikai genso* (Tokyo: Kokushokankokai, 1988), pp. 245–296.

2. *Direct Translation of the New National Reader*, No. 5, trans. Motoki Tadao (Tokyo: Bunseido, 1891).

3. Such major writers of Meiji Japan as Tsubouchi Shoyo and Mori Ogai are among the earliest introducers and translators of Poe's works, although the translations were not always complete and they appeared without the translators' names. See Kimura, "Poe to Meiji-Taisho bundan," pp. 403–470.

4. Ibid., pp. 424–427.

5. Lafcadio Hearn, "Notes on American Literature" and "Poe's Verse," in *Interpretations of Literature*, ed. John Erskine (New York: Dodd, Mead, 1915), vol. 2, pp. 150–166.

6. Ueda Bin, "Eibei no kinsei bungaku," *Myojo* (March 1902).

7. *Tanizaki Junichiro zenshu*, 30 vols. (Tokyo: Chuokoron-sha, 1981), vol. 13, p. 360.

8. Noguchi Yonejiro (1875–1947), a Symbolist poet who wrote poems in English during his stay in the United States after 1893 as an immigrant, was criticized for plagiarism of Poe by American critics (*The Story of Yone Noguchi Told by Himself* [Philadelphia: Philadelphia Press, 1896]). He introduced Poe to Japan as a Symbolist in the line of Hearn-Bin's introduction of Poe. The influence of the introduction of Poe by Hearn-Bin was continued through Sakutaro by Hinatsu Konosuke (1890–1971) and Nishiwaki Junzaburo (1894–1982), Japan's representative Symbolist poets and scholars of Western poetry.

9. For the influence of Western writers on Sakutaro, see Tsukimura Reiko, "Hagiwara Sakutaro," in *Kindai nihon: hikaku bungakuteki kosatsu* (Tokyo: Shimizu Kobundo, 1971), pp. 164–190; Okada Takahiko, *Nihon no seikimatsu* (Tokyo: Ozawa Shoten, 1976). For Sakutaro and Poe, see Satoya Shigenobu, "Poe to Sakutaro no Shinrei Bigaku," in *Poe no meikai genso*, pp. 215–230; Matsuyama Akio, "Poe to Hagiwara Sakutaro," *Bulletin of the College of General Education* 27 (1977): 23–42.

10. Hagiwara Sakutaro, *Jojo shokyoku shu* (1925); *Hyoto* (1934), in *Hagiwara Sakutaro shishu*, ed. Ito Shinkichi (Tokyo: Kadokawa Bunko, 1973).

11. Hagiwara Sakutaro, "Shi no honyaku ni tsuite" (1933), "Poe no kankei" (1936), in ibid.

12. For Poe's influence on *Shin seinen*, Japanese detective stories, and Edogawa Rampo, see Kimura, "Poe to Meiji-Taisho bundan," pp. 467–470; Satoya, "Nihon Kindaibungaku ni okeru Poe no eikyo," pp. 277–279. See also James Roy King, "Rich-

mond in Tokyo: The Fortunes of Edgar Allan Poe in Contemporary Japan," in *Papers on Poe*, ed. Richard P. Veler (Springfield, Ohio: Chantry Music, 1972).

13. A very popular detective story series *Hanshichi torimono cho* [Hanshichi detective story], written by Okamoto Kido, began to be serialized in 1917 in *Bungei kurabu*. Its seventh story is a work entitled "Hansho no kai" [A mystery of a bell], which is obviously based on Poe's "The Murders in the Rue Morgue." *Hanshichi torimono cho*, one of the earliest series of indigenous detective stories in Japan, is extremely popular to this day, having been made into several film series and television drama series. See also Edogawa Rampo, *Tantei shosetsu no yonju nen* (Tokyo: Kodansha, 1961); the book is an important document not only on Poe and Rampo but also on Poe and the Japanese detective story in general.

14. On Poe and Akutagawa, see Eguchi Hiroko, *Essays on Edgar Poe — Akutagawa and Edgar Poe* (Tokyo: Tokyo Women's Christian University, 1968). According to Eguchi, the number of references to Poe in Akutagawa totals twenty.

15. See Mizuta Lippit, "Natsume Soseki on Poe," *Comparative Literature Studies*, 14.1 (March 1977): 30–37. See also Kimura, "Poe to Meiji-Taisho bundan," pp. 453–454; Satoya, "Nihon kindaibungaku ni okeru Poe no eikyo," pp. 264–266; Ikeda Mikito, "Soseki and Poe," in *Hikaku bungaku kenkyu* (Tokyo: Tokyo U, 1978), vol. 33, pp. 138–158.

16. For *Seito* and literary feminists, see Mizuta Lippit, "*Seito* and the Literary Roots of Japanese Feminism," *International Journal of Women's Studies* (March/April 1979); Ushiyama Yuriko, "*Seito* to Poe no yakubun," *Mugen* 25 (1969) (special issue on Poe).

17. For Haniya's references to Poe, see Haniya Yutaka, "Poe ni tsuite," introduction to vol. 1 of *Poe zenshu* (Tokyo: Sogensha, 1969); "Poe ni tsuite," *Hato yo* 9.8 (August 1991) (special issue on Poe). For Haniya and Poe, see Satoya "Nihon kindaibungaku ni okeru Poe no eikyo," pp. 281–284; Takemura Naoyuki, "Poe and Haniya Yutaka," in *Poe no uchu kan* (Tokyo: Tsurumi Shoten, 1994), pp. 119–170.

18. For Hanada's references to Poe, see Hanada Kiyoteru, "Kyumen sankaku-Poe" *Bunka soshiki* (December, 1941), "Shumatsu kan-Poe" *Roningyo* (1941), "Tantei shosetsu ron" *Bunka soshiki* (1941), "The Spirit of the Renaissance" (1947), "The Avant-Garde Art" (1954), collected in *Hanada Kiyoteru zenshu* (Tokyo: Kodansha, 1980).

19. For Hanada and Poe, see Nakamura Tohru, "Nihon de no Poe," *Bulletin of the College of General Education* 25.14, (1986): 239–258; Satoya, "Nihon kindaibungaku ni okeru Poe no eikyo," pp. 283–284.

20. Mishima Yukio, "Chisei no danmatsuma," introduction to vol. 3 of *Poe zenshu*.

21. Shimada Kinji, *Poe, Iwanami koza*, vol. 12 (Tokyo: Iwanami Shoten, 1933); Shimada Kinji, "Nihon ni okeru Edgar Poe," in *English and American Literature* (Tokyo: Rikkyo University, December 1954), vol. 15, pp. 121–141; Shimada Kinji, "Poe and Baudelaire: A Study in Comparative Literary History," *Tokyo Evening Star*, 1948; Tanizaki Seiji, *Edgar Allen Poe — hito to sakuhin* (Tokyo: Kenkyusha, 1967). Tanizaki Seiji, a younger brother of Tanizaki Junichiro, was one of the most committed trans-

lators and introducers of Poe in Japan. Tanizaki Junichiro, Sato Haruo, and Edogawa Rampo owed much to Seiji for the information on Poe; Yagi Toshio, *Edgar Allan Poe no kenkyu: hakai to sozo* (Tokyo: Nanundo, 1979).

22. Tatsumi Takayuki, *Edgar Allan Poe wo yomu* (Tokyo: Iwanami Shoten, 1995); Motoyama Chitose, *Poe wa Doracula daro ka* (Tokyo: Keiso Shobo, 1989); Takemura, *Poe no ucho kan.*

# *Poe in China*

SHENG NING AND DONALD BARLOW STAUFFER

While many American writers, such as Mark Twain, Jack London, Theodore Dreiser, and Ernest Hemingway, were widely translated and read in the People's Republic of China after 1949, the works of Poe underwent a total eclipse for more than thirty years, until the reopening of Chinese-American relations in the 1980s. An entire generation thus remained ignorant of Poe and unaware of the fact that he was not only one of the first American writers whose works were introduced into China but also was an important influence on the work of most major fiction writers and poets writing in the 1920s and 1930s.

Zheng Zhen-duo, a leading member of the New Culture movement, wrote in his *An Outline of Literature* in 1926: "Washington Irving made American literature first recognized in Europe, while it is Edgar Allan Poe who first made American literature greatly influence European literature. In 1909, the year of Poe's centennial, the whole of Europe, from London to Moscow, and from Christiania to Rome, claimed its indebtedness to Poe and praised his great success."[1] Zheng's description of Poe's European reputation could also be applied to the situation in China in the 1920s, when Poe was constantly mentioned in the leading periodicals whenever there was an article about American literature. He was praised as the greatest nineteenth-century American writer, the founder of the short story, and an extraordinary genius. At the same time his works were being continuously translated into Chinese. It is no exaggeration to say that almost all the leading writers of the time, in one way or another, showed some interest in Poe.

In fact, China's most famous and respected modern writer, Lu Xun, and his brother, Zhou Zuo-ren, were the first to introduce Poe's works into the country. In 1903 Lu Xun went to Japan to study medicine. There he found a copy of "The Gold-Bug" annotated in Japanese, which he sent home to his brother. Zhou Zuo-ren, as he later recalled, found the tale exquisitely beautiful, and he translated it into Chinese, calling it "The Story of a Jade-Bug." Not long after the publication of "The Story of a Jade-Bug" Zhou Zuo-ren translated "Silence — A Fable," which was first published in a student magazine, *Honan*, and reprinted in Tokyo in *A Collection of Foreign Fiction* (1909).[2]

In 1917 Zhou Shou-Juan translated and edited a three-volume collection, *Short Stories by Famous European and American Writers* (1917). This collection included "The Tell-Tale Heart" as well as a brief introduction about the author. Lu Xun warmly praised the anthology.[3] A few years later (1920) "The Tell-Tale Heart" was retranslated by the editor of *Short Story Monthly*, Shen Yan-bing, later to become one of modern China's most famous writers as Mao Dun. The tale first appeared in a popular magazine, *Eastern Miscellany*, and was then reprinted in the *Collection of Modern English and American Short Stories* published by Shangwu Publishing House.[4]

One might ask why a mystical writer like Poe should be of interest to Chinese readers in the 1920s. As early as 1920 *Eastern Miscellany* started to publish articles commenting on "Neo-romanticism," which emphasized the presence of mystical elements that were seen as a revival of the tendencies of Romanticism. The authors of these articles shared the belief that "the artists are now longing to explore the unknowable, which seems to be more profound and lasting than real life . . . to step into the realm of the instinct, and to extract meanings from the mystical unknown."[5] *Short Story Monthly*, *Literature Ten Daily*, and other periodicals published articles written by such prominent critics and authors as Xie Lu-yi and Yan Ji-cheng dealing with this new literary trend. The literary atmosphere, in which the drama of Maeterlinck and the fiction of Andreyev were fashionable, was also favorable to Poe.

Aestheticism was another important influence on two different literary coteries of the 1920s, the Creation Society and the Crescent Society. The former was founded by the poets Guo Mo-ro, Yu Da-fu, Chen Fang-wu, and others. It adopted the principle of "art for art's sake" in opposition to "art for life's sake," advocated by the Literary Association, still another coterie founded by Shen Yan-bing and others. The Crescent Society, headed by Xu Zhi-mo and Wen Yi-do, espoused a similar kind of Romanticism in order to establish the independence of art from politics. These literary groups introduced Walter Pater, Oscar Wilde, Dante Gabriel Rossetti, the French Symbolists, and Poe into China. In 1924 *Short Story Monthly* published Poe's "The Poetic Principle," an event that influenced the early stages of development of the New Chinese Poetry.

Poe's poems were not translated as extensively as his tales. His most famous poem, "The Raven," first appeared in 1923, followed by "Annabel Lee" and "The Bells."[6] It is noteworthy, however, that "The Raven" was repeatedly translated into different versions and by different literary coteries. The first translation, a pell-mell piece of work that appeared in *Literature Weekly*, was, in the opinion of Guo Mo-ro, "extremely absurd." The Creation Society's *Creation Weekly* then published another version by Zhan Bai-fu, which was revised by Guo Mo-ro himself.

To counterbalance the influence of the Creation Society, *Critical Review* also published a translation of "The Raven" that was entirely different in style and diction. The title was changed to "The Song of the Owl" because, as the editor Wu Mi explained, the owl is also a bird of omen, and the change was intended to remind Chinese readers of the classical poem bearing the same title.

Wu Mi, the editor of *Critical Review*, was a professor at Qinghua University in Beijing who had studied at the University of Virginia, where he visited Poe's old room. In his "Notes on English Poetry" printed in the *Quarterly* run by Chinese students in America, he showed his admiration for this "poetic genius."[7] In 1920 Hu Xian-su, one of the Nanjing professors of the *Critical Review* group, pointed out that "it is Poe who made the short story a literary form. His writing techniques have been followed by the later short story writers."[8] In 1926 *Short Story Monthly* published "The Angel of the Odd," translated by Fu Dong-hua, together with a picture of Poe and his autograph.[9] In February 1927 "The Gold-Bug" appeared in the *Morning Daily Supplement* in installments retranslated by Tong Ye (pseudonym).

In that same year Zheng Zhen-duo finished his complete history of world literature from preclassical times to the present, entitled *An Outline of Literature*. Chapter forty was devoted to five nineteenth-century American writers: Cooper, Irving, Hawthorne, Stowe, and Poe; in it he made a number of good judgments about the tales of ratiocination and about "Ligeia" and "Shadow."[10] Another important piece of criticism appeared in the *Morning Daily Supplement* in 1928. "The Art of Short Fiction" by Ren Qiu (pseudonym) gives a detailed account of the growth of short fiction beginning with Poe, in the course of which various aspects of Poe's theories on short fiction are closely examined in relation to his best-known tales.[11]

In 1925 the Sunken Bell Society was established, with a special interest in Poe. In July 1927 the society published a special issue of its magazine devoted to Poe and E.T.A. Hoffmann. It included three of Poe's tales, "Ligeia," "Eleonora," and "The Black Cat," translated by Chen Wei-mo, and two poems, "The Bells" and "The Raven," translated by Yang Hui. Chen Wei-mo also wrote a critical review, "Edgar Allan Poe's Fiction," for this issue.[12] At about the same time, Poe's tale "The Assignation" was translated by Zhu Wei-ji and later collected into *The Daffodils*, an anthology of foreign poetry and prose published by the Guanghua Publishing House in 1929.[13]

The first collection of Poe's short stories in book form appeared in 1934. Wu Guang-jian, one of the earliest professional translators in China, translated three of Poe's tales: "The Tell-Tale Heart," "The Pit and the Pendulum," and "The Purloined Letter." In his preface Wu calls Poe "the greatest literary genius in America" and "the inventor of the short story." [14] Not long afterward, "The Fall of the House of Usher" and "The Tell-Tale Heart" were translated into Chinese by Jian Xian-ai and Chen Jia-ling for the World Library Series, edited by Zheng Zhen-duo, and *Literature Quarterly* published another translation of "The Pit and the Pendulum," by Bai He (pseudonym). [15]

General interest in Poe went into a decline in the 1930s, for several reasons. Poe's works, which were detached from social reality, could be enjoyed only by that very small circle of readers who regarded literature as a mere pastime, and following the outbreak of the War of Resistance against Japan in 1937, translation and publication of Poe's works virtually came to an end. Poe's star shone once more in China, however, before a blackout of more than thirty years. In the autumn of 1949 two books by Poe were published: one was *Selected Tales*, containing "The Black Cat," "The Mystery of Marie Rogêt," "The Gold-Bug," and "Lionizing"; the other was *The Narrative of Arthur Gordon Pym*, all of which were translated by Jiao Ju-yin. By this time, Poe's major works had been translated into Chinese. These two titles belong to the twenty-volume American Literature Series, a project sponsored by the famous historian John K. Fairbank in which many well-known Chinese literary figures took part; it is now recognized as a significant event in postwar Sino-American cultural relations. Unfortunately, the timing was bad. Immediately after its publication Sino-American relations reached their lowest ebb, and the entire series was soon forgotten. As we recall this series today, though, it becomes apparent that up until 1949 Poe was regarded in China as one of the major nineteenth-century American writers. [16]

In the 1920s, after the "May Fourth Incident" of 1919, China's New Literature movement flourished, particularly in the short story. In this decade there were more writers of short fiction than ever before in the history of Chinese literature. These writers were influenced by the large amount of Western literature that had been translated, and as a result Chinese fiction was changing in both form and content. Poe influenced this short fiction in three different ways. First, some of his well-known tales were used as models, and their technical devices and structure were widely imitated. Second, the elements of Aestheticism, Symbolism, and Mysticism in his work made him the spiritual kinsman of those Chinese writers under the influence of the so-called Neoromantics. The third and most common kind of influence was his use of certain kinds of emotional effects and his psychological probing into people's minds.

Three writers in particular were influenced by Poe in these various ways. The first is Chen Xiang-he, who in the early 1920s left Fudan University in Shanghai to join his friends in Beijing, including Feng Zhi, Yang Hui, and Chen Wei-mo. This group later founded the Sunken Bell Society, which worked for more than eight years to promote the new Chinese literature. Chen Xiang-he had a special interest in Poe, and he was temperamentally susceptible to the dream and Gothic elements in Poe's fiction. Two of his short stories bear traits of Poe's style. "The Mourning" concerns the repentance of Mr. B., the narrator, a worshiper of Poe, who is full of sorrow and regret over having killed his wife. He decides to sell all of his books to redeem his crime, but the only books he has left are "a thick volume of tales by E. A. Poe and three or four plays by Strindberg." He regards these two writers as "the most beloved and most admirable sages." [17] Poe inspires other elements in the tale; like the narrator of "The Black Cat," Mr. B. is a victim of the imp of the perverse, and the appearance of Mr. B.'s wife is similar to that of Poe's Ligeia.

"The Eyes," also by Chen, is a first-person narration of the incoherent thoughts of a monomaniac. Obsessed with the beautiful eyes of a nurse, Mr. N., the narrator, becomes insane and is hospitalized. Every time he is on the verge of regaining consciousness the only thing that looms large in his mind's eye is that pair of beautiful eyes. "The Eyes" is typically Poesque, highly imaginary and highly symbolic. The plot resembles that of "The Pit and the Pendulum," if we see it as the visionary account of a man in a state of half consciousness, half swoon. Mr. N.'s obsession with the woman's eyes reminds us of Poe's obsessed narrators in such tales as "Ligeia," "The Tell-Tale Heart," and "Berenice."

A second prominent author under Poe's influence was Li Jian-wu. Best known as a leading playwright in the 1930s and 1940s, Li began his career writing short stories in the 1920s. "The Last Generation of the Guan Family" (1926) is in fact an imitation of "The Fall of the House of Usher." The protagonist of the tale lives in a cluster of tumbledown houses situated in a secluded resort in the suburbs of Beijing. He likes to sit by himself for long hours, lost in a sort of reverie, dreaming either about the past glories of his forefathers or about that day in the future when his bankrupt family will be revived. The narrator pays a visit to the house of the Guan family, where, to his surprise, he finds his friend lying on his deathbed, shrieking spasmodically in a sort of delirium. The tale ends in a way similar to "The Fall of the House of Usher," with the narrator rushing out of the house, "hearing, amid the howling north wind, a high-pitched, long yell of despair." Other grotesque tales by Li Jian-wu that show Poe's influence are "The Shadow" (1927), "The Last Dream" (1929), and "Before the Second Lover" (1930).[18]

A third writer influenced by Poe was Yu Da-fu, one of the founders of the Creation Society. Yu Da-fu considers death and sexual desire basic topics for literature, an idea akin to Poe's notion of the death of a beautiful woman as the best subject for poetry; and he is interested in "the abnormal, the eccentric and the irrational." "The Silver-Grey Death" is generally regarded as his masterpiece.[19] The narrator is young, melancholy and dissipated; he finally dies from a cerebral hemorrhage caused by alcohol poisoning. Those familiar with the popular version of Poe's biography will readily recognize the image of Poe lurking between the lines. Reminiscent of Poe's child-bride, Virginia, the narrator's wife is a young morbid beauty who dies of consumption, vomiting blood from time to time. Another story by Yu Da-fu, "The Thirteenth Night," is like Li Jian-wu's "The Last Dream" in its resemblance to Poe's "The Fall of the House of Usher" both in structure and effect. Like "Usher," "The Thirteenth Night" depicts the doom of a monomaniac or paranoid painter, narrated by an observer, but the story seems more human and the effect less weird. In Yu Da-fu's tale, Mr. Chen, the painter, is obsessed with the beautiful phantom girl he thinks he has met in the wild mountains. Driven by their obsessions, both retreat more and more into themselves until, in the end, they have identified themselves with the phantom object. The appearance of Mr. Chen seems to be a self-portrait of the author, just as the features of Roderick Usher resemble those of Poe.

In addition to those writers who consciously imitated Poe's style and those who resembled him in temperament or aesthetic aims, there is another category of writers who were merely interested in his writing techniques. China's most famous modern writer, Lu Xun, is a case in point. To awaken the Chinese people ignorant of their oppression and exploitation, he resorted to symbolic methods. He would project an image of the Chinese people not in their normal proportions but with some exaggerations that would startle his readers. Lu Xun therefore chose an insane man to be the protagonist of his first creative work, "A Madman's Diary," a title taken from Gogol. "The White Light" also deserves our attention, as it, too, is a tale about a monomaniac and resembles Poe's "Berenice" in many ways. Chen Shi-cheng, the central character, fails the county examination, destroying in one blow his dream of advancing in the social hierarchy. Delirious, he suddenly remembers a legendary saying that his ancestors had buried a large number of silver dollars somewhere under the courtyard. Guided by the light of the full moon he gropes his way, digging here and there, first in his own yard, then outside, then in the mountains. He finally unearths a rotten skull with some teeth still attached to it. This episode is very similar to the one in Poe's "Berenice" in which the monomaniac protagonist Egaeus sneaks into the tomb of his cousin at night and extracts the teeth from the still-living body.[20] Another recurring Poe theme is premature burial and suspended animation. Lu Xun uses these devices in a prose poem called "After Death," in which the narrator finds that after the paralysis of his motor nerves, his sensations still remain. Lying by the roadside he hears the cries of magpies, then of crows.[21] However, the story is not an exploration of the fear of death as Poe's tale is. Lu Xun borrows the theme of premature burial in order to ridicule and denounce his enemies.

Mao Dun has always been regarded as the chief representative of the realistic school of modern Chinese literature; therefore there is generally little in common between his writing and Poe's. But one "essay" of his, actually a prose poem, is remarkably similar to "The Tell-Tale Heart," which he once translated. "Knocking at the Door" describes the working of a very sensitive mind, from its hypnagogic state to reverie and from reverie to wakefulness. Mao Dun once remarked that those "visionary, unearthly things" in Poe's works would very often "impinge upon our souls." This "essay" illustrates the way Poe's works impinged upon his own.[22]

Other writers possibly influenced by Poe include Fang Guang-tao, whose tale "The Death of Melan" is about the death of a black cat as well as its effect on the human psyche. In the tales and short plays of Deng Gu, written in the 1920s, there are also Gothic elements and descriptions of abnormal mental states that recall both Poe and Maeterlinck.

Poe's influence on modern Chinese poetry is less direct. Many of the theories and techniques reflecting his influence were filtered through the French Symbolists; some Chinese poets came into contact with the poetry of the French Symbolists when living in France and Japan.

Toward the end of the Qing dynasty in the late nineteenth century, many young poets were calling for reform and were rebelling against the restraints of classical Chinese poetry. In 1919 some young poets, including Hu Shi, Liu Fu, and Shen Yin-mo, began publishing poems that cast off the shackles of the classical poetic conventions for the first time. Soon the New Poetry was sweeping the country, as others began writing in new forms, particularly in free verse. But as to content, the poems were heavily didactic, reflecting the current interest in ideology.[23] As a reaction to this didacticism, Zhou Zuo-ren promoted a shorter poem, following the models of the Japanese haiku and tanka.[24] The Japanese poets attempted to support their rationale for short poems by referring to Poe's criticism. Zhou also told his readers that owing to Poe's influence, the French Symbolists, such as Baudelaire, Mallarmé, and Verlaine, all favored the short poem. The trend of writing short poems continued for about three years.

When Wen Yi-do returned to China from three years of study in the United States he joined the Crescent Society. He and other poets — Xu Zhi-mo, Zhu-Xiang, Rao Men-ken, Liu Meng-wei, and Yu Geng-yu — opened up a new column in the Beijing *Morning Daily* called "Shi Juan" [Poems engraved], declaring that its sole purpose was "to bring out something new" and "to discover new forms and new syllables and meters."[25] At almost the same time, Xu Zhi-mo, the best-known poet of the time, was also putting forth similar views of "word music," and Rao Meng-kan published articles on "The Rhythm and Rhyme of the New Poetry."[26] The emphasis of these poets on the musical effects of poetry derives mainly from the nineteenth-century English Romantics — Coleridge, Wordsworth, Byron, Shelley, and Keats — but it also comes partly from Poe's "The Poetic Principle." Wen Yi-do made some serious attempts to put Poe's theory into practice. To enhance the musical effects of his narrative poem "The Yuyang Strains," he imitated the onomatopoeia of Poe's "The Bells." "The Goddess of Love" also seems indebted to Poe, since there are parallels in structure and theme with "The Haunted Palace."

Xu Zhi-mo was an even better known poet than Wen Yi-do at that time, although his theories were not as influential. He was most active in importing and experimenting with new poetic forms.[27] The immediate task for writers of the New Poetry, he held, was to "discover new rhythms and new rhymes" for a new kind of "pure word music."[28] For this he turned to Baudelaire, translating "Une Charogne," which he described as "the most vicious and the most grotesque flower in *Les Fleurs du Mal*." In a long introduction to this translation, he elaborates on the musical effects of poetry in general in a passage that echoes not only Baudelaire but Poe's "The Poetic Principle."[29]

As the New Chinese Poetry was developing in the 1920s, another school of poets emerged who had studied in either France or Japan and wrote poems in the French Symbolist manner. One such writer was Li Jing-fa, who wrote poems that were free verse in form but classical Chinese in diction, which made them even more difficult to understand than the old forms of classical Chinese poetry.

Among the Symbolist poets of the 1920s, Yu Geng-yu stands nearer to Poe than do the rest of his contemporaries. Even the titles of his collections reveal his idiosyncratic characteristics: *Before the Dusk, Roses above the Skeletons,*

*Demons' Dance,* and *The Lonely Soul.* In poetics, Poe remains one of Yu Geng-yu's idols. In "The Art of Poetry," one of his twelve essays on poetics, he declares himself to be on the side of Coleridge, Poe, and Yeats, and Poe's definition of poetry as *"The Rhythmical Creation of Beauty"* lies at the heart of his argument.[30] He maintains that poetry should be "an independent art" and the poet should write poems "solely for the poem's sake," and in his essays he cites "The Raven" again and again as a model for lyric poetry.[31] In his close attention to style Yu Geng-yu seems to be a faithful disciple of Poe's. But even though he inherited much from Poe, the poetic forms he used do not resemble Poe's at all.

We must keep in mind, then, that Poe's influence on these Chinese Symbolists was indirect, through the French Symbolists. Two poets of the so-called later-stage Creation Society, Mui Mu-tian and Wang Du-qing, published some articles in *Creation Monthly* in an exchange of views on Symbolist poetics. According to Mu, a poem must preserve its "unity," and "the lack of unity is a fatal blunder to poetry in general." "A poem," he believes, "should be kept to one idea; and the content of a poem must be the content of one idea. . . . Poe's 'The Raven' is a perfect example."[32] These ideas of unity are probably derived from Poe's ideas on unity of effect in "The Poetic Principle."

Mui Mu-tian, Wang Du-qing, and a third Symbolist, Feng Nai-chao, shared these ideas, and they decided to advocate *la poésie pure* as an ideal remedy for prosaism in the New Poetry movement. Unfortunately, their poetical ability seems to have fallen short of their ambition. Moreover, with the development of the revolutionary situation, a political split between them became inevitable, and pure poetry was out of the question.

As we have seen, conventional Chinese literary form and aesthetics had become outworn by the beginning of the twentieth century. Writers and poets of the 1920s could have turned back to classical tradition for inspiration, but instead they looked to the West and to Poe among others. Poe was admired for several reasons, among them as the founder of the short story and as the precursor of aestheticism. His "neurotic genre" was accepted by modern Chinese short story writers, who moved away from old conventions that merely presented a series of events to new experiments that employed psychological themes. Writers using abnormal psychological states were able to use veiled hints and indirection instead of writing directly, and readers could respond to these hints using their own imagination.

Poe's theories on the musical qualities of poetry, on the suggestiveness and undercurrents in a poem, and on the unity of effect were also of interest in the development of the New Chinese Poetry. Although the type of poetry that was influenced by Poe disappeared for almost forty years, it is worth noting that in the late 1970s a new group of poets appeared who are called "the poets of ambiguity." Deprived of formal education in the ten-year Cultural Revolution, they acquired a cultural background entirely different from that of the old generation. Their poems are therefore quite different, not only in subject matter but also in symbolism and imagery. One of the young poets writes: "Who is walking there in the distance? / The Pendulum. / He is hired by Death / to measure Life." Depicting the scenery along the Lia-ling River, he writes: "The collapse has stopped. / On the riverbank, are piling high / the skulls of the giants. / The mourning sailing boats / slowly, slowly pass by, / Unfolding their dark yellow shrouds." [33]

To those familiar with Poe, these lines are sure to strike a chord. Perhaps the influence of Poe is not entirely a thing of the past.

NOTES

1. Zheng Zhen-duo, "An Outline of Literature," *Short Story Monthly* 17 (1926).

2. Du Ying (pseudonym for Zhou Zuo-ren) trans., *Honan* 8 (1908); rpt. *A Collection of Foreign Fiction* (Tokyo, 1909).

3. Zhang Jing-lu, *Historical Data Concerning Publication in Modern China* (Shanghai, 1954), pp. 321–322; see also Zhou Xia-shou, *Lu Xunde gujia* (Hong Kong, 1962).

4. Zhang Jing-lu, *Historical Data*, p. 314.

5. Xi Chen, "Neo-Romanticism in Modern Literature," *Eastern Miscellany* 17 (1920).

6. *Literature Weekly* 100 (1923); *Literature Weekly* 17 (1925).

7. Gu Qian-ji, trans., *Critical Review* 45 (1925).

8. Hu Xian-su, "The Latest Tendency in European-American Modern Literature," *Eastern Miscellany* 17 (1920).

9. *Short Story Monthly* 17 (1926).

10. Zheng Zhen-duo, "Outline."

11. "The Art of Short Fiction," *Morning Daily Supplement* 2168–2171 (1928).

12. Chen Wei-mo, "Edgar Allan Poe's Fiction," *Sunken Bell* (special issue).

13. Zhang Jing-lu, *Historical Data*, pp. 316–317.

14. Wu Guang-jian, *Tales by Edgar Allan Poe* (Shanghai, 1934).

15. Zheng Zhen-duo. ed., *Shije wenku*, vol. 4 (Shanghai, 1936); Bai He, trans., *Literature Quarterly* 3 (1935).

16. Zhao Jia-bi, "Around the Publication of the *American Literature Series Books*," *Book Review* 10 (1980): 90.

17. Cheng Xiang-he, "West Wind at My Pillow — A Record of My Dreams, Written to Yang Hui" and "The Mourning," *Sunken Bell* (1926) (one-volume edition).

18. The three tales are included in Li Jian-wu's collection of short stories entitled *Tanzi* (Shanghai, 1931).

19. Dong Yi, "A Preliminary Study of Yu Da-fu's Fiction," *Literary Review* 5 (1980).

20. Lu Xun, *Nahan* (Beijing, 1973), p. 136.

21. Lu Xun, "After Death," in *Wild Grass* (Beijing, 1974).

22. Mao Dun (Shen Yen-bing), "My Own Reminiscence," in *Mao Dun's Own Selection* (Shanghai, 1933).

23. Zhu Zi-qing, preface to the *Collection of Poems, Series Books of Chinese New Literature* (Shanghai, 1933), p. 2.

24. Ibid., p. 4.

25. Ibid., p. 5.

26. Xu Zhi-mo, "A Letter to Ouyang Lan," quoted from Ouyang Lan, "Semantic Symmetry," *Literature Ten Daily* 53 (1924).

27. Zhu Zi-qing, preface, p. 6.

28. Xu Zhi-mo, "A Letter to Ouyang Lan."

29. Xu Zhi-mo, "Translation of Baudelaire's 'La Charognc,'" *Thread of Talk* (December 1, 1924).

30. Yu Geng-yu, "Art of Poetry (Part II)," *Huayan Monthly* 1 (1929).

31. Yu Geng-yu, "Art of Poetry (Part I)"; Yu Geng-yu, "The Power of Poetic Creation," *Morning Daily Supplement*, February 28, 1927.

32. Mu Mu-tian, "On Poetry: A Letter to Guo Mo-ro," *Creation Monthly* 1 (1926).

33. Quoted from Gu Gong, "Two Generations," *Shikan* 10 (1980).

# *Poe in India*

D. RAMAKRISHNA

Among the many Poe tales translated into Indian languages, "The Gold-Bug" appears the most frequently. In the late 1960s Sadanand R. Pavnaskar carried out an extensive research project that identified forty-three stories by Poe translated into six Indian languages, including Assamese, Bengali, Hindi, Marathi, Kannada, and Malayalam.[1] The largest edition in Hindi contains twenty-five tales and an introduction to Poe's life and works written by Ramnath Suman, editor of the volume. Suman concludes his essay with the remark that Poe occupies a place of honor among the litterateurs of the world.[2] In the preface to the Kannada translation of fifteen tales, Dhanvanta describes Poe as primarily a storyteller capable of handling horror themes with marvelous dexterity.[3] Poe's popularity as a detective fiction writer is evident among Malayalee readers, who find three of Poe's tales of ratiocination in two editions translated into Malayalam. Editors and translators of the Marathi edition describe Poe as the originator of modern terror, science, and mystery fiction.[4]

Poe is recognized in the various Indian translations as principally a writer of mystery and detective novels. "The Purloined Letter" and "The Murders in the Rue Morgue" are especially popular among Indian readers, both general and academic. While some general readers are acquainted with Conan Doyle's Sherlock Holmes, most of them are not aware of the fact that Dupin was the model for the British detective. Several detective writers in Indian languages have used Poe's tales as models, but they do not openly acknowledge their indebtedness to the American writer. In an unpublished paper entitled "Poe and Tamilvaanan: An Analysis with Particular Reference to 'The Murders in the Rue Morgue' and *Shankaral in Paris*," S. Savitri maintains that Tamilvaanan, a major detective-fiction writer in Tamil during the 1970s, appears to have drawn heavily from Poe. Shankarlal, Tamilvaanan's detective hero, bears striking resemblances to Poe's Dupin, particularly in Dupin's unique ratiocinative powers but without his eccentricities. Besides modeling his hero on the lines of Poe's, Tamilvaanan weaves his plot around a mystery that is eventually unraveled by the hero. The depiction of the police official as less ingenious and imaginative than the hero is yet another common factor between Poe and Tamilvaanan.[5]

Although Poe's tales have been translated into a number of Indian languages, his poetry has received less attention. Sadanand R. Pavnaskar rendered three of Poe's poems into Hindi, the only ones known to have appeared in an Indian language.[6] Poe's essays on poetry and his influence on the French Symbolists are the subject of discussion among Indian academics and creative writers. Consciously or unconsciously, poets in several Indian languages use Symbolist techniques in their poems.

The academic interest in Poe since the 1960s has focused on a few tales and poems. A high degree of involvement and freshness of approach to Poe is evident among the present generation of Indian scholars. Since the founding of the Indian Chapter of the Edgar Allan Poe Society of Baltimore at the American Studies Research Center in India in 1993, Poe scholars from India and the United States have come together each year to participate in seminars that I have organized. Some of the papers presented at the Poe seminars show interest on the part of the younger Indian scholars, who analyze Poe's work in light of recent developments in critical theory. B. Mendonca, in his paper entitled "The Reign of Madmen: The Hue of Sanity in Poe's 'The System of Doctor Tarr and Professor Fether,'" reads the tale in light of Postmodernist notions of text and history. In an interesting parallel between Poe's "The Man of the Crowd" and Joyce Carol Oates's "Stalking," P. Sreelakshmi points out numerous intertextual references. Nandana Dutta, in her article entitled "The Real House of Usher," reads the tale within the aesthetic parameters of Romanticism, specifically the Romantic dilemma of reality as presence and reality as construct. She believes that Poe never completely resolved this dilemma, preferring instead to present the tale as a balancing act. Manju Jaidka, in "Orang-Outang in *The Waste Land*," studies the influence of Poe's detective fiction on T. S. Eliot. According to Jaidka, Eliot's "Sweeney Erect" and "Sweeney among the Nightingales" are strongly indebted to Poe's "The Murders in the Rue Morgue." Connecting Poe with India, I argue in "Poe's *Eureka* and Hindu Philosophy" that Poe is expressing (without acknowledging it) the essence of the Emersonian Transcendentalist ideal, which is also the essence of Hindu philosophical thought.[7]

A number of recent doctoral dissertations on Poe's works by scholars at Indian universities attest to the fact that Poe is a writer who fascinates both academics and general readers. In a collection of my own essays, *Explorations in Poe*, I treat many different topics that show the wide range of interest Poe inspires among readers in India today.[8] *Perspectives on Poe*, published in New

Delhi, brings studies by American scholars to Poe readers in India.[9] While general readers continue to enjoy Poe's tales translated into their own languages, Indian scholars explore the American writer's connections with other literatures and themes.

NOTES

1. Sadanand R. Pavnaskar, "Indian Translations of Edgar Allan Poe: A Bibliography with a Note," *Indian Journal of American Studies* (January 1971): 103–110. An expanded version of this bibliography by the same author but without the notes is found in "Poe in India: A Bibliography, 1955–1969," *Poe Studies* 5.2 (1972): 49–50.

2. *Rahasyapoorna Kahaniyan*, ed. and trans. Ramnath Suman, (Delhi: Rajpal & Sons, 1969).

3. *Savige Munche Samadhi mattu Itara Kathegalu*, ed. and trans. Dhanvanta (Bangalore: H. N. Rao & Brothers, 1955), i–iv.

4. *Soneri Bhunga*, trans. S. R. Devale (Poona: Chitrashala Prakashan, 1956); *Teen Chittatharak Katha*, trans. Kamale Phadke (Bombay: Majestic Book Stall, 1965).

5. Tamilvaanan, *Shankaral in Paris* (Madras: Manimekala Press, 1976).

6. Sadanand R. Pavnaskar, trans., *Ankan* 4.1 (1970): 27–29.

7. D. Ramakrishna, "Poe's *Eureka* and Hindu Philosophy," *Emerson Society Quarterly* 47:2 (1967): 28–32.

8. D. Ramakrishna, *Explorations in Poe* (Delhi: Academic Foundation, 1992).

9. D. Ramakrishna, ed., *Perspectives on Poe* (New Delhi: Associated Publishing, 1996).

PART TWO

*Poe's Influence*

*on Major World*

*Writers*

# Charles Baudelaire

LOIS DAVIS VINES

A precursor of the Symbolist movement, Charles Baudelaire (1821–1867) is best known for his collection of poems *Les Fleurs du mal* [*Flowers of Evil*] (1857). He believed in the creation of art through patient calculation, refusing to give undue credit to instinct and inspiration. During the last twenty years of his life, he translated Poe's tales, literary essays, and *Eureka*.

Charles Baudelaire was twenty-six when he discovered Poe's life and works, an encounter he described as a "shock of recognition." Not only did he find parallels with his own life but also poems and stories he had thought about. In a letter to literary critic Armand Fraisse dated 1860, Baudelaire recalled the excitement that led to his Poe obsession:

> In 1846 or '47 I came across a few fragments by Edgar Poe. I experienced a singular shock. His complete works were not assembled into a single edition until after his death, so I had the patience to make contact with Americans living in Paris to borrow from them collections of newspapers edited by Poe. And then — believe me if you will — I found poems and short stories that I had thought of, but in a vague, confused, and disorderly way and that Poe had been able to bring together to perfection. It was that that lay behind my enthusiasm and my long years of patience.[1]

Baudelaire's comments in this letter reveal three important aspects of his discovery of Poe. First, by indicating the approximate dates, he offers clues to Poe's works that caught his attention early on. Baudelaire scholar W. T. Bandy is convinced that the French poet had read Isabelle Meunier's translation of "The Black Cat," which appeared in *La Démocratie pacifique* on January 26, 1847.[2] On October 15, 1846, a twenty-page article on Poe by E.-D. Forgues, a journalist who also translated tales from American and English sources, appeared in *Revue des deux Mondes*.[3] Forgues lauded Poe's talent as an author of captivating tales. After recounting "A Descent into the Maelström," Forgues points out Poe's "peculiar lucidity of intellect, a miraculous power of observation."[4] Since Baudelaire mentioned in his letter that he "came across a few fragments" by Poe, he is no doubt referring to Meunier's translations and probably to Forgues's article.

The second important point is that Baudelaire made contact with Americans living in Paris who were able to lend him press accounts published in the United States. Through circumstances still unknown, he made the acquaintance of an American journalist by the name of William Mann, who just happened to have copies of the *Southern Literary Messenger*, a monthly literary periodical published in Richmond, Virginia, where Poe served as editor from mid-1836 to January 1837. The editions in Mann's possession contained an obituary of Poe written in November 1849 by John R. Thompson, editor of the magazine. Even more important, Baudelaire found a long review article by John M. Daniel, which was one of the most complete studies of Poe's life and works to appear in an American periodical until that time. As Bandy remarks, "Baudelaire could not have been more fortunate than to come by this extraordinary article."[5] When Baudelaire wrote a major essay on Poe in 1852, he seems to have relied heavily on the two articles. Bandy devotes most of his 1973 study to the subject of Baudelaire's American sources, pointing out that twenty-five of the forty pages of Baudelaire's article are translated almost word-for-word from Daniel's review.[6] Bandy also shows that portions of Thompson's obituary were paraphrased by Baudelaire and incorporated into his essay. While using the American accounts in his own article, Baudelaire was careful to leave out any derogatory comments. Thus Baudelaire's 1852 article, which became the source of Poe's reputation in Europe and beyond, appears to be an altered version of pieces from the American press.

The third significant point in Baudelaire's letter is his remark that he found in Poe's work "poems and short stories that [he] had thought of . . . and that Poe had been able to bring together to perfection." This admission has inspired much debate with no definitive answers. Peter Wetherill wrote a detailed study showing striking similarities between specific poems by Baudelaire and Poe, observing that "one cannot deny that by the tone and detail, [Baudelaire's] Sabatier cycle seems to be an imitation of Poe."[7] Baudelaire's first biographer, Charles Asselineau, argues that some of these poems were written before Baudelaire read Poe but were published later, thus supporting Baudelaire's remark that in Poe he found poems he had thought of himself before discovering the American poet. Another Baudelaire contemporary, Ernest Prarond, mentions that the poet constantly rewrote his poems and could have included lines inspired by his reading of Poe.[8] A detailed comparison of Baudelaire's "Le Flambeau vivant" ["The Living Torch"] and Poe's "To

Helen" reveals that eight of the fourteen lines in Baudelaire's poem seem to be translations from Poe.[9]

Well aware of the similarities, Baudelaire was annoyed by suggestions that he had incorporated lines from Poe into his own poetry. Just two years before his death he complained in a letter to a friend: "I lost a great deal of time translating Edgar Poe and the great benefit it brought me was to make some kindly souls say I'd borrowed *my* poems from Poe — poems I'd written ten years before I knew Poe's works."[10] Baudelaire translated only four poems: "The Raven," rendered in French prose in his version of "The Philosophy of Composition"; "To My Mother," a sonnet serving as a dedication to *Histoires extraordinaires*; "The Conqueror Worm," included in the tale "Ligeia"; and "The Haunted Palace" in his translation of "The Fall of the House of Usher." The task of translating Poe's poetry was taken up later by Stéphane Mallarmé.

Between 1848, when Baudelaire published his first Poe translation, the tale "Mesmeric Revelation," and his death in 1867, he produced five volumes of Poe translations along with articles and prefaces that would become the source of Poe's renown in many European countries and throughout the world.[11] Although his first translation probably did not attract much attention, Baudelaire's article on Poe that appeared in the March and April 1852 issues of the *Revue de Paris* made the American writer's name known to a broader reading audience in France. The long article, entitled "Edgar Allan Poe, sa vie et ses ouvrages" ["Edgar Allan Poe, His Life and Works"], gives a detailed description of Poe's sad life, which had not been recounted earlier in Forgues's article.[12] In addition, Baudelaire praised the originality and intellectual quality of Poe's work. His 1852 article, containing both an analysis of Poe's work and biographical material (including several errors), became the source of information for future French authors and was widely translated around the world. Another article by Baudelaire, published in 1856 and bearing a similar title, is for the most part a revision of the 1852 essay.

Poe's literary essays made a strong impression on Baudelaire, who read them early in his writing career. He translated "The Philosophy of Composition" (giving it the French title "La Genèse d'un poème") and "The Poetic Principle." The latter piece is an example of Baudelaire's total intellectual merging with Poe. We find Poe's essay almost verbatim, without quotes or credit to the author, embedded in Baudelaire's 1857 preface to the translation of Poe's tales. The unsuspecting reader would have no reason to believe the ideas expressed are other than Baudelaire's. Valéry recognized that Baudelaire considered the Poe essay "his own property," remarking that "this plagiarism would be open to discussion if its author had not himself, as we shall see, drawn attention to it."[13] Valéry goes on to explain that in an article on Théophile Gautier, Baudelaire cited a whole passage from the purloined essay, saying that he was quoting from his own work.

What are the principles in Poe's literary essays that had such a profound influence on Baudelaire and, subsequently, on writers in many countries who admired the French poet? Baudelaire was particularly impressed by what he considered the psychological conditions of a poem, meaning that the poet consciously determines the effects the poem will have on the reader. In order to create a calculated effect, the poet must keep in mind the length of the poem, which must be short. But most important, Baudelaire credited Poe with the idea of eliminating from poetry subjects that can best be treated in prose, such as history, science, and morality. Valéry defines the aspect of Poe's work that changed Baudelaire's destiny: "Poe was opening up a way, teaching a very strict and deeply alluring doctrine, in which a kind of mathematics and a kind of mysticism become one."[14] This "doctrine," as Valéry calls it, was to have a profound influence on three generations of French poets.

American scholar Patrick Quinn set out to find an answer to the question, Is the Poe honored in France only a mythical construction of the French imagination? "With an entirely lukewarm appreciation of Poe's writings," he remarks, "I began my investigation into Poe's immense reputation in France. I thought that my inquiry would take me back to the origins and up through the history of a great misunderstanding, or even a hoax. . . . But now, some years later, I have rather different proposals to make."[15] Quinn immersed himself in Baudelaire's translations, compared them to the English originals, and participated intellectually in the French response to Poe. He discovered that Baudelaire's acumen as a literary critic paid off in his judicious selection of forty-five of the seventy-one tales that had been published. The stories Baudelaire chose to translate are generally recognized as among Poe's best and have withstood the test of time. In addition, Baudelaire had a keen sense of marketing. As he mentions in a letter to the critic Sainte-Beuve, he organized the tales into two volumes, the first of which "was designed as bait for the public: tricks, divination, leg-pulls, etc. . . . the second volume is of a loftier kind of fantastic: hallucinations, mental illness, pure grotesque, supernaturalism, etc."[16] The plan worked. Baudelaire's volumes of Poe's tales, *Histoires extraordinaires* (1856) and *Nouvelles Histoires extraordinaires* (1857), enjoyed a wide readership worldwide and inspired many critical studies.

Quinn addressed a question that is often raised concerning Baudelaire's translations: Did the French poet improve on the original versions? Using precise examples too numerous to cite here, Quinn shows that in specific cases

Baudelaire's French improved or even corrected Poe's faulty syntax and vocabulary; in other cases Baudelaire mistranslated certain expressions that are particularly obscure for a non-Anglophone. After careful examination of the evidence, Quinn concludes that "this or that detail may have been overlooked, or improved, or weakened in translation. But there is no full-scale transmutation. Baudelaire did not melt down these stories, remove their dross, and recast them in the pure gold of his French." [17] The fact remains, however, that Poe's tales were translated into French by one of France's greatest writers and were then rendered into many other languages from Baudelaire's version. Had an author of lesser talent attempted such an ambitious undertaking, Poe's fate might have been quite different.

Baudelaire's fate might also have taken a different turn had he not discovered Poe. Valéry beautifully describes this fortuitous encounter, observing that Baudelaire had a "critical intelligence allied to the gift of poetry. To this rare combination Baudelaire owes a capital discovery . . . the good fortune of discovering in Edgar Allan Poe a new intellectual world. . . . So many original views and extraordinary promises bewitched him; his talent was transformed, his destiny splendidly changed." [18] Poe and Baudelaire did indeed, in the words of Valéry, "exchange values" in one of the most remarkable literary connections between two writers who never met or corresponded. In exchange, Baudelaire offered Poe to the world.

NOTES

1. Rosemary Lloyd, ed. and trans., *Selected Letters of Charles Baudelaire: The Conquest of Solitude* (Chicago: U of Chicago P, 1986), p. 148.

2. For a detailed account of Baudelaire's discovery of Poe, see W. T. Bandy, *Edgar Allan Poe: Sa Vie et ses ouvrages* (Toronto: U of Toronto P, 1973). Although the title is in French, the book is in English.

3. The complete article translated into English can be found in Jean Alexander, *Affidavits of Genius: Edgar Allan Poe and the French Critics, 1847–1924* (Port Washington, N.Y.: Kennikat, 1971), pp. 79–98. A condensed version of the same article in English is in Eric W. Carlson, *Critical Essays on Edgar Allan Poe* (Boston: G. K. Hall, 1987), pp. 41–49.

4. Carlson, *Critical Essays*, p. 45.

5. Bandy, *Edgar Allan Poe*, p. xxv.

6. In "New Light on Baudelaire and Poe," *Yale French Studies* 10 (1952): 65–69, Bandy describes his discovery that much of Baudelaire's 1852 article came from Daniel's review. Bandy gives a detailed comparison in *Edgar Allan Poe*. The French critic Claude

Richard in *Poe: Journaliste et critique* (Paris: Klincksieck, 1978) juxtaposes Baudelaire's text and those of Thompson and Daniel. He compares the texts in detail, bringing to light similarities that add to Bandy's earlier analyses.

7. Peter M. Wetherill, "Edgar Allan Poe and Madame Sabatier;" *Modern Language Quarterly* 20 (1959): 344–354. Wetherill includes a similar analysis in French in his *Charles Baudelaire et la poésie d'Edgar Allan Poe* (Paris: Nizet, 1962).

8. Asselineau and Prarond both quoted by Léon Lemonnier, *Edgar Poe et la critique française* (Paris: P.U.F., 1928), pp. 18–26.

9. See Wetherill, *Charles Baudelaire*, pp. 136–137.

10. Lloyd, *Selected Letters of Charles Baudelaire*, p. 221.

11. These include *Histoires extraordinaires* (1856), *Nouvelles Histoires extraordinaires* (1857), *Aventures d'Arthur Gordon Pym* (1858), *Eureka* (1863), and *Histoires grotesques et sérieuses* (1865). For a list of the contents of the three volumes of short stories, see Charles Baudelaire, *Baudelaire on Poe*, ed. and trans. Lois Hyslop and Francis E. Hyslop Jr. (State College, Penn.: Bald Eagle, 1952), pp. 167–168.

12. English translations are included in Baudelaire, *Baudelaire on Poe*, pp. 37–86, and in Alexander, *Affidavits of Genius*, pp. 99–121.

13. *The Collected Works of Paul Valéry*, 15 vols., ed. Jackson Mathews (Princeton, N.J.: Princeton UP, 1956–1975), vol. 8, p. 206.

14. Ibid., p. 207.

15. Patrick F. Quinn, *The French Face of Edgar Poe* (Carbondale: Southern Illinois UP, 1957), pp. 4–5.

16. Lloyd, *Selected Letters of Charles Baudelaire*, p. 84.

17. Quinn, *The French Face of Edgar Poe*, p. 134.

18. *The Collected Works of Paul Valéry*, vol. 8, p. 194.

# Stéphane Mallarmé
# and Paul Valéry

LOIS DAVIS VINES

An English teacher by profession, Stéphane Mallarmé (1842–1898) became the leading figure of the Symbolist movement in France. He set off for London in 1863 to perfect his English, an experience that determined his career and inspired him to translate Poe. His most important poetic works are "Hérodiade" (1871) and "L'Après-midi d'un faune" ["A Faun's Afternoon"] (1876).

Best known as a poet, Paul Valéry (1871–1945) was also an essayist, philosopher, and literary critic. A unifying theme in his work is an obsession with knowing how the mind works. He considered his long poem *La Jeune Parque* [*The Young Fate*] (1917) and his collection of poetry *Charmes* [*Charms*] (1922) as mental exercises. His ideas on numerous subjects, including literature, painting, and dance, contributed to his influence on European intellectual life.

Stéphane Mallarmé never met Charles Baudelaire, although he once caught a glimpse of the poet at a bookstall but did not have the courage to approach him. Through Baudelaire's translations and reading Poe in English, Mallarmé developed a great admiration for the American writer, which inspired him to continue the translation task to which his predecessor had devoted so much time and work. Mallarmé translated thirty-six of Poe's poems selected from fifty that had been published. In the dedication to the Vanier edition in 1889, Mallarmé wrote: "To the memory of Baudelaire, whose death alone prevented him from completing, by translating all of these poems, the magnificent and fraternal monument dedicated by his genius to Edgar Poe."[1]

Although Mallarmé knew Poe's poems well, there is only scant evidence that they had any influence on his own poetry. Cambiaire compared Mallarmé's poem "Pour votre chère morte" [For your dear deceased] to "The Raven," pointing out that the subject is essentially the same.[2] In a dreary ambience at midnight, the lonely lover mourns his lost beloved while gazing at the dying embers of a pale fire. Jean Alexander reveals connections between Poe's "For Annie" and Mallarmé's *Nuit d'Idumée* [*Night of Idumea*].[3] Poe as a poet inspired one of Mallarmé's most beautiful poems. In 1876 to commemorate the twenty-fifth anniversary of Poe's death, Mallarmé expressed his admiration in a sonnet entitled "Le Tombeau d'Edgar Poe" ["The Tomb of Edgar Poe"].[4] The first line of the poem, "As into Himself at last eternity changes him," is one of the most often quoted from Mallarmé's poems. The line is especially poignant when considered in the context of Mallarmé himself. His poetry was deemed unfathomable during his lifetime but much admired after his death. Valéry saw in this line the essential connection with Baudelaire: "That transcendence which changes the poet into himself, as in Mallarmé's great line, that was what Baudelaire's action, his translations, his prefaces, assured for the miserable shade of Edgar Allan Poe."[5]

It was in Poe's essays that Mallarmé found the ideal he wished to attain. He believed that poetic creation is a conscious process that has an intended effect on the reader. The ideas Poe expressed in "The Philosophy of Composition" and "The Poetic Principle" became his guide as he spent many hours creating a single poem. He remarked in a letter to a friend: "The more I work, the more I will be faithful to the strict ideas that my great master Edgar Poe bequeathed to me. The remarkable poem 'The Raven' was created according to his ideas. And the soul of the reader responds absolutely as the poet intended."[6] Mallarmé was also impressed by Poe's views on the relationship between poetry and music, which he found in "The Poetic Principle" and in "Letter to B——," one of Poe's essays that Mallarmé read in English. In the latter piece Poe states that "music, when combined with a pleasurable idea, is poetry; music without the idea is simply music; the idea without the music is prose from its very definitiveness."[7] As a poet Mallarmé became obsessed with refining the use of language in order to produce musical effects through poetry. Like Poe, he envisioned pure poetry with beauty as its ultimate goal, rejecting political, social, or moral subjects as themes in his poems. Mallarmé believed that with conscious effort, language could be refined to the point of writing the perfect poem, an idea to which he devoted his artistic life.

From Baudelaire and Mallarmé, Valéry inherited excellent translations of Poe's tales, poems, literary essays, and *Eureka*, along with a sense of great admiration for the American author.[8] At the age of eighteen, Valéry wrote to Mallarmé, describing himself as a young man "lost in the provinces" and "deeply imbued with the cunning doctrines of the great Edgar Allan Poe — perhaps the most subtle artist of this century!" (CW 8: 406–407). The extent to which Valéry was immersed in Poe early in his career is evident in an essay written in 1889 entitled "On Literary Technique," which is an obvious rehash of "The Philosophy of Composition." His opening line states that "literature is the art of playing upon the mind of others" (CW 7: 315). He goes on to explain that the primary concern of the poet is to create an effect upon the listener which is calculated from the very beginning. Left unpublished, the manuscript was found among Valéry's papers after his death. When Valéry went to live in Paris in 1893, he frequented Mallarmé's Tuesday evening literary circle and developed a personal relationship with the poet that lasted until Mallarmé's death in 1898. Valéry recalled that at their first meeting, the subject of Poe brought them together as kindred spirits.

While Valéry was also devoted to perfecting language through poetry, he differed with Mallarmé on an essential point. Valéry was more interested in the mental process that goes on while writing a poem than in the poem itself. When he read "The Philosophy of Composition," he saw a mind observing itself in the act of artistic creation. In a letter to a friend written in 1912 but referring to his mental state in 1892, Valéry describes the effect of reading Poe: "I was brought to feel [Mallarmé's] power most by a reading of Poe. I read in him what I wanted and caught that *fever of lucidity that he communicates. Consequence*: I gave up writing verse. That art, which became impossible for me from 1892, was simply an exercise" (CW 8: 421). In his *Cahiers* [Notebooks], Valéry refers to Poe as this "demon of lucidity."[9] Although he continued to write poetry, he did not publish his poems during a twenty-year period (1897–1917).

Valéry observed his own mind to learn how it dealt with mathematics and the sciences and to figure out how it functioned during the creative process. A phrase in his 1894 notebook shows that he was reading Poe's tales, which suggested to him a possible literary project entitled "The Life and Adventures of Ch. Auguste Dupin" (C 1: 50). A close examination of Valéry's prose piece *La Soirée avec Monsieur Teste* [*The Evening with Monsieur Teste*] reveals numerous similarities between Valéry's main character and Poe's Dupin.[10] The aspect of Dupin that captured Valéry's imagination was the detective's ability to observe his own analytical faculties, a goal Valéry had set for himself. In Monsieur Teste Valéry created a superbrain, a mind that was not only intelligent but also capable of understanding its own mental operations. As in Poe's Dupin tales, Valéry uses a narrator to describe and react to the main character. But unlike Dupin, Teste does not need to show off his superior intellect; his greatest pleasure is observing the functioning of his own mind. Valéry once remarked that Teste "is a caricature of someone who might have been invented by Poe."[11]

During the period when Valéry was working on the prose piece that became *Monsieur Teste*, he was invited to write an article about Leonardo da Vinci for

*La Nouvelle Revue*, which was published on August 15, 1895. His approach to the subject was suggested to him by his reading of Poe. He made the following observation in his notebook: "Criticism consists of posing new problems. Poe was the first to consider mental mechanism as the producer of works. No one followed him" (C 6: 717). In his article "Introduction à la Méthode de Léonard de Vinci" ["Introduction to the Method of Leonardo da Vinci"], Valéry imagined how the mind of the great artist operated as it came to grips with science and art. Valéry's original approach was so different from the familiar historical and biographical criticism that he began his essay by laying out his method, an explanation that sounds like a paraphrase of "The Philosophy of Composition." Valéry writes: "Many an error that distorts our judgment of human achievements is due to a strange disregard of their genesis. We seldom remember that they did not always exist. This has led to a sort of reciprocal coquetry which leads authors to suppress, to conceal all too well, the origins of a work" (CW 8: 8). In one sense, Valéry wrote the article suggested in "The Philosophy of Composition," where Poe states: "I have often thought how interesting a magazine paper might be written by an author who would — that is to say who could — detail, step by step, the processes by which any one of his compositions attained its ultimate point of completion" (T 14). Instead of writing about himself, Valéry re-created the modus operandi of Leonardo. Valéry mentions the "coquetry" of authors as a reason to hide the origins of a work, an idea that Poe suggests by using the term "autorial vanity" (T 14). In his analysis of Leonardo's mind, Valéry imagines Leonardo dealing with the effects he wanted to create rather than producing art as a personal statement. Valéry was convinced that Poe was the first to see these "mechanics of effect." At the end of his Leonardo article, it is evident that Valéry had Poe in mind: "Edgar Poe, who in this century of literary perturbation was the very lightning of the confusion, of the poetic storm, and whose analysis sometimes ends, like Leonardo's in mysterious smiles, has clearly established his reader's approach on the basis of psychology and probable effects" (CW 8: 61–62). Poe not only had a direct influence on Valéry's Leonardo article but in a broader sense he confirmed Valéry's approach to literary criticism in general. Rather than examining biography or morality in a work, Valéry insisted that the literary critic must examine the relationship between what the author intended and how well these intentions are carried out in the work itself. When he spoke of "psychology and probable effects," he had in mind Poe's "The Philosophy of Composition," in which we see the author's mind calculating the effects on the reader.

Valéry's published comments on Poe are found in two essays connected with Baudelaire. In "The Place of Baudelaire," Valéry's analysis of Poe's influence on the French poet reflects his own admiration for both his predecessors. "On Poe's *Eureka*" is the only published piece that Valéry devoted entirely to his American mentor. Baudelaire translated *Eureka* but mentioned that he could not write a commentary on it. Valéry's essay was written as an introduction to the 1921 edition of Baudelaire's translation of Poe's cosmogony, thus fulfilling a task Baudelaire was unable to complete. Although Valéry found weak points in *Eureka*, he refers to the work as an abstract poem constructed on mathematical foundations. The aspect he admired most in Poe's attempt to explain the origin of the universe was the noble effort of the mind to come to grips with its own genesis. Again, he was mainly interested in observing the mental process by which the human intellect attempts to construct the concept of a universe. Valéry admired Poe's scientific knowledge and found in *Eureka* a synthesis of Poe's creative talents and his love of science.

Poe's literary essays had an influence on Valéry by confirming his own thinking about poetry and poem-making. Valéry's definition of a poem as "a machine for producing the poetic state of mind by means of words" (CW 7: 79) is very similar to Poe's description in "The Philosophy of Composition." For Valéry, inspiration played only a small role in poetic creation. "A good head is needed," he remarked, "to make full use of inspiration, to master the happy chance, and bring things to a finish" (CW 12: 46). Valéry credits Poe with having moved poetry away from didactic and moralizing elements. He saw poetry as having nothing in view but itself, stating that "such a preparation of poetry in its pure state had been accurately predicted and advocated by Edgar Poe" (CW 7: 40). In his essay "Pure Poetry," Valéry drew much of his inspiration from "The Poetic Principle," especially when he describes his concept of pure poetry as an ideal and the role of music in poetry.

Among Valéry's poems there is only one that seems to have been directly inspired by Poe. The little-known poem "Disaster" brings to mind Poe's description of Pym as he lay in the hold of the whaling ship *Grampus*. James Lawler studied the early manuscripts of the poem and pointed out the parallels between Valéry's poem and *The Narrative of Arthur Gordon Pym*.[12]

Valéry continued to read Poe throughout his life, as can be seen in brief references in his *Cahiers*. Although some direct influence on Valéry's work is evident, the French writer sought in his reading of Poe a mental approach to creative endeavors that confirmed his own conscious method of seeing beauty in science and calculated procedures in writing poetry. He believed that in science and literary creations there must be a leap of the imagination followed by tedious, calculated work. Valéry's mentor Mallarmé discovered in Poe the inspiration to pursue the elusive perfection of poetic language. But for Valéry, writing poetry was only a mental exercise that offered insights into how his mind worked. In one of his early notebooks Valéry mentioned an idea in connection with Poe that would become the driving force in his intellectual development and literary production: "Poe — or some demon — whispers: the very limit of analysis — where?" (C 1: 809). This question became an obsession for Valéry. While observing the functioning of his own mind in an attempt to unveil its secrets, he discovered what he considered to be the most poetic of all themes: the beauty of the human brain in operation. No writer before or after Valéry has given poetic expression to the drama of the intellect as a dominant theme in poetry and prose.

NOTES

1. Stéphane Mallarmé, *Oeuvres complètes*, ed. Henri Mondor and G. Jean-Aubry (Paris: Gallimard, 1961), p. 1526. My translation.

2. Célestin Pierre Cambiaire, *The Influence of Edgar Allan Poe in France* (New York: Stechert, 1927; rpt. 1970), pp. 131–132.

3. Jean Alexander, "Poe's 'For Annie' and Mallarmé's *Nuit d'Idumée*," *Modern Language Notes* 77 (1962): 534–536.

4. See Lois Davis Vines, *Valéry and Poe: A Literary Legacy* (New York: New York UP, 1992), pp. 36–38, for the French and English versions and for a discussion of the poem.

5. *The Collected Works of Paul Valéry*, 15 vols., ed. Jackson Mathews (Princeton, N.J.: Princeton UP, 1956–1975), vol. 8, p. 304; hereafter cited as CW.

6. Stéphane Mallarmé, *Correspondance 1862–1871*, ed. Henri Mondor and Jean-Pierre Richard (Paris: Gallimard, 1959), vol. 1, p. 104. My translation.

7. *Edgar Allan Poe, Essays and Reviews*, comp. G. R. Thompson (New York: Literary Classics of the United States, 1984), p. 11; hereafter cited as T.

8. For a detailed study of Poe's influence on Valéry, see Vines, *Valéry and Poe*.

9. Paul Valéry, *Cahiers*, 29 vols. (Paris: Centre National de la Recherche Scientifique, 1957–1961); hereafter cited as C.

10. See Vines, "Dupin-Teste: The Poe Connection," in *Valéry and Poe*, p. 77–103.

11. Paul Valéry, *Lettres à quelques-uns* (Paris: Gallimard, 1952), p. 98.

12. James R. Lawler, *The Poet as Analyst: Essays on Paul Valéry* (Berkeley: U California P, 1974), pp. 32–33.

# Valery Brjusov and Konstantin Bal'mont

ELOISE M. BOYLE

Valery Brjusov (1873–1924), poet, scholar, editor, and leader of the Russian Symbolist and Decadent movements, devoted his editorial career to ensuring that French Symbolism, and with it Edgar Allan Poe, found a place in Russian literary life. His best-known poetry is collected in *Urbi et orbi* and *Stephanos-venok* [Stephanos-wreath].

Konstantin Bal'mont (1867–1942) is one of the most celebrated translators in the history of Russian literature. A poet himself, Bal'mont was a committed Decadent, dressing and acting the part throughout his youth. Along with his translations, Bal'mont published several collections of his own poetry, including *Budem kak solnce* [Let us be like the sun] and *Tol'ko liubov'* [Nothing but love].

Edgar Allan Poe's influence on the lives and works of Valery Brjusov and Konstantin Bal'mont is easily discerned, from the time they met in 1894, through the poetry of their youth, and into their later philosophical and critical writings. Though Brjusov and Bal'mont were friends for several years, their paths diverged as Brjusov gained confidence as a critic and editor. It was Poe and poetry that united the two men. Together they shaped the reputation of Poe in Russia, a reputation that has as much to do with personality as it does with poetry.

Brjusov discovered Poe through his own readings of the poems and tales and through the enormous influence Poe had on French Symbolism, which captivated Brjusov. His first attempts at publishing the Symbolists were three volumes entitled simply *Russkij simvolizm* [Russian Symbolism], in which the original work of Russian poets is supplemented by translations of French Symbolist poets and Edgar Allan Poe.

Joan Grossman, a Brjusov scholar who has also done pioneering work on the history of Poe in Russia, shows that much in Brjusov's work was strongly affected by Poe, even to the point of "influence bordering on imitation."[1] Poe's influence on Brjusov is evident not only in the themes of many of his works (perversity, the notion of utopia, and a morbid preoccupation with disease, illness, suicide, and death) but also in his technique of constructing a short story. Brjusov himself points to Poe as an influence when describing the narrative techniques he used in several of his short stories. One work in which the hand of Poe is seen is the story "Respublika južnoj kresti" ["The Republic of the Southern Cross"], which contains echoes of the journalistic style used by Poe in "The Unparalleled Adventure of One Hans Pfaall" and employs a similar matter-of-fact narration of fantastic events. Although much of Brjusov's short fiction is centered, as is Poe's, around the psyche of his main character, one important distinction to be made between Brjusov's heroes and Poe's, as Grossman points out, is the overt eroticism of the Russian's characters.

Poe is evoked in many of Brjusov's poems. Grossman has assessed the influence of Poe on Brjusov's poetry as essentially one of stylistics. For example, the rhythmic and sound composition in Poe's "Ulalume" and Brjusov's "Svidanie" [Rendezvous] clearly belong to the same family (G 129). "Snega" [Snows] shares with Poe the motifs of memory and melancholy. In the poem "V otvet na odno priznanie" [In answer to a certain declaration], Brjusov invokes Poe's image in the midst of passions and dreams. "The imp of the perverse" is dropped into the 1922 poem "Iskuščenie gibeli" [The seduction of death]. In Brjusov's poem "Domovoj" (a house spirit that can wreak havoc if offended), the following lines recall Mount Yaanek in Poe's "Ulalume": "In a dark crowd — I am the dark house, / where there are volumes, shadows, dreams and portraits; / The Yaanek of Edgar — that is I; under the ice / of lava, burning with memory."[2] Other heroes from Poe's poems and tales appear throughout Brjusov's long poetic career, and there is no mistaking the influence of Poe on his musicality, his versification techniques, and his dark, perverse themes.

Poe's presence is also keenly felt in Brjusov's literary criticism. As early as 1894 he was consumed with the artistry of Poe. Known as a man of psychological extremes, of being unafraid of crossing the limits of experience, Brjusov was nevertheless a sober critic and editor. "Why search for that which is already found, or use something worse, when something better already exists?" he asks when commenting on Poe's use of meter in "The Raven."[3] By 1903 Brjusov was claiming a place for Poe alongside the giants of Russian literature, mentioning his name in the same company as Puškin, Lermontov, Fet, Gogol, and Solov'ev. The connection of Poe with the Russian Romantic Lermontov is especially cogent, given Poe's own affinity for the Romantic notions of mystery, melodrama, and the exotic.

Fervently seeking ways to make Poe relevant to the Russian literary scene,

Brjusov turned his critical skills to analyzing Poe in light of Russian literature. In an essay on Gogol, for example, Brjusov finds that many of Gogol's characters in *Revizor* [*The Inspector General*] and *Mertvye dusi* [*Dead Souls*] resemble Poe's fictional heroes in that all of them exhibit monstrous souls or psyches.[4] Brjusov goes on to note that while Poe describes the physically grotesque, Gogol's characters are spiritually deformed, a distinction that carries great importance for a Russian audience.

Brjusov discusses the question of genre in relation to Poe's work. While praising Poe's skill as a horror writer and insisting that the detective novel is the highest form of puzzle, he goes on to discuss the complexities of poetry and prose and the convergence of their devices, a tremendously important question in Russian literature from the time Puškin wrote his "novel in verse" *Evgenij Onegin* [Eugene Onegin]. Brjusov maintains that "in poetry the word is all; in prose the word is merely a means."[5] Yet if an author forces words to submit to specific restraints, he continues, then the creation is poetic, even if expressed in prose. Brjusov praises Poe for his use of "the living word" in his tales. He sees Poe's texts as "poems in prose" because they are endowed with rhythmicality. Thus a strong link is made between Poe and several of the Russian masters. Brjusov continued to analyze Poe and his craftsmanship until his death in 1924.

For Bal'mont, Poe was an all-consuming passion. All aspects of Bal'mont's life, from his behavior and dress to his own poetry and translations, reflect his desire to pay homage to the American master. It is important to note, however, which "version" of Poe influenced Bal'mont most intensely. Brjusov pointed out in a 1903 essay on Bal'mont's collection of poetry *Budem kak solnce* [Let us be like the sun] that Bal'mont was fascinated by "'the mad Edgar,' the creator of Usher." He later indicates that Bal'mont was attracted to Poe because the American "loved and knew how to express the entire impetuous character of an isolated man, of those living life at ten times its normal rate."[6]

Grossman is convinced that Bal'mont genuinely and deeply identified with Poe. Bal'mont and other members of his circle mimicked Poe in ways they imagined to be the most decadent: by creating "mad Edgar" doubles of themselves, dressing in black, indulging in narcotics, and devoting themselves to literary and editorial endeavors. Bal'mont was obsessed with the cult of Poe: it was a source of inspiration for his own poetry, although the echoes of Poe in Bal'mont's poetic works are, as Grossman puts it, "all of [an] unearthly sort" (G 161). The poem "Edgar Po" from Bal'mont's 1917 collection *Sonety solnca, meda i luny* [Sonnets of the sun, honey and moon] describes Poe as a man with a penetrating soul who senses the movement of the earth and hears night approaching while the rest of humankind merely sees such phenomena.[7] The poem is constructed out of dark and mystical images, with Poe as the "meteorite" who lights the world, thus suggesting an image used by both Baudelaire and Mallarmé.

Most illuminating in our understanding of this case of influence is Bal'mont's essay on Poe, "Genij otkrytija" [The genius of discovery], which begins with two epigraphs, one from "The Oval Portrait," the other from "The Masque of the Red Death."[8] Both quotes, significantly, touch upon madness. In Poe, Bal'mont found enormous intellectual power, incredible meticulousness in his choice of artistic effects, precise "miserliness" in his use of words, an unquenchable "greediness of soul," and a "wise sang-froid." Bal'mont saw Poe as the consummate artist, the genius of "the mad gaiety of inescapable horror."[9]

The most important aesthetic concept that Bal'mont appropriated from Poe was the ideal of beauty. For all the Decadents and Symbolists touched by Poe, this ideal was utmost in their assimilation of his poetics. Bal'mont expresses this idea in his essay on Poe: "Behind his poetry lies the thirst for a more mad beauty than that which the earth provides us, and Edgar Poe strove to quench that thirst through the creation of unearthly images. His landscapes are dreamscapes."[10] For Bal'mont, Poe is a genius precisely because he touches that other world, because he dares to gaze on that which repels and frightens others.

For all his fascination with Poe, Bal'mont did not assimilate much of the American poet into his own work, although Martin Bidney points out traces of Poe's influence in individual poems by Bal'mont.[11] But overall, Bal'mont responded to Poe as a fellow innovator in poetry, as a kindred soul, and as a poet unappreciated in his own time and banished because of his genius.

Bal'mont will always be most closely associated with the American writer through his translations of Poe's poetry. His 1894 rendition of "The Raven" was followed in 1895 by *Edgar Po, Ballady i fantazii* [Edgar Poe, ballads and fantasies], then in 1900 by his greatly expanded version of "The Bells." Between 1906 and 1912 Bal'mont published four volumes of Poe's work, including a selection of his tales, essays, and letters, thus earning him the title "the Russian Baudelaire."

Critics have been debating the quality and success of Bal'mont's translations since the day they appeared. Lack of restraint seems to have been the most prominent characteristic of Bal'mont's writings and personality, yet he was a natural translator for Poe. His own technique and craftsmanship include rich alliteration, complex sound patterns, repetition, and musicality. Many critics, Brjusov among them, both praise the skill of Bal'mont's Poe translations and criticize his transformation of Poe's language into "Bal'montian" language and Poe's verses into original Russian poems.

Martin Bidney discusses Bal'mont's most important translation of Poe's poem "The Bells," which is rendered into Russian as "Koloko'čiki i kolokola" [Little bells and bells]. Bidney notes several examples in Bal'mont's own poetry, such as in "Smertiju smert" [Let death die], and in the essay "Rubinovye kryl'lja" [ "Ruby Wings" ], where images from "The Bells" are evoked, expanded upon, and transformed. Bidney sees this poem as the centerpiece of the work of Poe's greatest Russian translator: "As Bal'mont transforms Poe's 'Bells' into a requiem plus symbolic biography of Poe as seer, he works out (in the poem and in related essays) a new scheme of imagery that includes not only the new themes of the visionary gaze, but also a dialectic of aspiration and oblivion." [12]

Thus is Edgar Allan Poe — the man, the writer, and the critic — rendered into Russian by Konstantin Bal'mont, one of the finest yet most controversial translators in Russian history, and promoted by the genius of organization, Valery Brjusov. Poe's reputation in Russia rests primarily on the efforts of these two men and continues today to be a source of scholarly and artistic inspiration.

NOTES

1. Joan Delaney Grossman, *Edgar Allan Poe in Russia: A Study in Legend and Literary Influence* (Wurzburg: Jal-Verlag, 1973) p. 11, hereafter cited as G; Joan Delaney Grossman, *Valery Brjusov and the Riddle of Russian Decadence* (Berkeley: U of California P, 1985).

2. Valery Brjusov, *Sobranie sočinenij v semi tomax* (Moscow: Xudožestvennaja literatura, 1975), vol. 3, p. 198. My translations.

3. Brjusov, *Sobranie sočinenij*, vol. 6, p. 474.

4. Brjusov writes: "Edgar Poe has a story in which two sailors arrive in an empty city devastated by the plague. They enter a house in which a monstrous society is feasting. . . . One has an enormous forehead, another an unbelievably huge mouth. . . . All of Gogol's characters recall these phantoms . . . they are all monstrous; one aspect of their souls, their psyches, is disproportionately developed. Gogol's creatures are bold and terrible caricatures . . . , a reflection of Russian reality." Ibid., p. 137.

5. Ibid., p. 379.

6. Brjusov comments: "Bal'mont . . . was particularly attracted to foreign poets [such as] Calderon and the creator of Usher, the 'mad Edgar.'" Ibid., p. 255.

7. Konstantin Bal'mont, "Edgar Po," in *K. Bal'mont: Izbrannoe* (Moscow: Xudožestvennaja literatura, 1980), p. 351.

8. Bal'mont, "Genij otkrytija," in *Izbrannoe*, pp. 589–593.

9. Ibid., p. 590.

10. Ibid., p. 592.

11. Martin Bidney, "Fire and Water, Aspiration and Oblivion: Bal'mont's Re-Envisioning of Edgar Allan Poe," *Slavic and East European Journal* 35.2 (1991): 193–213.

12. Ibid., pp. 194–195.

# Ola Hansson and
# August Strindberg

BJÖRN MEIDAL

Ola Hansson (1860–1925) was a poet, novelist, writer of short stories, and essayist. His departure from Naturalism was marked by a series of essays on French Naturalist writers published in the magazine *Framåt* [Forward] from 1885 to 1887 and in his own pamphlet *Materialismen i skönlitteraturen* [Materialism in literature] (1892). His most well known works are the collections *Sensitiva amorosa* (1887) and *Ung Ofegs visor* [The songs of Young Unafraid] (1892).

August Strindberg (1849–1912) is known primarily as a Naturalist playwright (*Fadren* [*The Father*], 1887; *Fröken Julie* [*Miss Julie*], 1888) and as a pioneer of the twentieth-century Modernist theater (*Till Damascus I–III* [*To Damascus I–III*], 1898–1904; *Ett drömspel* [*A Dream Play*], 1901; *Spoksonaten* [*The Ghost Sonata*], 1907). In addition, he is one of Sweden's most important poets and prose writers. Today he is also recognized as a painter and as an important representative of early experimental photography.

Ola Hansson was the first in Scandinavia to criticize the supremacy of tendentious Naturalism. He thereby sought an alternative to the theories of Georg Brandes and was intrigued by the "night side of the soul." His collection of prose-poem sketches, *Sensitiva amorosa*, in which images of eroticism and mystical correspondences are shaped, was very negatively received by contemporary critics. This rejection contributed to Hansson's decision to leave Sweden and move to Germany, where he attempted to work as a German writer.

In 1888 Hansson discovered Poe, who immediately became his master. Poe's importance for Hansson, as well as for Strindberg, has been described in the excellent study *Poe in Northlight* (1973) by the American scholar Carl L. Anderson.[1] Poe helped Hansson overcome the harsh criticism of *Sensitiva amorosa* and provided him with arguments for the value of "psychological-artistic" literature. Poe's influence immediately left its marks on Hansson's subsequent collection of short stories and sketches, *Parias* [Pariahs] (1888), which is characterized by the Naturalist interest in criminology and the nature of crime. The protagonists are all criminals who commit their crimes under the influence of inexplicable impulses. Several of the short stories, in particular "En modermördare" [A mother-murderer], are more or less a direct application of Poe's idea about the "perverse" impulses. It should be kept in mind, however, that Poe's influence can be difficult to measure in greater detail, since Hansson was also strongly influenced by his study of contemporary scientific literature, especially the works of psychiatrists such as Mosso, Maudsley, and Ribot and the criminologist Lombroso.[2]

Hansson's determination to remain within the boundaries of scientific Naturalism also characterizes the three essays he wrote about Poe during this period. In the longest, "Edgar Allan Poe," the American writer is heralded as the man of the future. Following Baudelaire's account, Hansson sees Poe as a prophet and martyr and an intuitive genius who also suffers from madness. After describing Poe's relationship to German Romanticism, Hansson gives a short sketch of Poe's life. Most important, though, is Hansson's thesis that Poe's capacity for reasoning was a necessary precondition for his visionary talent. Hansson ignored the growing interest in Poe among the French Symbolists. He also disregarded Poe's theories about the music of poetry and about art as a ritual. The main point of the essay is that Poe anticipated modern psychiatry, the "mental pathology."[3]

In the shorter essays, "Andliga produktionssätt [Methods of literary composition] and "Suggestion och diktning" [(Hypnotic) suggestion and poetry], Hansson — with the help of Poe — attempts to distinguish between different types of literary creation. In the first essay he distinguishes between the "inspirational" (Strindberg, the Romanticists) and the "systematic" (the Naturalists). Poe is seen as one of the few exceptions who in one person combined both categories.[4] In the latter essay, Hansson writes about "the classics" and "the others"; among "the others" Poe is presented as the clearest example of "impressionist suggestionists."[5]

Poe's influence on Hansson's further writing was slight. With the help of Strindberg, Poe was replaced after a short period by Nietzsche. But, most important, Hansson played a major role in introducing Strindberg to Poe. Hansson's short story "Parias" had caught Strindberg's attention, and Strindberg invited him to dramatize it for his experimental theater in Copenhagen.[6] During the years 1888 to 1891 the two authors had an intensive correspondence, with an exchange of many mutually fruitful impulses.[7] Since Hansson was not interested in the proposal to dramatize "Parias," Strindberg took on the project himself. Hansson had described a forger who in a state of somnambulance commits a crime. Strindberg transformed the story into a "battle of the brains," a struggle between the "strong" and the "weak," with many detective-like elements. He mentions in a letter to Hansson that he had already read Poe: "On the night between Christmas Day and Boxing Day I read Edgar Poe for the first time! And noted in my diary! I'm astounded! Is it possible that he [died] in '49, the year I was born, and could have smoldered down through hosts of spirits to me!" [8] In the same letter Strindberg continues: "And 'The Gold-Bug'? You know, I immediately associated it with your fascinating 'Pariah'! Do you remember that you mentioned Edgar Poe by name last time! And that I was captivated by your 'Pariah'? My whole body was uneasy for many days until, with nothing else in my mind, I obtained the book from you! Once I got to read 'The Gold-Bug,' I was delivered! Your 'Pariah' isn't there, but the butterfly net — everything that enticed and attracted me — is. . . . I've so much new in the way of psychology to talk over, and I think I ought to be able to take Edgar P. a lot further. I reckon I could find treasures without ciphers and the like — come here one day and I'll tell you how!" (R 301).[9]

Strindberg's reaction to Poe was thus enthusiastic and in many ways typical of his temperament. He informs Hansson that Poe not only "inspired Bourget, Maupassant (in *Pierre and Jean*), and Rosmersholm" but also his own drama *The Father*, "not to speak of all mind readers and hypnotists! The future belongs to E.P.!" (*Brev* 218). He even refers to his own drama *Gillets hemlighet* [The Secret of the guild], which he had already written in 1880. This reference conceals a complicated thought: praise of Poe becomes a vehicle to emphasize Stringberg's own position and importance. Strindberg had thereby himself participated in launching Symbolism, a long time before Ibsen, Bourget, and Maupassant. Thus the joking occult hypothesis that Poe's soul had taken its place in Strindberg in 1849 can be given a broader, literary political meaning.

Strindberg's correspondence with Hansson in 1889 literally explodes with admiration for Poe. Not only had Poe inspired the Symbolists, writes Strindberg, the American writer had influenced his own earlier writing. Strindberg goes so far as to discover Poe in the works of many writers who interested him, including Shakespeare: "*Lear* has something of Edgar Poe! Read the bit where Gloster [*sic*] believes he's fallen down the mountain, and Edmund [*sic*] is afraid this notion could have the same effect as the fall itself" (R 303).

Yet ambivalently, the influence of Poe is also denied. Strindberg characterizes his own historical novel *Tschandala* (1888) as follows: "This is Poe before Poe! Entirely!" (*Brev* 247; R 303). He adds that the novel is "not as good as it could have been, partly because I had to leave reality and present time; and partly because I hadn't yet read Edgar Poe" (*Brev* 273). [10]

Similar to the protagonists in his novels and plays, Strindberg involves him-

self in his own "battle of the brains" in his correspondence with Hansson. It
is Strindberg who is aggressive. Although Hansson introduced him to Poe,
Strindberg now wishes to prove that it is he who has the most legitimate
claims. He describes his one-act *Samum* [Simoom] as "a brilliant Edgar-Poer"
(*Brev* 272; R 310), and his novel *I havsbandet* [By the open sea] is announced
as "a modern novel in Nietzsche's and Poe's footsteps" (*Brev* 347). Strindberg
was so impressed by Legrand's brilliant solution to the cipher in "The Gold-
Bug" that he challenged Hansson to a mental duel. Strindberg writes to Hansson: "Let us try a simple mind-reading! Solve this! Fjabkvebcjmsffhp! It is
Edgar Poë! And let me know how much time you needed! Then send me a
similar one! If you are frightened, just say to me that you *have* understood"
(*Brev* 241). Hansson declined the offer, and it may be superfluous to note that
even later criminologists have not succeeded in deciphering it.[11]

During the years 1888 to 1889 Poe thus undeniably came to play a central
role as a Symbolist guide for Strindberg, even becoming his "real literary
ideal." [12] Poe also served as a perfect instrument for Strindberg's planned departure from Zola. There was an inner logic to this shift. Strindberg had once
praised Zola as "the great father of Symbolism";[13] this hero was now to be
replaced by the "Naturalist Symbolist" Poe. As so often is the case with Strindberg, such changes were more of a shift or a transformation of old ideals than
a dramatic rupture. From Poe Strindberg learned how to create atmospheres
of terror and death in which the concept of the "battle of the brains" also
could be combined with mysticism. It is likely, furthermore, that Poe inspired
Strindberg to abandon fiction during this period.[14]

But did Poe leave any lasting marks on Strindberg? The difficulty is, of
course, to distinguish the influence of Poe from that of the mainstream French
Symbolists. It was the mysticist Emanuel Swedenborg who subsequently was
to become Strindberg's new ideal. It is probable that Poe had a substantial
importance for Strindberg's dream play technique.[15] In his chamber plays,
Strindberg ironically toys with the conventions of the classical detective novel.
In *The Ghost Sonata*, the sharp-eyed old man Hummel unmasks everybody's
secrets but is then immediately subjected to the same treatment himself. In
*Pelikanen* [*The Pelican*], the process of unmasking is not accompanied by tri-
umphant smiles but rather by compassion. The crimes and secrets unveiled in
these works of Strindberg are, however, no longer punishable according to the
law. The legal or psychological author-detective of the 1880s has now become
a theologist. The analogies and correspondences may be difficult to decipher
for the uninitiated, but if interpreted in a proper sequence, they indicate a
divine order. Strindberg's interest in speculation about languages is predomi-

nant: "Languages are therefore codes, and he who finds the key can understand all the languages of the world," he writes in *The Ghost Sonata*.[16] It is
tempting to compare the mummy who is unmasked in *The Ghost Sonata* with
the protagonist in Poe's "Some Words with a Mummy." Even more striking is
the multifaceted symbol of the house that Strindberg uses so often in his works
from the turn of the twentieth century: the tower in *Dödsdansen* [*Dance of
Death*], the growing castle in *A Dream Play*, and the childhood home in
*Brända tomten* [*The Burned House*]. The parallels between *The Ghost Sonata*
and Poe's "The Fall of the House of Usher" might have become even greater
if Strindberg had been able to realize the intentions outlined in his original
draft of the play. Theater machinery at this time was not capable of letting the
walls of the house collapse in the final scene, engulfing the stage and theater
in a glowing shower of light.[17]

Poe was undoubtedly one of the important guides for Strindberg's dramatic
creations, which in turn inspired the theater of cruelty and of the absurd. In a
lasting tribute to Poe, Strindberg named two of the characters in *Dance of
Death* Edgar and Allan.

NOTES

1. Carl L. Anderson, *Poe in Northlight: The Scandinavian Response to His Life and
Work* (Durham, N.C.: Duke UP, 1973). The description of Hansson's relation to Poe in
this chapter is largely based on Anderson's work.

2. Ibid., pp. 93–95. Hansson's story was first published in a Danish translation in
the journal *Ny Jord* in November 1888.

3. Ibid., pp. 64–72. An English translation of Hansson's essay "Edgar Allan Poe"
appears in Anderson, *Poe in Northlight*, pp. 167–217. Anderson includes a history of
publication (p. 164), indicating that the essay was first printed in an abbreviated German translation (1889), in Danish (1890), in Norwegian (1893), in Polish (1905), and
finally in the complete original Swedish version in 1921.

4. Ibid., pp. 96–97.

5. Ibid., pp. 97–102.

6. Strindberg, in a letter to Hansson, 1888, *August Strindbergs Brev*, ed. Torsten
Eklund (Stockholm: Albert Bonniers förlag, 1961), vol. 7, p. 164, hereafter cited as *Brev*;
all letters cited from this point are from Strindberg to Hansson and dated 1889 unless
otherwise indicated. The part on Strindberg and Poe in this chapter is based on Björn
Meidal, "Författaren som detektiv. August Strindberg och Edgar Allan Poe. Några be-
röringspunkter," in *Läskonst Skrivkonst Diktkonst. Till Thure Stenström den 12 april
1987*, ed. Pär Hellström and Tore Wretö (Vänersborg: Askelin & Hägglund, 1987),
pp. 147–160.

7. The correspondence is published in *August Strindbergs och Ola Hanssons brev-växling 1888–1892* (Stockholm: Bonniers, 1938).

8. This letter is quoted from Michael Robinson's translation, *Strindberg's Letters. Vol. I 1862–1892* (London: Athlone P, 1992), p. 300; hereafter cited as R.

9. In "The Gold-Bug" there is, as in Hansson's story, an entomologist, but no butterfly net is mentioned in Hansson's tale. In Strindberg's play *Paria*, Mr. Y makes his appearance with a butterfly net and a vasculum.

10. In a letter to Hansson (1889), Strindberg writes: "It is peculiar that I wrote the entire novel *Tschandala* before I had read Poe!" (*Brev* 348). Hans Lindström points out in *Hjärnornas kamp. Psykologiska idéer och motiv i Strindbergs åttiotalsdiktning* (Uppsala: Natur och kultur, 1952), p. 193, that Strindberg on the one hand could have revised the novel after having read Poe's short stories; on the other hand, he had already studied many of Poe's disciples. Anderson, *Poe in Northlight*, pp. 132–133, is skeptical about the idea that Strindberg's reading of Poe influenced *Tschandala*.

11. Hansson to Strindberg (1889), *August Strindbergs och Ola Hanssons brevväxling 1888–1892*, p. 26. See also, Anderson, *Poe in Northlight*, p. 129.

12. Gunnar Brandell, *Strindbergs infernokris* (Stockholm: Bonniers, 1950), p. 205; *Strindberg in Inferno*, trans. Barry Jacobs (Cambridge: Harvard UP, 1974), p. 224.

13. August Strindberg, "Begränsningen," in *En blå bok*, in August Strindberg, *Samlade skrifter* (Stockholm: Bonniers, 1918), vol. 46, p. 167.

14. See, for example, Strindberg's letter to Hansson (1889): "Don't you see yourself that you're moving away from synthetic literature towards the psychological essay? This is a transitional form like Poe — towards the essay pure and simple!" (*Brev* 248; R 305).

15. Erik Vendelfelt compares Poe's torture scene in "The Pit and the Pendulum" with the imprisoned characters in *Dance of Death* and the death scene in this play with Poe's "Loss of Breath." See Vendelfelt, "Edgar Allan Poe och Strindbergs drömspel," *Meddelanden från Strindbergssällskapet* No. 26 (1960): 7–10.

16. August Strindberg, *Samlade Verk*, ed. Gunnar Ollén (Stockholm: Norstedts, 1991), vol. 58, p. 205. The translation is from Evert Sprinchorn, *August Strindberg, Selected Plays Volume 2. The Post-Inferno Period* (Minneapolis: U Minnesota P, 1986), p. 768.

17. For more details on Strindberg's *The Ghost Sonata* drafts, see Göran Stockenström, "The Journey from Isle of Life to the Isle of Death: The Idea of Reconciliation in *The Ghost Sonata*," *Scandinavian Studies* 50.2 (1978): 138.

# Arno Schmidt

THOMAS S. HANSEN

During his life Arno Schmidt (1914–1979) had a small readership in Germany, but he has posthumously gained a secure place in the canon of German literature. Schmidt's early novels depict postwar misery; a spirit of cultural and material deprivation pervades the works of the 1940s and 1950s. His protagonists protest the rearmament of Europe, the Cold War, and the devaluation of literary standards. By the 1970s Schmidt defended the isolation of the writer from social concerns, and his late experimental texts are dense, multicolumn works rich in linguistic and cerebral play.

Edgar Allan Poe's influence is obvious in Arno Schmidt's early writings of the 1940s to his Postmodern experiments of the 1970s.[1] There is truly no aspect of this remarkable oeuvre that is untouched by the power of his American "lodestar," as he called Poe. Poe provides Schmidt with a nexus of allusions for his literary texts, scholarly speculation for his essays, a translation project, and the material for a monster of a novel, *Zettels Traum* [Bottom's dream] (1970). Three encounters with Poe's works were particularly formative. The first was the purchase of a small secondhand German volume of Poe's tales when he was still a teenager in Görlitz (Silesia).[2] This reading experience had a power that he likened to first love. His mature understanding of Poe, however, began much later when he had access to texts of Poe in English. On a trip to London in 1938 he discovered the four-volume Edinburgh edition (1874–1875) edited by John Henry Ingram. This volume, an antiquarian curiosity, remained Schmidt's primary source for Poe's texts throughout his life. The next great encounter came in 1945 when, at age thirty-one and in a British prisoner-of-war camp, Schmidt discovered a fragmentary copy of Poe's stories in German that nonetheless contained the complete text of "The Fall of the House of Usher."

It was not the aura of terror in Poe's texts that Schmidt found compelling but rather a personal, temperamental affinity. Schmidt sensed an innate congruence. First, there was his identification with Poe, the great outsider to his own generation, the seer neglected by his contemporaries — certainly a one-sided picture. By emphasizing this aspect of Poe's biography, Schmidt nursed his own resentment toward the literary establishment, which took little notice of him. Second, Schmidt identified with Poe's sacrifice of creative intellect to hack work. Economic necessity had forced Schmidt to translate American detective fiction before his reputation as a translator allowed him to choose his own material. Schmidt saw an analogy in Poe's time-consuming work as reviewer and editor. A further autobiographical detail — apart from the near correlation of their birthdays (Poe born on January 18, Schmidt on January 19) — is a military parallel. Both did military service with the artillery, a fact that made Schmidt, as he put it, "almost predestined to sympathize" with Poe.[3] Both writers were, furthermore, autodidacts whose formal studies had been interrupted. This formative detail lies behind their tendency to develop normative theoretical systems, as in Poe's "The Poetic Principle" or Schmidt's theory of subconscious linguistic associations. In the works of both men, islands, astronomical phenomena, and mathematical logic are frequent enough to document a further thematic affinity. Each exploits the fictional convention of setting works a century in the future. Schmidt's *Gelehrtenrepublik* [*The Egghead Republic*] (1957) is set in 2008 and *Die Schule der Atheisten* [*The School of Atheists*] (1972) in 2014, a technique suggested by Poe's "Mellonta Tauta" (set in 2848) and by the letter "quoted" in *Eureka* from the same year.[4]

The posthumous publication of Schmidt's *Dichtergespräche im Elysium* [*Poets' Conversations in Elysium*] (written in 1940) made Poe's early influence clearly discernible. In this collection of twelve dialogues with the dead, figures of world literature, including Schopenhauer, Homer, Shakespeare, Hölderlin, and Coleridge, exchange views on literary subjects in the afterlife. Poe is the first and last to speak, thereby framing the entire fiction. Homer says how much he would have liked to own a book in Poe's handwriting, while the German philosophers have their joke about the "The Philosophy of Furniture." The picture of Poe is somewhat hackneyed, as evidenced by his supposed preference for dreary, rainy evenings over morning sunshine. In an outright devaluation of two tales, Poe admits he has been elected to Elysium despite aesthetic transgressions like "The Facts in the Case of M. Valdemar" and "The Black Cat."[5] Schmidt's text goes beyond casual clichés when the book's final pages relate Poe's last feverish hours in a style imitating his own narrative voice:

> The enchantment of stone had entered me. As a stone possesses the deepest, most fundamental level of spirit — gravity — which it both follows and

exerts, thus I sensed currents in the gravitational field of my body. I measured time in the orbits of the most distant stars which tugged at me, yet which I pulled from their paths. Thus I lay active in space and gave my body over to the elements.[6]

This literary pastiche imitates a particular type of Poe narrative: a vortex of movement engulfing a helpless narrator (as in "MS. Found in a Bottle" and "A Descent into the Maelström"), while content and structure follow closely "The Colloquy of Monos and Una."

This early form of outright imitation of Poe is not the model for Schmidt's later use of the American author. As Schmidt outgrew his early devotion, his texts from the 1950s frequently refer to Poe haphazardly. Three passages are typical of the allusions in Schmidt's stories and novels before 1970. The first, "I uttered the venerable name . . . Poe Trismegistos (Eureka)" from *Leviathan* (1949), has no symbolic resonance with its context but simply engages the reader on a plane external to the fiction. Two other references to Poe, however, demonstrate how Schmidt focuses his allusions: "Rain was already touching the barracks of our heads, haunted palaces —";[7] similarly, "*In the snowy reaches of her breasts*" ("A Tale of the Ragged Mountains").[8] These two passages share a common denominator: Poe references provide anatomical correlatives in which the body is no longer nature's landscape but essentially literary topography created by intertextuality. Texts beget texts as Poe exerts authority over fiction, desexualizing the body and establishing an authority of allusion. In the 1960s Schmidt developed a psycholinguistic theory of reading that drew heavily on the theories of Freud and the wordplay of James Joyce. He applied this technique to the German writer of adolescent literature Karl May and revealed that, at the word level, May's texts held encrypted messages of homosexuality and voyeurism.[9] For the rest of his life Schmidt refined and applied this method (which he called the "etym theory") to works of literature, particularly to Poe.

In 1963 Schmidt began work both on his magnum opus, *Zettels Traum*, as well as on the Poe translations, which are the background and accompaniment to the novel, where they are thematized in the plot.[10] Schmidt's German versions of Poe's tales excited critical responses from admiration to opprobrium because of a startling technique that may be termed "archaizing neologism." This paradoxical method uses sentence rhythms and poetical devices to approximate Poe's style in the German of his generation. At its worst, the result is an oddly antiquated Americanized German; at its best, it is a blend of powerful, rhythmical syntax and an innovative, poeticized lexicon.[11]

Schmidt's grandiose monument to Poe, the novel *Zettels Traum*, is certainly the most intricate and eccentric document of Poe reception in the twentieth century.[12] A 1,334-page, seventeen-pound tome in which three columns jostle for space down each crowded typescript page, *Zettels Traum* may be penetrated only by the intrepid. But behind its complexities lies a simple plot. During the course of one day the reclusive Poe expert Dän (Schmidt's persona) receives guests, Paul and Wilma Jacobi (husband and wife) and their seductive teenage daughter, Franziska, who engages in a salacious flirtation with Dän. The center column of the text depicts the group browsing among books, strolling through the summer countryside, swimming, and engaging in learned discourse about Edgar Allan Poe as Dän expounds on scholarly problems to his guests. The left column prints passages from Poe's works; the right column, a broad spectrum of references to world literature.

*Zettels Traum* produces, on one level, a playfully absurd psychobiography of Poe that is more reductionist than any orthodox Freudian method. The picture that emerges is bound to win few converts among Poe scholars, namely the image of Poe as an impotent, fetishistic voyeur whose perversity can be discerned from his texts. Dän/Schmidt deduces this view at the word level using etyms. The subconscious meanings of etyms inhere at the core of words and reveal, by acoustical association, the taboo spheres of sexuality and excrement. One must deconstruct a word into discrete signifiers to discern this hidden code. Two fairly innocent examples, "Eddy-Poe's Complex" and "POE de Chambre," manifest psychological and excretory dimensions "sublimated" in Poe's texts (according to Dän). At the simplest level etyms represent punning. But this wordplay can cross language boundaries to trigger associations in all Indo-European languages, thus re-creating a sort of Esperanto of subconscious urges. Using this reading method, Dän predictably finds repressed sexual and excretory fantasies virtually everywhere.[13]

As a psychological treatise on Poe, *Zettels Traum* remains as disturbing as it is fascinating. The lasting achievement of the work lies neither in Schmidt's theory of etyms nor in the hypothesis of Poe's damaged psyche but rather in its abundance of critical thought on sources and analogues for Poe's works. Schmidt's broad learning places Poe in the context of world literature as no other treatise does and rewards the diligent reader with insights and opinions that go far beyond his idiosyncratic readings. Despite the formidable erudition of *Zettels Traum*, its remarkable passages of ribald humor and memorable erotica remind the reader that Schmidt's ultimate achievement is one of linguistic invention rather than scholarship.

Idiosyncrasies aside, Schmidt has had an impact on Poe studies. His hypothesis about a German source for "The Fall of the House of Usher" has led (with additional refinement) to a clarification of the Germanic material behind that tale,[14] and one German work on Poe, Heinrich Kerlen's *Edgar Allan Poe; Elixiere der Moderne [Edgar Allan Poe: Elixir of modernism]* (1988), recognizes in Schmidt an intelligent translator and interpreter whose insights into Poe derive from the mutual comprehension of a doppelgänger.[15]

NOTES

1. For a more complete treatment of this topic, see Thomas S. Hansen, "Arno Schmidt's Reception of Edgar Allan Poe: Or, the Domain of Arn(o)heim," *Review of Contemporary Fiction* 8.1 (Spring 1988): 166–181 (special issue on Arno Schmidt, ed. F. Peter Ott).

2. Arno Schmidt, *Vorläufiges zu Zettels Traum* (Frankfurt: Fischer, 1977), p. 12. This was probably the collection of "Seltsame Geschichten" in the 1925 translation by Wilhelm Cremer.

3. Arno Schmidt, *Der Triton mit dem Sonnenschirm: Grossbritannische Gemütsergetzungen* (Karlsruhe: Stahlberg, 1969), p. 426.

4. For further discussion of Schmidt as autodidact, see Wolfram Schütte, "Die unbekannte Grösse. Arno Schmidt — unsere Gegenwart, seine Nachwelt," *Merkur* 35.397 (June 1981): 558–573.

5. Arno Schmidt, *Dichtergespräche in Elysium* (Zurich: Haffmanns, 1984), p. 11.

6. Ibid., p. 138.

7. "Schon betastete Regen die Baracken unserer Köpfe, haunted palaces — ." In Arno Schmidt, "Seelandschaft mit Pocahontas" (1955), in *Bargfelder Ausgabe* 1/1.2, p. 434.

8. Arno Schmidt, *The Egghead Republic*, ed. Ernst Krawehl and Marion Boyars, trans. M. Horovitz (London: M. Boyars, 1982).

9. See Arno Schmidt, *Sitara und der Weg dorthin; Eine Studie über Wesen, Werk und Wirkung Karl Mays* (Frankfurt: Fischer Taschenbuch, 1963).

10. The project was a collaboration with the gifted novelist and translator Hans Wollschläger. Volume 1 of the translations was published in 1966; volume 2 in 1967; and volume 3 in 1973.

11. See L. Černy, "Die abbildende Übersetzung. Klang und Rhythmus in Arno Schmidt's übersetzung von Poes 'Ligeia'," *Lebende Sprachen* 36.4 (1991): 145–151.

12. The title puns on *Zettel*, the German name for Bottom the Weaver in *A Midsummer Night's Dream*, and the word for index card. Schmidt's method of composition was to amass trays of thousands of such cards and then assemble them into prose.

13. For a discussion of this technique applied to *The Narrative of Arthur Gordon Pym* as presented in *Zettels Traum*, see Hansen, "Arno Schmidt's Reception of Edgar Allan Poe," pp. 175–177.

14. See Thomas S. Hansen, "The 'German' Source for 'The Fall of the House of Usher,'" *Southern Humanities Review* 26.3 (Spring 1992): 101–112.

15. See Thomas Krömmelbein, "Verhinderte Erwachsene; Poe und Schmidt in einer neuen (Poe-)Biographie," *Der Haide-Anzeiger; Mitteilungen zu Arno Schmidt* 24 (July 1988): 12–14.

# Bolesław Leśmian

FRANK KUJAWINSKI

Born in Warsaw, Bolesław Leśmian (1877/78 –1937) completed his secondary and university studies in Kiev, then traveled extensively in western Europe, sojourning in Paris for three years before returning to Poland. He became cofounder and director of the Warsaw Experimental Theater in 1911 and the following year published his first collection of poetry, *Sad rozstajny* [Orchard at crossroads]. Best known as a poet, he was elected to the Polish Academy of Literature in 1933.

Bolesław Leśmian's early reading of Poe is mentioned by one of his schoolmates, Henryk Hertz-Barwiński, who noted Leśmian's "interest in Russian literary criticism, philology, psychology, and folklore, and . . . his admiration for Poe and Baudelaire."[1] Some years later, Leśmian was asked by the Muzy publishers to translate some of Poe's tales, a request he was to fulfill by way of Baudelaire's French edition. In a 1934 interview Leśmian again mentioned the effect of the two writers: "As regards the French poets, the only one which truly influenced me was perhaps Baudelaire. Later I was under the influence of Edgar Allan Poe, but these influences are somehow not evident."[2] The influence of Poe is not directly evident inasmuch as the psyche of each was equally tuned to the same undercurrents of the subconscious. Leśmian, coming later, did not copy Poe, but neither could he deny the kinship of sensibility and the particular insights of methodology garnered from his reading and translation of Poe's works.

For his own introduction to the Polish edition of Poe's works, Leśmian borrowed much, if not most, of Baudelaire's rendition of Poe's life and works. The adulatory tone, the quasi-biographical method, and even the nervous, high-strung style that Baudelaire had used so often in his Poe essays were adopted by Leśmian for the major portion of his introduction. After this extensive borrowing, Leśmian's discovery of his own Poe becomes dramatically clear in the last four paragraphs of his essay, where an abrupt change in both style and content alerts the reader to the fact that Leśmian is presenting a new and quite different understanding of Poe's work. The first sentence is both a departure from Baudelaire and a summary foreshadowing Leśmian's own artistic development: "These are Poe's works — frenzied verisimilitudes of barely perceptible visions in which the feverish parallelism of sleep and wakenings recasts the attributes of reality into the rainbow of dreams."[3] In his tales and narrative poems, Leśmian parallels many of the themes that haunted Poe. We find descent, journey, death, and nothingness. The destruction that takes place in Leśmian's tales and narrative poems are no less vicious, no less terrifying than those Poe described. Leśmian peels away the psychic layers of many of his characters, stripping them of their metaphysical moorings as they wander far beyond the real world into an unknown realm of newness and dreams. At times, even the comfort of death is denied because for Leśmian there was a further journey to be made beyond the destruction of death.

Leśmian stopped writing prose works around 1913 to concentrate on poetry. Many of his tales were published during his lifetime and in a collection that appeared posthumously in 1956. All of these tales are taken from or constructed on the traditions of folk narratives/folk myths and incorporate the strange, mysterious, and magical. Elements similar to those fundamental to Poe are present, especially the centrality of nonlogical modes of cognition. Conscious reality is progressively overwhelmed by the upheaval of subconscious or nightmarish happenings.

In Leśmian's *Legendy tęsknoty* [Legends of longing] (1904), the first legend, "Baśń o rycerzu panskim" [The tale of the lord's knight] contains the following narrative voice: "I don't know whether this story was a real, remembered happening, or the creation of a feverish delirium, or indeed a dream which ought to have materialized had not a strong wind snatched it away."[4] A second tale, "Błędny ognik" [Errant flame], includes this introductory comment: "The nameless author sketched here, undoubtedly in hours of reverie, dreams gone astray which held back, timidly and unwillingly, at the threshold of materialization. And this book was for him the mirror of these dreams, a mirror which reflects objects distant or nonexistent."[5] Thus it was that Leśmian indeed began with a sensibility akin to Poe's, of the unknown and unexplored in the subconscious and in dreams, even though later he would develop it in directions properly unique to himself.

The early period of his prose tales was a significant apprenticeship for Leśmian. The narrative nature of the folk tales provided him with the means to break the bonds of contemporary Symbolist practice, to assert the vitality of his own vision. He emphasized the importance of narration in his poetry in a letter to Przemycki in 1904: "Each image of mine is created and is called into being by narration, . . . the kind of writing by means of which the author relates that which he might or might not be able otherwise to bring out of his inner self into the light."[6] Leśmian's appreciation of the narrative method and going beyond the bounds of reality and logic were reinforced by his reading of Poe. In 1899 Leśmian spoke of a new kind of story, "an epico-lyric, poetical novel, not a Symbolist short story, but a psychological one with realistic action."[7] Both Poe and Leśmian wrote tales that draw upon the mental powers ignored by the Rationalists. For Poe, these are his tales of "Arabesques" and "Grotesques"; for Leśmian, they are the *Klechdy sezamowe* [Sesame tales], the *Klechdy polskie* [Polish tales], and the corpus of poems that followed. Both writers probe the middle ground between reality and sleep, between dream and wakening. Leśmian's statements in his introduction to Poe's translated works reveal a dimension of understanding of Poe that parallels his own artistic goals. Speaking of Poe's works he wrote: "Dream borders on reality, reality on dream. Moreover, the difference between them joyfully disappears in the moment when an enigmatic and indivisible wholeness absorbs them. The object and its reflection seem identical truths on earth and similar privileges in heaven. . . . To dream — and to see one's dream, and to bring it under the ruthless control of a ruthless artistry, and to secure for it a miraculous right of existence in surrounding space — behold this is the only deed to which a poet should bestir himself."[8] For Leśmian, the cognitive vistas opened up to the imagination by the newly found respect for dreams were endless.

In Poe Leśmian recognized an aesthetic appreciation for a concept that is represented by the Polish word *baśń*, meaning the ideas of dream, of myth and mythmaking (legend, story, and ritual), and of knowing. There is no word in English that conveys the same sense of mystery, age, and secret knowledge. The more technical term "mythopoeic" suggests a similar range of cognitive involvement but without encompassing the quasi-mythical accretions of the Polish word, which Leśmian attempts to define: "this *baśń* moreover plays an important role in our thought: the role of rainbow-bridge, which joins us to the non-logical domain of existence, with the precipitous bluffs of its mystery, whose face is not similar to the human face. This *baśń* is always the product — of intuition, instinct, concerning which logic says that it is blind since it has eyes of a color other than its own. It sees that which logically speaking ought not to be visible."[9] Leśmian understood the creative domain that Poe inhabited, a domain that Poe alluded to — one way or another — in the passage of his main characters from reality to vision by dream, drug, or nervous temperament.

A close reading of Poe shows that whatever their insights or discoveries, his travelers never return whole from their experiences. Some disappear, others die, and still others return transformed. Here is where Leśmian's tales and poems are different from Poe's; Leśmian most always writes of a unified experience, of a sailor who is not lost, of tragedies that in the overall view of things can be overcome, of the man who finds himself whole in the universe. It was Leśmian's faith in the primordial life force, in the rhythm of life, that allowed him to complete what Poe and Baudelaire could not.

Poe wrote in "The Philosophy of Composition" that "there is little possibility of variety in mere *rhythm*," recommending instead devoting one's powers of composition to varieties of meter and stanza which, he says, "are absolutely infinite." [10] Leśmian's approach was fundamentally different; he eschews metric innovation while expanding the discussion of rhythm from the area of prosody to that of metaphysics. He writes: "Rhythm, intoxicating thought with its wine brimming over onto our lips, teaches us trust and faith in the powers existing beyond us, which we are not capable of enclosing in the dense and tight curls of logic, but in which we can always celebrate and sing our hearts out." [11] His conception of rhythm provided him with the theoretical foundation necessary for his poetic insights. Rhythm became a unifying principle in his art and in his thought. "The creative endeavor," he wrote, "is much the same as — and even primarily — a rhythmic one." [12]

While Poe emphasized rhythm as a poetic device, Leśmian found in it the aspect of prosody and metaphysics that would make his works the expression of a comprehensive unity in human experience. Poe struggled an entire life for a unifying principle to his dream tales; Leśmian found that principle much earlier and made it an integral, even essential, part of his narrative/lyrical poetry. Leśmian's heroes go beyond descents into maelstrom and destruction toward, at the very least, hope and promise. Descent is only one part of the terrible and awesome journey into the unknown; for Leśmian, there is an ascent beyond, a completion — if often only projected — into a new heretofore unrealized wholeness. One of many possible examples of this basic difference is Leśmian's poem "Dwaj Macieje" [Two Matthews], which repeats the theme of double identity that has such fertile history in Western literature. It recalls Poe's tale "William Wilson," which is specifically mentioned in Leśmian's introduction. In Leśmian's poem we find the same pattern of identity: "One could not tell the one Matthew from the other." After the two Matthews work together to attain the sprig of immortality, and after they abandon it to *płaczybóg* [weeping god], the two must await their simultaneous deaths. But whereas in Poe the death of the one is the death of the other, Leśmian alters the trope so as to transcend death with the hint, almost promise, of something beyond, as we see in the concluding lines of the poem:

And already death drew near, to hamper them with sleep,
Not knowing which of them the first one to chill.
The world closed down in their eyes . . . , evil shivers ensued
And then the world was not, but they continued on . . .
One said: "Night is coming!" — The other: "Dawn's in the sky."
So did both the Matthews simultaneously die.

Poe's quest for unity was expressed in one of his last works, *Eureka*, subtitled *An Essay on the Material and Spiritual Universe*, which Leśmian was familiar with and which he mentions in his introduction to the Poe translations. While Poe could not find, for most of his life, the promise of an upward passage, Leśmian possessed early in his life a sense of wholeness that allowed him to go beyond where Poe left off.

NOTES

1. Quoted in Rochelle Heller Stone, *Bolesław Leśmian: The Poet and His Poetry* (Berkeley: U of California P, 1976), p. 6.

2. Bolesław Leśmian, *Szkice literackie*, ed. Jacek Trznadel (Warsaw: Państwowy Instytut Wydawniczy, 1959), p. 498.

3. Leśmian, "Edgar Allan Poe," in *Szkice literackie*, p. 465.

4. Bolesław Leśmian, "Legendy tęsknoty," in *Utwory rozproszone/Listy*, ed. Jacek Trznadel (Warsaw: Państwowy Instytut Wydawniczy, 1962), p. 119.

5. Ibid., p. 130.

6. Ibid., p. 277. English quotation from Stone, *Bolesław Leśmian*, p. 48.

7. Ibid., p. 234. English quotation from Stone, *Bolesław Leśmian*, p. 40.

8. Leśmian, "Edgar Allan Poe," pp. 465–466.

9. Leśmian, "Z rozmyślań o Bergsonie," in *Szkice literackie*, p. 31.

10. *Edgar Allan Poe, Essays and Reviews*, comp. G. R. Thompson (New York: Literary Classics of the United States, 1984), pp. 20–21.

11. Leśmian, "Rytm jako światopogląd," in *Szkice literackie*, p. 67.

12. Leśmian, "Z rozmyślań o poezji," in *Szkice literackie*, p. 84.

# Antun Gustav Matoš

SONJA BAŠIĆ

Storyteller, poet, essayist, critic, and journalist, Antun Gustav Matoš (1873–1914) grew up in Zagreb but spent most of his life as a wanderer, exiled from Croatia because he had deserted the Austro-Hungarian army. His art is a curious blend of vulgarity and refinement, of bluff and learning, of hack work and true masterpieces. His *Sabrana djela* [Collected works] in twenty volumes was published in 1973.

Extremely poor but fascinated by art and beauty, Antun Gustav Matoš was a hypersensitive, difficult person whose letters and personal writings are filled with complaints about poverty and appeals to friends and publishers for loans. Like Poe, his short life of just over forty years was dedicated to a pure aesthetic ideal that provided little in the way of material comfort. He felt a strong affinity with Poe throughout his adult life and adopted the title of Poe's tale "Hop-Frog" as one of his pseudonyms.

In an early, rambling feuilleton mourning the separation from his sweetheart, appropriately entitled *Impromptu* (1899), Matoš wrote: "While writing this . . . I remember the majestic, awe-inspiring poem 'The Raven' for which my only Decadent friend, the non-decadent Poe received a large fee — 10 dollars — . . . . How many times have I unwillingly whispered its desperate, ominous refrain Nevermore. . . . Is it necessary to starve, to poison oneself with wine and laudanum, to be an eternal orphan, to die in the street of delirium like a rabid dog in order to write 'The Fall of the House of Usher,' 'Ligeia' and Nevermore?" (CW 13: 32).[1] The refrain from "The Raven" returned to his mind several years later when Matoš lamented the death of a fellow poet: "And Lacko Vidrić died before I could see him again. And I will see him no more. Never. Never-more!" In the same essay he describes the asylum in which Vidrić died as "a dark chapter from the darkest Dostoevsky; green, dead eyes staring from a corner of Poe's alcoholic imagination, eyes silent and opaque on chaotic crossings where the seven paths of reason meet, where an enigmatic wind is blowing from a strange country beyond" (CW 4: 197).

Matoš gleaned details of Poe's biography and became acquainted with Poe's tales through his reading in German and French. Comments in his fifteen "Notebooks," amounting to about 1,500 typewritten pages, reveal that he had read German translations of Poe as early as 1898 and transcribed long passages from books on Poe in French by Emile Lauvrière and A. Barine, to which he referred on many occasions. Recognizable traces of Baudelaire's views on Poe begin to appear in Matoš's work in 1905, after he had duly copied excerpts from the French poet's prefaces to *Histoires extraordinaires*.

Fascinated by Poe's personal life, Matoš often cited even the most trivial details. In essay after essay he referred to "poor Israfel," the artist who died of privation, suffered abuse and neglect, and engaged in a "horrible struggle . . . between genius and the golden calf" (CW 4: 250, 277, 282). He obviously identified with Poe as a penniless genius unrecognized and neglected by his contemporaries, the same image Baudelaire created in his descriptions. The fact that the French had adopted Poe and that he was praised by a genius such as Baudelaire was for Matoš another argument supporting his thesis that "little cultures and semi-cultures like those of Croatia, Serbia, and Bulgaria should, in the interest of their own survival, arm themselves with cultural goods from abroad" (CW 4: 269).

Matoš frequently referred to characters, themes, and motifs from Poe's tales and poems. Of Baudelaire's female characters he observed that they are either disreputable or pure like Poe's Ligeia (CW 4: 65–66). He also chose the cat as Baudelaire's "symbolic animal," "a proud black cat . . . as terrible as Poe's" (CW 4: 68). Matoš often mentioned Poe in his reviews of Croatian and Serbian writers and artists. He notes that like Poe, the poet Sima Pandurović gives a specific erotic coloring to the theme of love after death (CW 4: 189); the conservatism of Stevan Sremac reminds him of Poe's contempt for democracy (CW 4: 146); and Djuro Deželić's "erudition" reminds him of Poe's (CW 4: 245). Writing about the painter Klement Crnčić, he finds that the sea in his paintings is "plastic in the first place. Sculptured. Without figures. Without man, as if Poe's recipe for landscape were known to him" (CW 4: 121). Finally, the characters in his own stories are also compared to figures from Poe's poetry and prose, for example, the man of the crowd, Annabel Lee, and others.

Poe states in "The Philosophy of Composition" that the most poetic of all topics is the death of a beautiful woman. Matoš took this theme to heart in his poem "Utjeha kose" [The consoling hair], a sonnet mourning the death of a beautiful young woman (CW 5: 56). Two lines from Matoš's poem, "Everything, everything was dead: your eyes, your breath, your hands, / Only your hair was still alive," are reminiscent of Poe's "Lenore": "The life upon the yellow hair but not within her eyes — / The life still there upon her hair, the death upon her eyes." This image must have deeply impressed Matoš because he transcribed in his notebook the same two lines from the German version of "Lenore."

Poe's influence is evident in several of Matoš's stories and essays. The tale "Zeleni demon" [Green demon] deals with the destructive force of alcohol and describes graveyards and people buried alive. In the same story, the detachment, logic, and clarity of the first-person narration are reminiscent of "The Black Cat." The cat as an instrument of evil also appears in the story "Bijeda" [Misery], which begins in a realistic mode with the description of a young mother whose child is dying from hunger and cold, then changes abruptly into extreme, fantastic Poesque horror: "The cat jumped on the child, fiercely scratching, tearing with its claws at the blue, bloodied eyes. Its hair rose stiffly while its cold, brilliant pupils pierced my bosom" (CW 2: 57).

But the tale that seems to have made the strongest impression on Matoš's imagination was "The Fall of the House of Usher." Although the motif of the haunted house appears several times throughout his work, it is particularly striking in his essay "Oko Lobora" [Around Lobor] (1908), in which the description of Lobor, an old Croatian mansion, seems to come directly from Poe: "In the twilight this old house seems strange and unfriendly like that of Eleonora. . . . In such an old mansion, in one of the remotest and oldest Anglo-Saxon parks, in sumptuous halls alive with unhappiness and old age lived the lover of the girl that died, Poe's mysterious aristocratic recluse Usher, waiting for the wind of madness, of fate, of rare and inexplicable catastrophe to sweep him away like a hurricane" (CW 4: 92). Matoš continues his description with acoustic effects that evoke "The Raven": "An impenetrable, tragic darkness descends upon the last of the Ushers and his haunted house, darkness is also falling, falling upon these old, aristocratic roofs from where two eyes . . . keep looking and looking at me — while something resounds in the draw-well, while ominous crows are croaking from the black wooden tower, while darkness and sorrow are descending from the clouds, the black, dull, wandering clouds" (CW 4: 92). The final part of this sentence appears to come directly from Baudelaire's translation of Poe's "The Fall of the House of Usher": "Les nuages pesaient lourds et bas dans le ciel" [the clouds weighed heavy and low in the sky]. Once inside the mansion, the narrator discovers "the demented, white and silken virgin dying in contemplation of the cold, green moonlight," whose cries are "imprisoned within the thickest walls" of the house, a clear echo of Madeline Usher (CW 4: 92).

"Oko Lobora" is perhaps the best example of the degree to which Matoš knew and used Poe, but the essay also shows the limits of Poe's influence. After the ghoulish "homage to Usher," Matoš goes on to describe Lobor with more than a reporter's objectivity, ending up with his opinions on the Croatian nobility, the European aristocracy, and the "morals of our time." In his own tales Poe remains consistently within the conventions of his phantasmagoric world, while Matoš nearly always returns from his excursion into the fantastic to deal with the living, pressing, actual matters of his day. This ambiguity of subject and tone is the reflection of a duality inherent in Matoš, who in his writings rarely succeeded in blending art and actuality, Aestheticism and fanatical patriotism into a harmonious whole. Still, art was his greatest, most sacred ideal, and Poe and Baudelaire were its high priests. In their lives and work he found not only kindred spirits and an artistic achievement that satisfied his craving for beauty but also a religion that enriched his own short life.

NOTE

1. All references to Matoš's work are from *A. G. Matoš. Sabrana djela*, 20 vols. (Zagreb: Jugoslavenska akademija znanosti i umjetnosti, Liber & Mladost, 1973); hereafter cited as CW. All translations of quotations are mine.

# Franz Kafka

GERHARD HOFFMANN

Born into a German-speaking Jewish family in Prague, then part of the Austrian Empire, Franz Kafka (1883–1924) received a law degree, which allowed him to earn a living as a bureaucrat while developing his avocation as a writer. He is considered one of the main representatives of European literary Modernism. His major works include the novels *Amerika* [*America*] (1912–1914; published in 1925) and *Der Prozess* [*The Trial*] (1914–1915; published in 1925). Among his major short stories are "Die Verwandlung" ["The Metamorphosis"] (1916), "Ein Landarzt" ["A Country Doctor"] (1919), and "In der Strafkolonie" ["In the Penal Colony"] (1919).

An overview of the similarities and affinities between Edgar Allan Poe and Franz Kafka must take into consideration the fact that Poe would not be seen as a major innovator if certain developments in the twentieth century had not made him, in hindsight, one of the precursors of Modernism. Max Bense, for example, remarks that Poe's "Maelzel's Chess Player" can be read as a "fundamental ontological commentary on Kafka's characters."[1] And Jorge Luis Borges states in his essay "Kafka and His Precursors" that "in the critics' vocabulary, the word 'precursor' is indispensable, but it should be cleansed of all connotation of polemics or rivalry. The fact is that every writer creates his own precursors. His work modifies our conception of the past, as it will modify the future."[2]

As to Kafka's view of Poe, Gustav Janouch recalls that he showed Kafka a selection of Poe's short stories and that Kafka acknowledged only a superficial acquaintance with Poe's works, stating: "Poe was sick. He was a poor man, defenseless against the world. This was why he sought refuge in drunkenness. Fantasy was for him only a crutch. He wrote unearthly stories in order to come down to earth. . . . I know the path he took in flight, his phantom. It is always the same."[3] Although there are doubts as to Janouch's reliability, Kafka's alleged remarks about his knowledge of Poe are corroborated by the fact that there is some reason to assume that one of the models for the episodic structure of Kafka's stories and novels was the beginning of Poe's *The Narrative of Arthur Gordon Pym*.[4] On the other hand, Max Brod always most vigorously denied any influence Poe might have had on Kafka. Still, he, too, sees a certain similarity in the motifs that both authors used, if not in the way they are depicted.[5]

The relationship between Kafka and Poe is one of influence and affinity in both a new kind of consciousness and fictional design. There is an indirect influence via Mirabeau and especially Dostoevsky in the depiction of perversity. Kafka can be seen as the end point in a development that began with Poe and progressed to the blurring of all borderlines. While for E.T.A. Hoffmann there was still enmity between reality and the imagination, Poe made reality the servant of the imagination, and the writers of fantastic fiction at the beginning of the twentieth century followed suit, as had the French Symbolists. For Poe the imagination was the aesthetic ability to construct, while for Baudelaire it was the capacity of the human mind to play creative intellectual games; for Alfred Kubin's spiritualism the "imagination" was "divine" and "the phantasies [were] simply realities."[6]

In Kafka we see the trend to finally radicalize this absoluteness of the imagination and, more important, to put it to practice in his fiction by fully abolishing the difference between everyday orderliness and the fantastically unusual and marvelous. Kafka writes: "All is imaginary — family, office, friends, the street, all imaginary, far away or close at hand."[7] But for Kafka this world is no longer a joy, as it was for Hoffmann, Poe, and the French Symbolists, but a burden he has to carry. He remarks that "the truth that lies closest, however, is only this, that you are beating your head against the wall of a windowless and doorless cell."[8] The imagination works, as with Poe, in the configuration of dreams, with their blurring of distinctions. All Kafka can indeed aim for is, in the famous words of his diary, to "portray my dreamlike inner life," to depict the immense world he has in his head.[9] But it is no longer a game. Just like Poe, Kafka has a price to pay, for he now has to sustain the split between himself and the world. As Kafka puts it: "The world . . . and my 'self' tear my body apart in unsolvable conflict."[10] The result is in both cases a neurotic relationship to the world and the self, and this split is promoted by writing, which itself leads to a systematic destruction of the self.

The structure of Kafka's works also has parallels in Poe. Poe's concept of "unity of effect" with its corollary, the "preestablished design," allows for various kinds of unity. Poe found suggestions for different models of effect in Schlegel's *Lectures*. Using the example of Homer's *Iliad*, Schlegel demonstrated that unity of action and effect can be attained not only by a cause-and-effect-oriented design or a logical sequence of time but also by an accumulation of impressions, each precise and separate, isolated and incongruous, but all pointing in the same direction.[11] Poe used this accumulative structure most successfully in "The Fall of the House of Usher." For Kafka's sense of isolation, futility, guilt, and uncertainty, such an accumulative but thematically integrated structure was exactly the form that was needed. The result was a kind of episodic, loose sequence of situation and incidents. Laura Hofrichter points out that "with the exception of 'In the Penal Colony', the action and plot of Kafka's works consist of two elements, namely a situation and the protagonist. More often than not all other persons are of a symbolical nature."[12]

Poe connected the elements of the narrative — space, time, character, and action — in the uncanny mood of the situation. He gave up the dominance of a single element like character or action in favor of the cooperation of all factors for the effect of totality. Kafka, however, abandoned all traces of the uncanny, which is based on the duality of the normal and the abnormal, and substituted for it a matter-of-fact equating of object and subject, animal and human being ("The Metamorphosis"), the living and the dead ("Jäger Gracchus" ["Hunter Gracchus"]), a method that has successfully leveled any dominance relationship among the fictional elements as did Poe's method of the uncanny. The fictional characters of both authors lose their individuality as a result of their being fully integrated into the fictional situation. They are passive and isolated. In the works of Poe and Kafka the protagonists scarcely ever act, and the basic situation never changes. The most a character will do is react, repeatedly and similarly, in an accumulative sequence of episodes.

The difference between the two authors is that though they both work with a kind of "mathematical," calculating imagination, they employ reverse methods. Poe introduces into a natural situation unnatural incidents, while Kafka uses an unnatural situation and works it out rationally or naturally. The result is that in Poe's case the natural and the rational remain the starting point and the norm of fiction, while in Kafka's method the unnatural is the norm and the only frame of reference, as can be seen at the beginning of "The Metamorphosis."

The theme of perversity is prominent among the German Romantics and with Poe. On the strength of his remarks on the psychic impulse of perverseness in "The Imp of the Perverse" and its depiction in stories like "The Tell-Tale Heart" or "The Black Cat," Poe indeed becomes one of the main reference points in the literary tradition of idées fixes and the general phenomenon of perversity. As Mario Praz has emphasized, Poe exercised an important influence on Dostoevsky, and through Dostoevsky, whom Kafka considered a "blood relation," also on Kafka.[13] Poe described the spirit of perverseness as "this unfathomable longing of the soul *to vex itself* — to offer violence against its own nature."[14] Dostoevsky, who admired Poe especially for his psychological insight and his "realistic" grasp, uses the motif of perverseness as Poe does (without, however, calling it perverseness). It is for him the sudden unexplainable banishment from the world of reason, predictability, and controllability into one of uncontrollable violence, criminality, and murder. Kafka discards the psychological aspect and makes the perverse the mark of a whole world, which is — paradoxically — perverse without being perverse. Perverseness becomes a kind of fictional paradox. There is no longer any normality against which perversity as the abnormal could be judged as such, so that the unnatural and perverse become the "natural" itself.

In both Poe and Kafka we find persons from outside drawn into abnormal situations (for example, "The Fall of the House of Usher," "In the Penal Colony," and "The Country Doctor"). With Poe such persons are affected by the sense of the unusual, drawn into its atmosphere against their will and better judgment, then frightened and generally affected by an overall feeling of uncertainty and insecurity. In Kafka's "In the Penal Colony," the person from outside accepts the unusual machine and the ritual of putting people to death (without trial and verdict or any given reason) matter-of-factly as an ordinary process.

Poe envisioned the state of the world as Kafka saw it and thus helped to create a new consciousness, for which he, like most of his contemporaries, still lacked the literary form to incorporate fully in fiction. At the end of "The Premature Burial" Poe remarks: "There are moments when, even to the sober eye of Reason, the world of our sad Humanity may assume the semblance of a Hell — but the imagination of man is no Carathis, to explore with impunity its every cavern . . . the grim legion of sepulchral terrors cannot be regarded as altogether fanciful . . . they must sleep or they will devour us — they must be suffered to slumber or we perish."[15] The difference between Poe and Kafka is visible in the language of this passage: Poe sees the terror of the soul, but he can still aestheticize it in the tone of his language and in the atmospheric effect of the narrative situation. Kafka's tales, however, as the story "Odradek" makes clear, reveal deformations of subjective perceptions and objective reality simultaneously; they also refer to the impossibility of describing or analyzing subjective and objective reality. Neither Odradek's "belonging to reality nor his representability" in the text is made manifest.[16] These absences reveal the "dissolution both of the laws of thinking and of picturing reality."[17]

Kafka clearly marks the extreme in Modernism as far as the experimental use of the fantastic is concerned. He is in his own words an "end" but also a "beginning" — an end in the development of the existential and cosmological fantastic in fiction, which devours and at the same time reestablishes the real as real; a beginning in the full fantasizing and metamorphosis of all elements of the narrative situation, which is the precondition for the Postmodern fantastic games that give up the cosmological and existential dimension of the fantastic and attempt to gain full liberation of the imagination from reality and from the rules of society, as well as from the burdens of individuality.[18]

NOTES

1. Max Bense, *Literaturmetaphysik: Der Schriftsteller in der technischen Welt* (Stuttgart: Deutsche Verlagsanstalt, 1950), p. 88.

2. Jorge Luis Borges, "Kafka and His Precursors," in *Franz Kafka: A Collection of Criticism*, ed. Leo Hamalian (New York: McGraw Hill, 1974), p. 20.

3. Gustav Janouch, *Gespräche mit Kafka* (Frankfurt: Fischer, 1968), p. 68. My translation.

4. See Theodor W. Adorno, "Aufzeichnungen zu Kafka," in *Theodor W. Adorno: Gesammelte Schriften*, ed. Rolf Tiedemann (Frankfurt: Suhrkamp, 1977), vol. 10, p. 274 ff.

5. Max Brod, *Über Franz Kafka* (Frankfurt: Fischer, 1966), p. 309.

6. Alfred Kubin, *Die andere Seite. Ein phantastischer Roman*, 2nd ed. (Munich: Rowohlt, 1973), p. 63 ff. My translation.

7. Franz Kafka, *Diaries, 1910–1923*, ed. Max Brod, trans. Joseph Kresh (London: Secker and Warburg, 1948), vol. 2, p. 197.

8. Ibid.

9. Ibid., p. 77.

10. Franz Kafka, *Hochzeitsvorbereitungen auf dem Lande und andere Prosa aus dem Nachlaß*, ed. Max Brod (Frankfort: Fischer, 1953), p. 123. My translation.

11. Henry A. Pochmann, *German Culture in America: Philosophical and Literary Influences 1600–1900* (Madison: U of Wisconsin P, 1957), p. 407.

12. Laura Hofrichter, "From Poe to Kafka," *University of Toronto Quarterly* 24 (1959–1960): 414.

13. See Eric W. Carlson, *The Recognition of Edgar Allan Poe: Selected Criticism since 1829* (Ann Arbor: U of Michigan P, 1966), p. 60 ff; S. B. Purdy, "Poe and Doestoevski," *Studies in Short Fiction* 4 (1967): 169 ff.; Hartmut Binder, *Kafka-Kommentar zu den Romanen, Rezensionen, Aphorismen und zum Brief an den Vater* (Munich: Winkler, 1976), p. 189 ff.

14. "The Black Cat," in *Collected Works of Edgar Allan Poe*, ed. Thomas Ollive Mabbott (Cambridge: Harvard UP, 1978), vol. 3, p. 852.

15. "The Premature Burial," in ibid., p. 969.

16. Rolf Günter Renner, "Kafka als phantastischer Erzähler," in *Phaïcon 3: Almanach der phantastischen Literatur*, ed. Rein A. Zondergeld (Frankfort: Suhrkamp, 1978), p. 156.

17. Rudolf Keis, *Die doppelte Rede des Franz Kafka: Eine textlinguistische Analyse* (Paderborn: Schöningh, 1967), p. 100.

18. Kafka, *Hochzeitsvorbereitungen*, p. 121.

# Fernando Pessoa

GEORGE MONTEIRO

Born in Lisbon and educated in South Africa, Fernando Pessoa (1888–1935) returned to Portugal as a young adult never to leave again. Cofounder of the important journals *Orpheu* and *Athena*, he contributed to all major literary and cultural genres. Writing in both Portuguese and English, Pessoa published much of his best work under heteronyms. During his lifetime he published one book of poetry in Portuguese, *Mensagem* [*Message*], in 1934, and, early on, several chapbooks in English, leaving behind at his death a large body of uncollected and unpublished work.

Among the five books Fernando Pessoa chose as part of the Queen Victoria Memorial Prize awarded him for the best essay on his college entrance examinations was the *Choice Works of Edgar Allan Poe, Poems, Stories, Essays* (1902). An introductory essay by Charles Baudelaire provided Pessoa with the context in which he would from then on view Poe's life and read his work. In the table of contents of his copy, which survives as part of the poet's library at the Casa Fernando Pessoa in Lisbon, Pessoa marked his favorite stories, including "The Gold-Bug," which he translated into Portuguese.[1] "Poe had genius," he said, "Poe had talent for he has great reasoning powers, and reasoning is the formal expression of talent."[2]

Pessoa was interested in all aspects of Poe's work. He valued the American writer as a theorist of poetic composition, as the inventor of the ratiocinative tale, as the practitioner of the horror story, and as a poet. He incorporated Poe's ideas into his own critical thinking, not only on the detective story (a critical history of which Pessoa intended to write but did not get beyond a brief beginning or two) but also on the mode of "horror" in fiction and the question of length in the detective story. Pessoa remarked that "it was one of Poe's critical triumphs that he foresaw the necessity of the shorter poems. This was one of his visions of a future, as the detective story was one of his anticipations of it."[3] He insisted that "the detective story must be short for there never is a problem that need take up very much space. Length in one of these stories is only admitted, when the reasoning demands it. Such is the 'Mystery of Marie Rogêt' of Edgar Allan Poe. Yet even this story is not long proportionally with its reasoning."[4] He goes on to state that "no detective story of to-day could be written in the style of *Tom Jones*."[5]

Pessoa also followed Poe in noting the impossibility, especially in modern times, of writing a long poem. "The tendency to brevity in modern literature — poetry — Poe," he wrote on a surviving scrap of paper, "our aesthetic sense is less keen than that of the ancients, but our intellectual sense keener." He projected and wrote versions of a dramatic poem entitled "Ligeia." Imitating Poe's fiction, he based his story "A Very Original Dinner" (which he attributed to his early English heteronym Alexander Search) on Poe's little-known story, "Thou Art the Man."[6] He began a story of his own, one clearly indebted to "The Man of the Crowd," written in the third person but centering on the old man pursued by Poe's narrator: "I became a man of the crowd. I never trusted myself to be alone."[7] Poe's text reads: "[He] is the type and the genius of deep crime. He refuses to be alone. *He is the man of the crowd.*"

In the first issue of *Athena* (October 1924), Pessoa published a magnificent translation of "The Raven" that, he prided himself, "conformed rhythmically to the original."[8] In the fourth issue (January 1925), he published under the title "Edgar Poe's Final Poems" his versions of "Annabel Lee" and "Ulalume."[9] Two years earlier he had published translations of several stories, including "The Masque of the Red Death" and "William Wilson." A note in the former states that Pessoa's translations of "The Gold-Bug" and "Ligeia" had also been published in the same series (by Editorial Delta), although it is not certain that these stories actually came out.[10] In addition to these poems and stories, Pessoa's papers (now at the Biblioteca Nacional in Lisbon) show that he tried his hand at translating "The Bells," "The Haunted Palace," and "MS. Found in a Bottle," while in his copy of Poe's *Choice Works* there are attempts at translating "For Annie" and "The City in the Sea."[11]

Pessoa speculated on the reasons for Poe's meager poetic production, ignoring Poe's explanation that his constant need for money forced him to turn to prose. Poe wrote "little poetry," Pessoa asserted, because in him "the critical faculty was developed at the same time as the poetic propensity. He wrote verse with ease while at college, but then neither his true imagination nor his intellect were [*sic*] developed. These were developed at the same time. Hence the critical faculty, the analytic mind, being ever on the watch, allowed not inspiration to take its free course." Although Pessoa once said that "not many are the poems of Edgar Poe, and of those few, not all of them are good" ("The Raven" not being among the good ones), he took Poe as poet seriously enough to speculate on what essentially differentiated him from Shelley: "Both Poe and Shelley were poets of the spiritual, but they have a great difference. Shelley describes the spiritual as the spiritual; Poe describes the spiritual as the not human. Shelley sees the grandeur, the joyous greatness of the problem of life; Poe sees this greatness also, but he sees none the less its horror. Shelley puts the great problem before us in reference to the soul that is warmed by its joyousness and its limitless love; Poe puts the problem before us in reference to the mind, which is crushed by its insolubility."

Two different but related aspects of Poe's temperament and work caught Pessoa's interest. He tried to define, first, the peculiar kind of fear that characterized Poe's work and, then, the American poet's almost preternatural fear of noise as well as his concomitant predilection for silence. This time he couched his comparison in terms of the French poet Maurice Rollinat. They are, he wrote, "both poets of fear yet each in a difft [*sic*] way. With Poe fear is more ethereal, more spiritual; it spiritualizes all things by its touch. With R. it materializes them, (distorts them at best). With P., however great his fear might be, it is but the chief manner of manifestation of his spirituality. With R., whatever spirituality he shows is a mode of manifesting his fear. This is why with P. fear is spiritual, & with R. spirit is material. Both are intensely dominated by the sentiment of terror." Pessoa attempted to explain elsewhere how this sentient terror resulted from Poe's obsession with silence and noise, as we see in "The Tell-Tale Heart" or "The Fall of the House of Usher," for example, and how Poe pervasively employs "silence." In a fragment labeled "Poe," he writes that closely linked to "the sentiment of fear" is "the auditory sensation": "A nervous person is startled, very little by touch & sight, and much by sound. To one who fears the storm . . . the thunder is the more terrible part. A child that blinks at a bright light cowers at a sharp sound. . . . Musicians are of all men the most nervous. . . . A very great susceptibility to music is accompanied . . . by a very great susceptibility to fear. . . . We know sufficiently Poe's sensibility to music & his perpetual dwelling on the rhythmic side of poetry." What is most suggestive in this fragment is the connection Pessoa makes between the musician's nervous susceptibility to music and humankind's generalized fear of noise. One thinks immediately of Roderick in "The Fall of the House of Usher" and of the title characater of "Ligeia." But of equal importance in the matter of Poe's influence on Pessoa is the reference to the notion that to those who fear storms "the thunder is the more terrible part." Pessoa feared thunder, even when one such storm inspired him, apparently, to write a story based on "The Man of the Crowd."

Related to this fear of noise, for Pessoa and Poe, is their preoccupation with madness. "Poe has of the world a view such as a man with senses perturbed, buoyant," writes Pessoa. "There is a sensation of surfeit in ecstasy. And a pain. . . . So to the eyes of the madman Poe the world is dilated, horrible." That Pessoa felt akin to Poe and his madmen is undeniable. "One of my mental complications — horrible beyond words — is a fear of insanity, which itself is insanity," he wrote clinically. "Impulses, criminal some, insane others, reaching, amid my agony, a horrible tendency to action."

Pessoa's interest in the American poet extended to the details of Poe's life that he learned from Baudelaire. Notably, Pessoa was struck by the French poet's apology for Poe's alcoholism. Poe's death occurred, decided Baudelaire, when he was "conquered by *delirium tremens*."[12] Just before his own death Pessoa wrote "D. T.," a poem about his own alcoholism that is not unrelated to "William Wilson" or "The Black Cat." His more characteristic view of alcohol, however, was that it had its good uses. "A stimulant is something that excites us to be ourselves; thus whisky has led many men to deeds wholly unconnected with barley," he wrote, echoing Baudelaire's defense of Poe as an alcoholic martyr to his work.[13]

If he admired Poe's work and was attracted to certain notorious aspects of his life, Pessoa also seemed to emulate that life. Baudelaire's words about Poe might be applied to Pessoa, that "the poet had learned to drink as a laborious author exercises himself in filling note-books," for "the works that give us so much pleasure to-day were, in reality, the cause of his death."[14] Appropriately, this is the theme of the painting used on the cover of the standard bibliography of Pessoa's work, in which appears a black bird perched atop an open chest containing the poet's books and, presumably, manuscripts.[15] When asked about this linking of poet, poetry, and bird, Pessoa's bibliographer explained that ravens held a strong personal meaning for Pessoa. The poet often did his drinking at shops run by *galegos* [Galicians], who customarily kept ravens in cages. As he drank their distinctive red wine, Pessoa amused himself by talking to their Poesque birds. "Disse o corvo, 'Nunca mais'" [Quoth the raven, nevermore].

NOTES

1. Maria Leonor Machado de Sousa, *Fernando Pessoa e a literatura de ficção* (Lisbon: Novaera, 1978), p. 11.

2. Fernando Pessoa, *Páginas de estética e de teoria e crítica literárias*, ed. Georg Rudolf Lind and Jacinto do Prado Coelho (Lisbon: Ática, 1966), p. 193.

3. Ibid., p. 207.

4. Fernando Pessoa Papers, Biblioteca Nacional, Lisbon. All quotations from Pessoa, unless otherwise indicated, are from this collection.

5. Pessoa, *Páginas de estética*, p. 221.

6. Machado de Sousa, *Literatura de ficção*, pp. 9–22. See also Maria Leonor Machado de Sousa, "Postface" to Fernando Pessoa, in *"Um jantar muito original" sequido de "A Porta,"* trans. Maria Leonor Machado de Sousa (Lisbon: Relógio d'Água, Editores, 1985), pp. 59–60.

7. Machado de Sousa, *Literatura de ficção*, pp. 15–16. My translation.

8. "O Corvo," *Athena* 1 (October 1924): 27–29.

9. "Os Poemas finais de Edgar Poe," *Athena* 1 (January 1925): 161–164.

10. José Blanco, quoted in *Fotobibliografia de Fernando Pessoa*, comp. João Rui de Sousa (Lisbon: Imprensa Nacional-Casa da Moeda/Biblioteca Nacional, 1988), p. 104.

11. Maria da Encarnação Monteiro, *Incidências Inglesas na poesia de Fernando Pessoa* (Coimbra: Coimbra Editora, 1956), p. 96.

12. *The Choice Works of Edgar Allan Poe, Poems, Stories, Essays*, intr. Charles Baudelaire (London: Chatto and Windus, 1902), p. 10.

13. Pessoa, *Páginas de estética*, p. 211.

14. *Choice Works*, pp. 18–19.

15. José Blanco, *Fernando Pessoa: Esboço de uma Bibliografia* (Lisbon: Imprensa Nacional-Casa da Moeda/Centro de Estudos Pessoanos, 1983).

# Rubén Darío

SUSAN F. LEVINE AND STUART LEVINE

Rubén Darío (1867–1916) was a major figure in Modernism, the important early-twentieth-century Spanish American literary movement that cohered around him. His extensive publications include poetry, prose poems, short fiction, novels, essays, and articles. Among his best-known works are *Azul* [Blue] (1888) and *Cantos de vida y esperanza* [Songs of life and hope] (1905).

The parents of Félix Rubén García Sarmiento separated before his birth. When he began to publish, he signed his works Rubén Darío, using a family name from his father's side. As Darío grew up in the home of a great aunt and her husband, he read extensively, from an early age transforming a wide variety of ideas and styles into his own. His precocious literary activity brought him the title "poeta niño" [child poet]. Still in his teens, he became a friend in El Salvador of the poet and translator Francisco Gavidia, who stimulated his enthusiasm for Victor Hugo and other French writers. Darío's literary interests broadened even more in 1886 when, working as a journalist in Chile, he became part of a group of young intellectuals who kept abreast of recent trends. There he is believed to have first read Poe, most likely in French and English. Darío's works suggest that throughout his career he continued to think about Poe.

Knowing the details of Poe's life, albeit from biographies now seen as largely unreliable, Darío must have been aware that he and Poe had much in common: their birthdays were only one day apart; they had been raised by people other than birth parents; they were curious, talented, and well-read; they were professional journalists as well as creators of poetry and prose fiction; they had melancholic tendencies and suffered the death of a wife, whom they presented in poetry as an "ideal woman." Both had difficulties with alcohol. Both, moreover, explored the occult and the realms of dream, fantasy, and mystery.[1] Each died relatively young, Poe at forty, Darío at forty-nine. More significant than these circumstantial coincidences are Darío's adoption of Poe's literary ideas and practices and his conception of Poe as an artist. Studies of Darío generally acknowledge his interest in Poe; those by John Englekirk, Enrique Anderson Imbert, and Ángel Rama are especially useful for understanding the relationship.[2]

Englekirk observes that there is much in "Darío's art . . . that both consciously and unconsciously has been patterned after Poe" (E 168). He notes the intensity with which Darío studied Poe's life and sees Poe in Darío's "spirit of restlessness," fascination with "the weird and the strange," and "interest in the occult sciences" (E 171, 173). He finds Darío similar to Poe in the affliction of melancholy and in the abuse of alcohol, which he attributes in part to "neurotic temperament" and in part to grief over the death of "Stella," Darío's wife, Rafaela Contraeras. Darío refers to "Stella," whom he identifies with Poe's women, in the essay on Poe in *Los raros* [The exceptional ones] (1896), in the essay "Stella," and in the poem "El poeta pregunta por Stella" [The poet asks about Stella]. He makes the connection explicit again in *Historia de mis libros* [The story of my books] (1905).[3] Englekirk shows that the first real evidence of Poe's influence on Darío is in Darío's use of the word "tintinabular" in an essay in 1889; in a later essay Darío also refers to the line in "The Bells" containing Poe's word "tintinabulation" (E 186). In addition to including Poe among *Los raros*, Englekirk observes that Darío frequently compares other authors to Poe: "references to him seem to . . . appear in almost every volume that follows *Los raros*" (E 190). Contending that much of Darío's symbolism is "directly traceable to Poe" (E 195), Englekirk discusses allusions to and the aura of Poe in numerous poems.

Anderson Imbert covers many of the same points, providing additional information on Darío's interpretation of Poe as a visionary and on references to "Stella."[4] Poe's Psyche of "Ulalume" influenced both Darío's "El reino interior" [The interior realm] (*Prosas profanas*, 1896) and "Divina Psiquis" [Divine psyche] (*Cantos de vida y esperanza*, 1905). "El reino interior" opens with an epigraph from Poe's "Ulalume": "with Psychis, my soul." "Divina Psiquis" contains a specific reference to Poe: "oh Psiquis, oh alma mía / — como diría / aquel celeste Edgardo / que entró en el Paraíso entre un son de campanas / y un perfume de nardo" [Oh Psyche, oh my soul / — as might have said / that celestial Edgar / who entered Paradise amidst a rumor of bells and perfume of tuberoses]. Darío's doubling of the poet into "I" (yo) and "soul" (alma), as "I" speaks with or about "soul," is similar to Poe's procedure in "Ulalume," where a conflict between the spiritual and the sensual also exists (AI 135).[5]

Anderson Imbert makes, in passing, an important observation about an aspect of both writers that is sometimes overlooked — humor in the grotesque. He finds, too, that some of Darío's stories leave the reader with the choice of rational or irrational explanations — madness or magic — a choice characteristic of Poe's stories as well (see, for example, AI 233–234).

Anderson Imbert finds that two of Darío's essays on theosophy and on Decadent literature have implications for his stories. "Onofroffismo: La comedia psíquica" [The psychic comedy] (1895), on theosophy, shows Darío's fondness for the supernatural. Its own tone and structure are reminiscent of Poe's colloquies. In "Richard Le Gallienne" (1894), Darío praises the Decadents, followers of Poe, for giving flight to the soul (psiquis) and for providing a defense against the dangers of scientific tyranny. In the essay Darío asks: "Who better than Poe and his followers have explored the dark realm of death?" (AI/B 103).

Darío, who experienced terrifying nightmares all his life, took dreams to be indications of the supernatural. In addition to dreaming of being approached by cadavers and supernatural beings, he had what he called "fantasticomatemáticas" [mathematical fantasies], nightmares involving disarming combinations or divisions of geometric constructions (AI/B 109). Contending that Darío had Poe in mind when he used the term, Anderson Imbert cites Darío's reference to "the algebraic nature of his [Poe's] fantasy" in *Los raros* and his comments in "Edgar Poe y los sueños" [Edgar Poe and dreams] on originality, alcoholic delirium, and nightmare in Poe's stories, in which "dream, mixed with that prodigious mathematical ability which makes the unbelievable obvious, is more commanding" (AI 234).

Rama further explores the importance of the dreamworld for Darío in his careful edition of Darío's *El mundo de los sueños* [The world of dreams] (1973), compiled from a series of articles in *La Nación* of Buenos Aires between 1911 and 1914. Rama calls the articles on Poe from 1913 "the crowning point of the investigation of dreams" (R 231). There Darío interprets Poe's visions as a way to reach "the other" and to recapture lost sacred knowledge.

As Darío's art evolves from an expression of his desire to create a beautiful work of art sufficient in itself to an expression of his philosophical, social, and political concerns, his interest in the occult, in Poe, and in other visionaries persists.[6] A comparison of Darío's treatment of Poe in *Los raros* and in *El mundo de los sueños* suggests that his respect for Poe as seer only increases.[7]

In *Los raros* Darío interprets Poe as a kindred spirit — an artist out of place in the noisy, stressful, materialistic culture of the United States, "a pale melancholic visionary" (LR 263) comforted by the lovely women emanating from his works, as Darío felt comforted by the memory of his wife when he found himself overwhelmed by New York City.[8] In *Los raros*, too, basing his judgments on the flawed Ingram biography, he describes Poe's important place in world literature, his noble lineage, his early loss of parents, his natural intelligence, and his physical beauty. He says that Poe was a dreamer possessed by dreams since childhood, dreams filled with "chimeras and cyphers like an astrologer's chart" (LR 267, 268).

Darío relates Poe's lack of religious faith or belief in the supernatural to his mathematical turn of mind. Not able to accept Poe as an unbeliever, he argues that although Poe said that he did not believe in the supernatural, in "Ligeia" he defines God as a great will pervading all things, and in "Mesmeric Revelation" Poe refers to God as "unparticled matter" (LR 270). Anderson Imbert explains Darío's surprise at Poe's position as follows: "The supernatural element in . . . [Poe's] stories was gratuitous; the note of gloom was owing more to a morbid curiosity about death than to religious or metaphysical concepts of reality" (AI/B 103). Of Darío's position, Anderson Imbert remarks: "In his own case imagination was inseparable from religious beliefs" (AI/B 103).

Darío's increased familiarity with Poe is apparent in the 1913 dream series essays, which include a general study, a study of Poe's poetry, and an analysis of Poe's fiction. Following his own interest in dreams and visions, Darío turns to Emile Lauvrière's study *Edgar Poe* (1911) and to Dr. Roger Dupouy's ideas regarding evidence of the effects of opium and alcohol in Poe's writing.[9] Darío still envisions Poe as a constant dreamer: "For him, as for Nerval, dreaming was part of his temperament, natural and innate: he lived dreaming" (R 180–181). He cites numerous dream sequences and characters in dream states in Poe's works. He finds Poe exceptional — "apart from common humanity" (R 183). Intoxicants, he says, are not the source of Poe's visions but rather the agents that release the transcendental visions of the genius within Poe.

At the beginning of the second essay, Darío observes that Poe, as dreamer, mystic, and visionary, had an exceptional understanding of himself and the universe. Darío notes that Poe dedicated *Eureka* to dreamers and cites examples of dream imagery from "Dreams," "Al Aaraaf," "The Valley of Unrest," "Irene," "Dreamland," "The Haunted Palace," "The Conqueror Worm," "The Raven," and "Ulalume," of which he says: "And when Psyche, his soul, spoke to him and entreated him to flee, he would tell her, 'This is nothing but dreaming'" (R 189).

Darío's reference to Poe's "prodigious mathematical faculty" cited earlier opens the third essay. Following Lauvrière, Darío gives examples of dream imagery from many Poe stories. He sees Poe as a dynamic mental force and notes the element of dream in Poe's cosmogony in *Eureka*. Darío marvels at Poe's ability to communicate visionary experience in language — perceptions from "the mystical realm and the empires of the shadow" (R 194). Darío places Poe among the "rarest" of artists: "He has expressions, ways of saying things, that can only be compared to those found in sacred texts" (R 194–195). Indeed, having in *Los raros* seen Poe as "an Ariel," and, along with Goethe, Byron, and Lamartine, as one of the beautiful sons of Apollo, here at the end of the third essay Darío calls Poe "the lyrical magus, the powerful Apolonida Trismegisto [Thrice Great son of Apollo]" (R 195).

NOTES

1. See Lucía Ungaro de Fox, "El parentesco artístico entre Poe y Darío," *Revista National de Cultura* 28.178 (1966): 81–83.

2. John E. Englekirk Jr., *Edgar Allan Poe in Hispanic Literature* (New York: Instituto de las Españas, 1934; rpt. New York: Russell and Russell, 1972); hereafter cited as E. Enrique Anderson Imbert, *La originalidad de Rubén Darío* (Buenos Aires: Centro Editor de América Latina, 1967); hereafter cited as AI. See also Enrique Anderson Imbert, "Rubén Darío and the Fantastic Element in Literature," trans. Anne Bonner, in *Rubén Darío Centennial Studies* (Austin: Department of Spanish and Portuguese, Institute of Latin American Studies, University of Texas at Austin, 1970), pp. 97–117, which contains in translation much of the material found in chapter 21 of the complete study; hereafter cited as AI/B. Rubén Darío, "Edgar Poe y los sueños," in *El mundo de los sueños*, Edición, Prólogo, Notas de Ángel Rama (Barcelona: Universidad de Puerto Rico, Editorial Universitaria, 1973), pp. 180–195, 231; hereafter cited as R. The 1917 memorial version of *El mundo de los sueños* is incomplete. All of Darío's articles in *La Nación* between 1911 and 1914 under that heading appear, texts corrected, in R.

3. Rubén Darío, *Historia de mis libros*, in *Obras completas* (Madrid: Afrodisio Aguado, S.A., 1950), vol. 1, p. 210.

4. The name was resonant for Darío. In El Salvador as a teenager, Darío had seen Gavidia's translation of Victor Hugo's "Stella." Rafaela had also published stories under the pseudonym "Stella." See AI 47.

5. See also E 193, 204–206; Humberto De Castro, "Whitman y Poe en la poesía de Rubén Darío," *Boletín Cultural y Biográfica* 10.1 (1967): 91–95; Rubén Darío, *Azul. Prosas profanas*, Estudio y Notas de Andrew P. Debicki y Michael J. Doudoroff (Madrid: Editorial Alhambra, S.A., 1985): p. 232, n. 45. For further discussion of psyche/soul in these poems, see Cathy Login Jrade, *Rubén Darío and the Romantic Search for Unity* (Austin: U of Texas P, 1983), pp. 62–65, 71–72.

6. For a full discussion of change in Darío, see AI 112 ff; R 39; Darío, *Azul*, pp. 25–26.

7. Rubén Darío, "Edgar Allan Poe," in *Los raros*, in *Obras completas* (Madrid: Afrodisio Aguado, 1950), vol. 2, pp. 255–270; hereafter cited as LR. Englekirk reports

that Darío's essay on Poe first appeared in *La Nación* in 1893 (E 90). *Los raros* was first published in 1896.

8. See Marjorie C. Johnson, "Rubén Darío's Acquaintance with Poe," *Hispania* 17.3 (1934): 274–276, for a discussion of Darío's use of Poe's language to describe Poe's women.

9. Darío is likely referring to Roger Dupouy, *Les opiomanes, mangeurs, buveurs et fumeurs d'opium: étude clinique et médico-littéraire* (Paris: Alcan, 1912).

# Jorge Luis Borges

GRACIELA E. TISSERA

Jorge Luis Borges (1899–1986) was born in Buenos Aires and died in Geneva, where he had studied from 1914 until 1919. Essentially a poet, he became a well-known author in the 1940s when three volumes of his short stories were published. Borges received many honorary degrees and international honors, including the Formentor Prize in 1961, the Jerusalem Prize in 1971, and the Cervantes Prize in 1980.

Jorge Luis Borges has been one of the strongest supporters of the Poe legacy in the literary world. If literature is a guided dream as Borges has postulated, it is easy to accept the Borgesean theory that "each writer *creates* his precursors."[1] In this concept of creation and constant enrichment lies the love of books and authors that Borges considers part of his personal baggage. Poe played a major role in this creative memory that Borges values.

Many aspects of these authors' lives have similarities that are difficult to overlook. John T. Irwin's comprehensive study of Poe and Borges, *The Mystery to a Solution*, presents numerous parallels between the lives and works of the two writers. As Irwin points out, both Borges and Poe can identify themselves with a southern zone, which for Borges defines a particular feeling: for him the South is the outskirts of Buenos Aires; it is myth more than history that flows into his love of the traditions of his homeland.[2] Although Poe was born in Boston, he grew up in Virginia and considered himself a southern gentleman, a detail that served to distinguish him from the literary world of the North. As young men, both writers aspired to a military life. Borges admired his military forefathers who bequeathed a line of conduct rooted in the ideal of discipline, logic, and love of one's country.[3]

To analyze the legacy of Poe in Borges is to return within the walls of the library where the Argentine writer was educated (CEB 24–25). An assiduous reader, he began his literary career by writing poetry, a passion he would never abandon except during a period dedicated to literary and philosophical reflections expressed through essays and stories. One of his literary concerns was the process of causality in a novel culminating in magic that is accepted as a part of reality. He recorded his thoughts on this subject in the essay "El arte narrativo y la magia" [Narrative art and magic] (OC 226–232), in which he includes an analysis of *The Narrative of Arthur Gordon Pym*. Borges uses Poe's novel to give an example of two causal processes, natural and magic, with magic being his favorite. Borges considers two different arguments: one that is immediate, the other one secret and only revealed at the end. The secret argument is the fear of the color white; the magic is the culmination of the cause. The act of not mentioning this color produces the suggestion and the effect in the reader of ascertaining something that is not named. This ability to suggest or to create in the reader the feeling of what is to come is the technique that Borges admired in Poe, and it became one of the American master's greatest influences in Borgesean works, which is expressed as a secret complexity.[4]

In Borges's judgment, Poe's work has value as a whole, although if his poetry and stories were considered individually there would undoubtedly be deficiencies. In a speech given at the University of Belgrano in 1978, Borges presented his most extensive evaluation of Poe under the title "El cuento policial" [The detective story].[5] It is obvious that Borges recognizes the validity of Poe's work, but he ranks him as a lesser Tennyson, while acknowledging Poe's historic importance and his influence on French writers.[6] Borges emphasizes the importance of Poe's poetic theory expressed in "The Philosophy of Composition." In contrast to Poe, Borges believed that poetry cannot be the result of a mere intellectual exercise;[7] his own definition of the creative process constitutes an irrefutable debt to the direct influence of the muse.[8]

Borges especially admired two creative aspects of Poe's work: the detective stories and fantastic literature. Although the American writer did not mix the two genres, Borges considered him the precursor of both science fiction and the detective story.[9] Even though the stories may be too exaggerated and grotesque for Borges's taste, he selected five of vital importance to the detective genre: "The Murders in the Rue Morgue," "The Mystery of Marie Rogêt," "The Gold-Bug," "Thou Art the Man," and "The Purloined Letter" (BO 75–76). Undoubtedly these stories influenced the Argentine writer, who himself tried to give a new direction to this genre in his tales "El jardín de senderos que se bifurcan" ["The Garden of Forking Paths"] (1941), "La muerte y la brújula" ["Death and the Compass"] (1942), and "Abenjacán el Bojarí, muerto en su laberinto" ["Ibn Hakkan al-Bokhari, Dead in His Labyrinth"] (1951).[10]

Although Borges the poet acknowledges a sense of order and the simplification of language in Poe's works, he dedicated his prose to what could be called a recovery of the detective genre, confronting the reader with a forced involvement in the work, creating anticipation and doubt. The game of logic and magic lies in this anticipation. Borges points out the characteristics of Poe's stories, emphasizing the principal aspect of the genre: the detective who resolves a problem through an intellectual operation. In Borges's view, the genre has to be a product of logic, that is to say, more than realistic it should be a game of intellect, not just imagination (BO 73). The strength of the story and its ability to surprise the reader lie in the element of the final solution. Borges followed in the tradition of Poe and faced the reader created by him. As in "The Murders in the Rue Morgue," where no one would think of an orangutan as the killer (BO 75), in Borges's "The Garden of Forking Paths" the reader does not find a solution until the end of the story. Borges's technique is similar to Poe's: to allow the reader to try to figure out the end by following the clues.

According to Borges, the creation of the character should also be a challenge for the reader, hence the portrayal of a distant person with whom the reader cannot find a means of comparison, someone who lives outside the reader's realm and has different habits so that imagination flows freely. Thus for American readers the first detective of the genre was French, Charles Auguste Dupin (BO 72). Continuing in this tradition in "Death and the Compass," Borges created the detective Erik Lönnrot, who "believed himself a pure reasoner, an Auguste Dupin, but there was something of the adventurer in him, and even a little of the gambler." [11] The reference to Poe is explicit; Borges creates the image of the other detective but with a difference: the insertion of chance into the story, which for Borges is synonymous with destiny. His detective is not simply going to follow the game of intelligence, but rather he will be subject to an inexorable *Fatum*.[12]

Although Borges follows Poe's techniques, he goes further by including the philosophical theories that are part of his aesthetic. Borges plays with the idea of destiny, cyclic repetition, time and space, pantheism, and the labyrinth-like quality of the universe.[13] Another aspect that Borges includes is the death of the detective. This element is essential in Borges, as the detective becomes part of the plot; he is transformed from a mere analyst of the situation into a participant.[14] Lönnrot is attracted to the center, to the trap, and is the axis of the tale. He was all along, although he did not know it. His death closes the circle of logic, where victim and murderer identify themselves as one.[15]

Borges dispenses with the closed room; the mystery grows with the consecutive crimes that contain the same characteristics. Clues add up, creating in the reader the impression that somebody has designed or carried out a plan. This idea makes us face the possibility of a divine plan in which the destiny of each person has been decided, a certain harmony that governs the universe beyond human understanding. The possibility of finding order in the universe leads the seeker to hopelessly confront a labyrinth that becomes the symbol for human life.[16] In contrast to Poe, Borges creates the terror of the closed room with the idea of infinity: the labyrinth. Therefore, a tentative solution does not mean the return of order as in Poe but rather establishes the human condition and its phantasmagoric quality in opposition to divine nature. What in Poe is a material mystery in Borges becomes a metaphysical mystery.[17]

In "Ibn Hakkan al-Bokhari, Dead in His Labyrinth," Borges establishes the same idea presented in "Death and the Compass": the victim who is attracted to the place of his death. The killer creates a maze from which the victim cannot escape. The trap is so obvious that it becomes invisible.[18] Dunraven, the narrator in Borges's story, and his friend Unwin argue the solution to the puzzle while they confront the reader with Poe's theory that mystery should be simple (OC 600).

The struggle between chaos and cosmos is the distinctive trait of Poe and Borges. Humans as imperfect and defenseless creatures possess an internal labyrinth in which they must begin their long voyage toward wisdom. From their internal being they must confront the projection of their own conflicted entity: the world. Moreover, they must unite their individuality and their external circumstance in order to face the universe, to arrive at the primary causes of all things. In Poe, the return of order amounts to the confrontation of a celestial plan where a perfect order exists, an idea he expresses in *Eureka*. In Borges, we face the order of disorder or risky chaos. There are only two ways that lead out of the labyrinth of the world: dreams and death. Borges, influenced by Idealistic and Platonic philosophies, states the concept of eternity through emotional apprehension (OC 762–766) and the concept of memory as the basic motion of the universe and of the human being's immortality (BO 41). Life, on the other hand, is a dead-end maze where humans wander to reach the double symbol of infinity and chaos. For Borges infinity is a more universal and dreaded concept than the concept of evil.[19] He summarizes this idea through constant multiplication of mirrors, of paths that repeat and divide, and of spatial and temporal vastness, and with cyclical repetitions that trap a person in innumerable labyrinths that make up the ultimate labyrinth of the universe.[20] According to Borges, the incessant quest for knowledge is the only hope.

One of Borges's last projects was the compilation of a personal library that would combine his preferred works.[21] In this incomplete effort, he left a list of authors based solely on the pleasure of reading, because this pleasure pro-

duces, in his view, the aesthetic act. Among the sixty-six prologues edited for
the project is one for the stories by Poe, whom he considered one of the
sources of current literature. Borges never lost his passionate interest in his
favorite American writer. During a visit to Baltimore in 1983, just three years
before his death, he remarked to John Irwin: "I have always had this fear that
some day I would be found out, that people would see that everything in my
work is borrowed from someone else, from Poe or Kafka, from Chesterton,
Stevenson, or Wells" (MS xxii). Although this remark does not do justice to
his own originality and literary achievement, Borges reveals the importance
he attributed to the creative influence of his precursors.

NOTES

1. See Jorge Luis Borges, *Obras completas* (Buenos Aires: Emecé, 1974), pp. 1022,
712; hereafter cited as OC.

2. John T. Irwin, *The Mystery to a Solution: Poe, Borges, and the Analytic Detective
Story* (Baltimore: Johns Hopkins UP, 1994), pp. 164–175; hereafter cited as MS. Jorge
Luis Borges, "Testimonio de mis libros," *Revista del notariado* 721 (1976): 3–9.

3. See Jorge Luis Borges, "An Autobiographical Essay," in *Critical Essays on Borges,*
ed. Jaime Alazraki (Boston: Hall, 1987), pp. 22–24; hereafter cited as CEB. Borges also
addresses the topic of military tradition with Fernando Sorrentino; see *Seven Conversations with Borges* (New York: Whitston Publishing, 1982), p. 35.

4. See the "Prólogo" to *El otro, el mismo* (1964) (OC 858). See also Ronald Christ,
*The Narrow Act* (New York: New York UP, 1969), pp. 125–130.

5. This lecture was later published in *Borges, oral* (Buenos Aires: Emecé, 1979),
pp. 65–80. Hereafter cited as BO.

6. Borges also mentioned this fact in "Pierre Menard, autor del Quijote"
(OC 447–448).

7. In "El cuento policial," Borges analyzes this essay with respect to the creation of
"The Raven." He concludes that although Poe conceived it intellectually, this argument is weak. See *Jorge Luis Borges. Textos Cautivos. Ensayos y reseñas en "El Hogar,"*
ed. Enrique Sacerio Garí and Emir Rodríguez Monegal (Barcelona: Tusquets Editores,
1986), pp. 113–114. Burton R. Pollin gives a list of Borges's references to Poe texts in the
previously mentioned book in "The Presence of Poe in Borges's Reviews in *El Hogar,*"
*Poe Studies* 25.1,2 (June/December 1992): 39. See also Georges Charbonnier, *El escritor
y su obra. Entrevistas de Georges Charbonnier con Jorge Luis Borges,* trans. Martí Soler
(México D.F.: Siglo XXI Editores, 1970), p. 43.

8. See OC 79, 976, and 1021. See also the "Prólogo" to *La rosa profunda* (1975) in
*Obra poética* (Buenos Aires: Emecé, 1977), p. 413.

9. See BO 68. See also "Sobre Chesterton," *Otras Inquisiciones* (1952) (OC 694).

10. The first two stories are included in *Ficciones* (OC 472–480, 499–507) and the third in *El Aleph* (OC 600–606). John Irwin explains Borges's intention of following the style of Poe's detective stories (MS 37). Borges also wrote detective stories in collaboration with Bioy Casares; see Jorge Luis Borges, *Obras completas en colaboración. 1. Con Adolfo Bioy Casares* (Madrid: Alianza Editorial, 1981).

11. See *Labyrinths*, ed. Donald Yates and James Irby (New York: New Directions, 1964), p. 29. For Borges's stories translated into English, see *The Aleph and Other Stories*, ed. Norman Thomas di Giovanni (New York: E. P. Dutton, 1970).

12. See Antonio Carrizo, *Borges el memorioso* (México D.F.: Fondo de Cultura Económica, 1982), pp. 229–230.

13. For a complete analysis of Borges's tales, see Jaime Alazraki, *La prosa narrativa de Jorge Luis Borges* (Madrid: Editorial Gredos, 1974).

14. See Alexander Coleman, "Notes on Borges and American Literature," in *Prose for Borges*, ed. Charles Newman and Mary Kinzie (Evanston: Northwestern UP, 1974), pp. 308–329.

15. See Jorge Luis Borges, "El tiempo circular" (OC 395). Borges also discusses the pantheist theory in "Nota sobre Walt Whitman" (OC 251). For an extensive analysis of this theme, see Maurice J. Bennett, "The Detective Fiction of Poe and Borges," *Comparative Literature* 35.3 (1983): 272–273.

16. See Waldemar Verdugo-Fuentes, *En voz de Borges* (México D.F.: Editorial Offset, 1986), pp. 130–132.

17. For the meaning of labyrinths in Borges, see MS 155–163.

18. Borges takes this characteristic of something too obvious to be discovered from Poe's "The Purloined Letter" (see BO 76). For an interesting analysis, see Julia A. Kushigian, "The Detective Story Genre in Poe and Borges," *Latin American Literary Review* 11.22 (1983): 27–39.

19. For the concept of evil in Poe and Borges, see Maurice J. Bennett, "The Infamy and the Ecstasy: Crime, Art, and Metaphysics in Edgar Allan Poe's 'William Wilson' and Jorge Luis Borges's 'Deutsches Requiem,'" in *Poe and Our Times: Influences and Affinities*, ed. Benjamin F. Fisher (Baltimore: Edgar Allan Poe Society, 1986), pp. 107–123.

20. For these concepts in Borges's fiction, see "El inmortal" (OC 533–544) and "La biblioteca de Babel" (OC 465–471).

21. See "Nota del editor," in Jorge Luis Borges, *Biblioteca personal (prólogos)* (Madrid: Alianza Editorial, 1988), pp. i–ii.

# Julio Cortázar

MARY G. BERG

Internationally renowned for his ten collections of short stories, five novels, four collections of poetry, and some ten books of essays and miscellanea, Julio Cortázar (1914–1984) was born in Belgium but lived in Argentina before moving permanently to France in 1951, the year his first book of stories was published. Once established in Paris, he spent his life as a writer, translator, and, in later years, as a spokesman for human rights. In 1953 and 1954 Cortázar translated Poe's complete prose works into Spanish, which were subsequently published in many editions, prefaced by his extensive biographical and critical studies of Poe.

Throughout his life, Julio Cortázar expressed great admiration for the works of Edgar Allan Poe. In dozens of interviews, speeches, and essays he spoke of his early fascination with Poe's stories and their enduring effect upon him. By the time he translated Poe's tales and most of his essays (1953–1954), Cortázar had written both long fiction, *El examen* [The exam] (1948–1950), and short stories, *Bestiario* [Bestiary] (1951), in which his profound empathy with Poe's topics and techniques are apparent. Cortázar's splendid translations have given Poe's prose an eminence and conspicuous presence within contemporary Spanish language narrative since the 1950s when they were published in Spain and Puerto Rico.[1] Five volumes were reissued by the Alianza publishing company in the 1980s and were widely distributed. The presence of Poe in Cortázar's own fictional and nonfictional prose has been analyzed by many critics, who seem to agree that his connection with Poe is a matter of extraordinary affinity rather than imitation. Cortázar himself was always very self-aware and articulate about the similarities in topics, techniques, and attitudes he shared with his favorite American writer.

Repeatedly throughout his life Cortázar recalled the profound effect Poe's stories had upon him at an impressionable age. In a 1984 memoir he spoke of how "from early childhood on I had to accept being all alone in that ambiguous territory where fear and morbid fascination made up my nighttime world.

I can trace this fear to a specific source: my clandestine reading, when I was eight or nine, of Edgar Allan Poe's stories. There the real and the fantastic (for instance, the Rue Morgue and Berenice, the Black Cat and Lady Madeline Usher) fused into a single horror which literally made me ill for months and from which I have never completely recovered."[2]

Cortázar has said that without being steeped in the magic of Poe's stories at such an early age he would not — could not — have written fantastic stories himself. He spoke of Poe's work as a totally assimilated, internalized, and essential influence that opened certain doors of possibility for his imagination. His readings of Poe offered him a way of conceptualizing and experiencing reality that seemed intuitively right to him. He remarked that "the traces of writers such as Poe are undeniable on the deepest levels of many of my stories, and I think that without 'Ligeia,' without 'The Fall of the House of Usher' I would not have found myself with this disposition toward the fantastic which assaults me in the most unexpected moments and which propels me to write as the only way to cross over certain limits, to install myself in the territory of *lo otro* — the Other."[3] Poe and Cortázar share a fascination with myth and archetypes and with moments of transcendence, as well as an obsession with ritual and the morbid.

Just before he undertook the lengthy enterprise of translating Poe's prose, Cortázar began to publish his own short stories. He commented that Poe's "stories fascinate us like fish aquaria or like crystal balls where, in their inaccessible centers, we behold a transparent, petrified scene."[4] Poe's tales are not mirrors of factual everyday reality, but rather they are like "those mirrors of so many children's stories which reflect only the strange, the unexpected, or the lethal."[5] Cortázar has said of his own stories that they, like Poe's, almost always "belong to the genre called, for lack of a better name, fantastic. They oppose that false realism which consists of believing that everything can be described and explained in the manner assumed by the scientific and philosophical optimism of the eighteenth century."[6]

In addition to identifying with Poe's personal life (both were fatherless boys who felt alienated from many aspects of their societies), Cortázar shared many of Poe's ideas concerning literary expression. Their theories of how the short story operates and what it can accomplish are similar. Cortázar particularly admired the tension and intensity of Poe's stories and wrote repeatedly of Poe's skill at evoking presence rather than simply describing exteriors: "In his best stories the method is frankly poetic: background and form are not distinguishable as such . . . we are put into the drama, we are made to read the story as though we were inside it."[7] A story is like a photograph, a closed form that captures a microcosm in all of its unity and complexity. Successful stories resonate with mythic forces and mental archetypes and from these resonances derive their effect.

Cortázar analyzed Poe's stories in essays and in extensive notes to his translations. He observed that Poe's stories and poems obey profound compulsions: "It is easy to see that Poe's *themes* surge from his own particular nature, and that in all of them the creative imagination and fantasy work with material from the unconscious. This raw material, which imposes itself irresistibly on Poe and *gives him the story*, providing him simultaneously with the compulsion to write it and the genesis of the topic, presents itself to him in the form of dreams, hallucinations, obsessive ideas and the influence of alcohol and especially of opium, facilitate its eruption on the conscious level.[8]

Cortázar speaks of how for both Poe and himself the creative process is one of exorcism of obsessions and anxieties; stories are born of the acute tension between the rational and the irrational and between conscious and unconscious compulsions. Literature for Poe and Cortázar was profoundly related to their personal searches for resolution, absolutes, and understanding. Cortázar's preface to *Eureka* describes at length the qualities he found aesthetically and spiritually moving, the poetic images that reveal the essence of things. For both Poe and Cortázar, literature was a vital and essential experience, an aperture of revelation and a fusion of opposites, a mystic experience beyond the rational.

Among the studies analyzing aspects of the relationship between Poe and Cortázar, Ana Hernández del Castillo's *Keats, Poe, and the Shaping of Cortázar's Mythopoesis* (1981) examines Cortázar's reshaping of powerful archetypal images in Keats's poetry and Poe's stories.[9] Hernández discusses how Cortázar's book-length study of archetypal structures in Keats (written from 1948 to 1952, just before he translated Poe) "ended by influencing his own perception of these in the works of Poe, who had remained as an unconscious, completely internalized model for Cortázar's works throughout his career."[10]

María Luisa Rosenblat's *Poe y Cortázar: Lo fantástico como nostalgia* [Poe and Cortázar: The fantastic as nostalgia] (1989) provides extensive analysis of Cortázar's deep attraction to Poe's writing, its profound influence on him, and the ways their affinities are expressed in their fiction.[11] Rosenblat analyzes Poe's *Eureka* and Cortázar's *Rayuela* [*Hopscotch*] as anxious inquiries into the nature of reason and logic. She sees Poe and Cortázar as hypersensitive to the tensions between reason and intuition, matter and spirit, self and the universal, reality and unreality, and science and art.[12] She describes both Cortázar and Poe as engaged in a lifelong search for transcendence and ultimate coherence.

Julio Rodríguez-Luis, in *The Contemporary Praxis of the Fantastic: Borges and Cortázar* (1991), explores definitions and dimensions of the fantastic and looks closely at many of Cortázar's stories.[13] He points out that Cortázar is "interested in depicting reality . . . in order to probe into it in search of an access to another dimension. . . . It is precisely his interest in reality that leads Cortázar to posit its disruption . . . and eventual transcendence. The latter aim links his work to that of some of the first practitioners of the fantastic, like Poe . . . , whose romantic impulse to negate everyday reality did not pass, as Cortázar's had to, through the sieve of psychological realism." [14]

Not only is there extraordinary affinity between Poe and Cortázar, but analyzing Poe allowed Cortázar to express many of his own concerns and theories. Similarities between the two are many, but particularly explicit ones include topics of yearning for perfection or unity for absolutes, and the metaphor of the house (or enclosed space: cellar, ship, cell, subway tunnel, traffic jam) as an extension of its occupants' horror or terror at the fusion of the irrational with the rational, the unconscious with the conscious, and the self-destructive (often sadistically or morbidly self-destructive) with the quest for meaning. Doubles and mirror images abound. The metaphors of the journey, of the expulsion from harmony, and of the descent into depths (pits, caves, maelstroms) are recurrent.

Almost all of Cortázar's stories contain elements of Poe's influence. "Queremos tanto a Glenda" ["We Love Glenda So Much"], like "The Oval Portrait," is about the sacrifice of living women to an obsession with perfection and about the tension between reality and the abstract purity of art. "Casa tomada" ["House Taken Over"], like "The Fall of the House of Usher," features a house that symbolizes the obsessions and limitations of its owners. The doubles of "Lejana" ["The Distances"], "Axolotl," and "La noche boca arriba" ["The Night Face Up"] recall aspects of "William Wilson." The interaction between the narrator and the jazz musician in Cortázar's "El perseguidor" ["The Pursuer"] is similar to the relationship between the narrator and Roderick Usher in Poe's story. Poe's interest in crime, obsession, and irrational compulsion ("The Black Cat," "The Cask of Amontillado," "The Imp of the Perverse," "The Tell-Tale Heart") has its counterparts in dozens of Cortázar stories, including "Circe," "Cuello de gatito negro" ["Throat of a Black Kitten"], and "El otro cielo" ["The Other Heaven"]. Cortázar's stories, such as "Las puertas del cielo" ["The Gates of Heaven"], recall some of Poe's tales of woman-centered obsession ("Ligeia," "Berenice," "Morella"); in "Las puertas del cielo," as in "Ligeia," the dead woman reappears. Women often represent access to the absolute in Cortázar's stories, as in "MS. hallado en una bolsillo" ["MS. Found in a Pocket"] (clearly a nod to Poe's "MS. Found in a Bottle"], "Cuello de gatito negro," or in the novel *Rayuela*, where La Maga is associated with poetry, magic, and the intuitive. The desire for love is a desire for completion, the fusion of all that is fragmented into oppositions and contradictions.

The voyages of Arthur Gordon Pym and the protagonists of Cortázar's novel *Los premios* [*The Winners*] are strikingly similar. Rosenblat analyzes the parallels and differences, finding that both books "develop some aspects and themes, and character motivations which are central in some of Poe's and Cortázar's stories: the journey as a search for knowledge, the topics of destiny and confrontation with a hidden order of reality, and the use of an ambiguous end." [15] Cortázar's "MS. hallado en una bolsillo" and "Texto en una libreta" ["Text in a Notebook"], stories told in the form of discovered manuscripts, recount journeys of subterranean exploration that end in horror. Cortázar placed Poe's sea stories in the category of "tales of terror," viewing the protagonists of "MS. Found in a Bottle" and "A Descent into the Maelström" as compelled by inexorable destiny to pursue adventures they would not choose, like the central character of "The Pit and the Pendulum." Many of Cortázar's stories, such as "Cefalea," depict mental states suspended between sleep and wakefulness, reality and fantasy, life and death.

More self-aware than Poe and infinitely more at ease in the world, Cortázar observed in an essay that all completely successful short stories "are products of neurosis, nightmares or hallucinations neutralized through objectification and translated to a medium outside the neurotic terrain . . . as if the author, wanting to rid himself of his creature as soon and as absolutely as possible, exorcises it the only way he can, by writing it." [16] In Poe, Cortázar seems to have found a lifelong soul mate who believed as he did in literature as a site for the expression of intuition, dreams, and the irrational as valid apprehensions of reality. Cortázar's summary of Poe's achievements could also represent his own when he says that "all of us, in some aspect of our personalities, are [Poe] and he was one of the great spokesmen of humanity." [17] Cortázar sees Poe's writing as both extratemporal and, in its ability to strip people bare, "so profoundly temporal that it lives in a continual present, seen both in bookstore windows and in the images of nightmares, in human evil, and also in human search for certain ideals and certain dreams." [18]

NOTES

1. These include *Obras en prosa*, 2 vols. (Madrid: Revista de Occidente, 1956); *Obras en prosa*, 2 vols. (Río Piedras: Editorial Universitaria Universidad de Puerto Rico, 1956; 2nd ed. 1969); *Eureka* (Madrid: Alianza Editorial, 1982); *Narración de Arthur Gordon Pym* (Madrid: Alianza Editorial, 1982); *Cuentos*, 2 vols. (Madrid: Alianza Editorial, 1983). For all of these, translation, prologue, and notes by Julio Cortázar. There are many subsequent editions of the Alianza volumes.

2. "Diario final," in "Papel literario," *El Nacional*, Caracas, Venezuela, February 19, 1984.

3. "The Present State of Fiction in Latin America," *Books Abroad* 50.3 (Summer 1976): 522–532. Also reprinted in *The Final Island: The Fiction of Julio Cortázar*, ed. J. Alazraki and I. Ivask (Norman: U of Oklahoma P, 1978).

4. Julio Cortázar, "El poeta, el narrador y el crítico," in *Edgar Allan Poe, Obras en prosa*, trans. Julio Cortázar (Río Piedras: U of Puerto Rico P, 1969), vol. 1, p. lxxxv.

5. Ibid.

6. Julio Cortázar, "Algunos aspectos del cuento," in *Literatura y arte nuevo en Cuba*, ed. Ignasi Rivera (Barcelona: Editorial Estela, 1971), p. 262.

7. Cortázar, "El poeta, el narrador y el crítico," p. lxxvi.

8. Ibid., p. lxxviii.

9. Ana Hernández del Castillo, *Keats, Poe, and the Shaping of Cortázar's Mythopoesis* (Amsterdam: John Benjamins B.V., 1982).

10. Ibid., p. 6.

11. María Luisa Rosenblat, *Poe y Cortázar: Lo fantástico como nostalgia* (Caracas: Monte Avila Editores, 1990).

12. Ibid., p. 52.

13. Julio Rodríguez-Luis, *The Contemporary Praxis of the Fantastic: Borges and Cortázar* (New York: Garland, 1991).

14. Ibid., p. 104.

15. Rosenblat, *Poe y Cortázar*, p. 111.

16. Julio Cortázar, "On the Short Story and Its Environs," in *Around the Day in Eighty Worlds* (San Francisco: North Point P, 1986), p. 161. The essay is about "the modern story begun, one might say, with Edgar Allan Poe, which proceeds inexorably, like a machine destined to accomplish its mission with the maximum economy of means" (158).

17. Cortázar, "El poeta, el narrador y el crítico," p. lvi.

18. Ibid.

# Carlos Fuentes

SUSAN F. LEVINE AND STUART LEVINE

Distinguished author of novels, short stories, plays, and essays, Carlos Fuentes (b. 1928) has also served as Mexican diplomat in France and has been a respected lecturer and teacher in the United States and other countries. Having established himself early with the novels *La región más transparente* [*Where the Air Is Clear*] (1958) and *La muerte de Artemio Cruz* [*The Death of Artemio Cruz*] (1962), as well as with short stories and novelettes, he has continued to write prolifically.

Carlos Fuentes's use of material from Poe is frequent, unusual, and significant for an understanding of both authors.[1] Although Fuentes alludes to Poe on numerous occasions and mentions that the American author played a part in the creation of his complex, all-encompassing worldview, his relationship to Poe does not really fit into any of the familiar categories of literary allusion, borrowing, or influence. As he explains in his critical writings, Fuentes uses Poe for reasons that illuminate not only his own work but Poe's as well. Fuentes has said that in his fiction he does not try to mirror actuality but rather to create new imaginative realities.[2] He wants the reader to perceive the world in unaccustomed ways, to discover hidden possibilities, a desire he attributes in part to his childhood acquaintance with authors such as Poe.

Fuentes's allusions to Poe often appear in contexts that superimpose figures from history, fiction, and myth from diverse times, places, and realities. The result is an ambiguity in fictional situations, an ambiguity that Fuentes says he needs if his fiction is to exemplify his social and aesthetic arguments. Seeing Poe against the backdrop of Fuentes throws into sharper relief certain qualities of Poe's writing of which modern readers were perhaps aware but had not considered in quite the same way. Poe begins to seem an important predecessor of certain stylistic tendencies in twentieth-century literature, for he, like Fuentes, juxtaposed times, places, and realities and mixed myth, history, and fiction. His fiction, like that of many authors writing today, was often ambiguous, synchronic, and open-ended.

A reader working chronologically through Fuentes's oeuvre might sense a Poesque mode from the earliest work but could hardly miss the affinity in the novelette *Aura* (1962), which Fuentes says was inspired by the Japanese film *Ugetsu Monogatari* (1953). *Aura* brings Poe to mind so forcibly that one critic says it recalls "a story that Edgar Allan Poe forgot to write." [3]

Consuelo's reincarnation in *Aura* strongly reminds the reader of Poe's tales of reincarnation, especially "Morella" and "Ligeia," because of congruities in theme: Fuentes stresses the merging of past and present and the efficacy of the human will. The daughter in "Morella" who comes to bear a "too perfect identity" with her mother suggests temporal ambiguity; if the daughter is the reincarnation of Morella, past and present seem to merge. What power there is in human will is a major theme in "Ligeia." We mention it in connection with *Aura* because, as in "Ligeia," it is ambiguous whose will is the source of the re-creation. [4] Fuentes's exploration of the other side of reality and his allusion to the concept of physical creation through an act of will in *Aura* initiate a dialogue with Poe that will continue, becoming more intense, in subsequent works.

Fuentes's references to Poe become more explicit in *Cambio de piel* [*A Change of Skin*] (1967), a richly complex metafiction. The narrator's name — Freddy Lambert — reflects Fuentes's interest in the concept of will. It combines, as Fuentes explains, the first name of Friedrich Nietzsche and the last name of Balzac's character Louis Lambert. [5] In the unusual combination, Fuentes, as he often does, mixes historical reality with fiction. Both names allude to the will. Balzac's Louis Lambert is a Swedenborgian who believes that it is possible to create physical form outside the body in reality just as it is in dreams. The role of the will in the work of Nietzsche is well known.

All of the names in *Cambio de piel* have interesting connotations, but the one that seems most closely related philosophically to Freddy is the nickname "Ligeia," used to refer to Elizabeth. Three times in the novel Fuentes cites part of the epigraph to Poe's story "Ligeia": "Man doth not yield himself to the angels, nor unto death utterly, save only through weakness of his feeble will." [6] At the end of Poe's story, the suggestion is that Ligeia's return is made possible through an act of will — perhaps hers, as a result of her studies, or perhaps the narrator's because of his desire to re-create her. Poe also leaves open the possibility that the narrator is mad and is imagining Ligeia's return. [7] This same kind of rational explanation is possible in the case of Felipe Montero in *Aura* or that of Freddy in *Cambio de piel*, in which Fuentes offers different versions of the same ending. Freddy, who in one version is in an insane asylum, may be imagining or dreaming everything.

The names Freddy Lambert and Ligeia are also related to the theme of madness. Nietzsche went mad in autumn 1888; Louis Lambert was considered insane by those who could not understand his ideas. The narrator in Poe's story, perhaps mad, is certainly unreliable, and Ligeia herself is unusual. By combining these figures, Fuentes seems to be exploring both the desire for power and the power of the will literally to create (or re-create) a parallel reality. Fuentes is trying to subvert the certainty of what he feels is an unacceptable reality. Creating ambiguities, uncertainties, and alternatives liberates the reader by offering the freedom to choose — or, for that matter, the freedom not to choose or to remain uncertain. Fuentes uses Poe to help achieve his ends: Poe is a wonderfully appropriate choice because his work, too, "Ligeia" especially, is ambiguous and "multiple."[8]

Fuentes's complex novel *Terra Nostra* (1975) takes as its referent Spanish history and the colonization of the New World. Fuentes makes extended allusions to Poe's sea narratives, "A Descent into the Maelström," "MS. Found in a Bottle," and *The Narrative of Arthur Gordon Pym*, in ways that demonstrate his intimate knowledge of Poe. At one point he re-creates the texture of Poe's prose in "A Descent into the Maelström" so convincingly in Spanish that even a reader familiar with Poe's works could momentarily mistake the passage for a good translation. The passage describing the Peregrino in the vortex is very similar to Poe's mariner's description of the maelstrom.[9] Poe's and Fuentes's narrators, while whirling in the vortex, are awestruck as they look at the sky far above them and the abyss below. Both, however, recover their wits enough to make rational observations. Each measures the progress of the descent.

Fuentes's and Poe's protagonists observe surrounding objects in the whirlpool, note which sink and which stay afloat, and call upon their powers of observation to formulate a means for their salvation. After intense observation, Poe's character becomes aware that cylindrical objects tend to rise; acting on this knowledge, he lashes himself to a water cask. Fuentes's narrator makes similar observations, which lead to a similar course of action. Like Poe's fisherman, Fuentes's narrator concludes that salvation lies in being tied to an appropriately shaped object.

In his description of the narrator's "rational" behavior in the vortex, Fuentes's prose takes a humorous turn when the narrator says, "I counted with my fingers, I counted forty seconds for each turn — I counted them even when my fingers were hurting from counting them" (TN 370; 364). Although Poe does not introduce this kind of humor of deliberate incongruity into "A Descent into the Maelström," it frequently appears in his tales, for example, in "Metzengerstein" and "A Predicament."

Poe's young man with white hair suggests an ambiguity of time similar to that experienced by some of his other characters. The narrator of "Ligeia" does not know how long he knew her. The narrator in "Mystification" tells us that the Baron Ritzner Von Jung was "of no particular age; — by which I meant that it was impossible to form a guess respecting his age by any data personally afforded" (SF 456). And several of Poe's tales involve movement into different epochs: "Four Beasts in One; The HomoCameleopard," "Mellonta Tauta," and "Some Words with a Mummy." In *Terra Nostra* all times are one time.

Fuentes incorporates his extended allusion to Poe's tale completely into the context of his novel, making the experience in the vortex an entry into and an exit from a timeless New World. As the vortex carries the Peregrino to the New World, life and death come together. The Peregrino embodies the conflict of good and evil tendencies inherent in both indigenous Mexican and Spanish cultures. Such themes, of course, are entirely Fuentes's and not at all Poe's; Fuentes is using Poe for his own ends.

In *Terra Nostra*, when the Peregrino falls in a vertiginous descent into the center of the volcano, he passes from a region of blackness to one of whitest whiteness (TN 448–450; 441–443). There he sees two "shimmering white" figures — a woman and a man — and at their feet, a heap of white bones. The movement from black to white and the white figures are reminiscent of Poe's *The Narrative of Arthur Gordon Pym*.

As in Poe's sea tales, the vortex and the journey in Part Two of *Terra Nostra* are related to the idea of a rebirth, a mystical moment of awareness. When black and white, hot and cold, fire and ice, life and death meet, an epiphany occurs. Thus the fisherman in "A Descent into the Maelström" has his great insight, sees how to save himself, only after he has been terrified beyond despair into the state in which he perceives the "terrific grandeur" of the place in which he is to die. Pym has his dazzling vision at what seems to be the moment of his death (yet survives, apparently, to tell the tale); the narrator in "MS. Found in a Bottle," as we shall see, comes through doom to discovery.

Fuentes in *Terra Nostra*, like Poe in *Pym*, is writing both an adventure and a metafiction. The tales of adventure in *Terra Nostra* are contained within several layers of narration; the book involves telling and retelling stories in a way akin to, though much more complex than, Poe's use of a double narrator in *Pym*. Its tales of adventure, moreover, like Pym's, are of a "positively marvelous" nature.

A dimension of the metafictional aspect of *Terra Nostra* is related to the work's most obvious allusion to Poe — reference to the manuscript in a bottle. Poe confines "MS. Found in a Bottle" to one bottle containing one manuscript that relates the events in the tale. Fuentes uses a multiplicity of manuscripts and bottles, in groups of three.

In the intricate pattern of allusion in Fuentes's novel, the reference to manuscripts in bottles also serves to relate Poe to Columbus. This connection may or may not be conscious on Fuentes's part; whatever the case, reflections of works by Poe and Columbus appear together. Fuentes's prose descriptions of the Peregrino's arrival in the New World, after he is caught in the vortex, echo certain passages in Columbus's *Diaries*: for example, the description of his sense of wonder (TN 374; 368) and the description of the hair and color of the indigenous people (TN 383–384; 377).

Burton Pollin has pointed out that Poe and his contemporaries knew well the books of Bernardin de Saint-Pierre, in whose *Études* Columbus is said to have put a message in a bottle; Pollin believes that Poe is referring to Columbus in his tale.[10] If Pollin is correct (he generally is), this means that in "MS. Found in a Bottle," Poe, like Fuentes, was combining references to history (Columbus) and to folklore (the Flying Dutchman). Like Fuentes's contemporary narrator in *Terra Nostra* who meets historical, fictional, and mythological figures from different periods, Poe's contemporary narrator in "MS. Found in a Bottle" meets a phantom crew from another time. The mystic word that appears upon the sail of Poe's Flying Dutchman is "Discovery," a word certainly suggestive in the contexts of Columbus and of manuscripts in bottles.

It would be inaccurate to claim that the patterns of juxtaposition of time and place in the works of the two authors, however striking or similar, mean precisely the same thing. Poe's juxtapositions are for irony, effect, or play. Fuentes's are more pointedly part of a unified social and aesthetic theory. But the congruence in the use of the juxtapositions is so strong that we suggest it is another reason for Carlos Fuentes's fondness for Poe: he feels for him both a spiritual and technical affinity.

A curious effect of our examination of Fuentes's use of Poe is an altered perception of Poe's work. Borges suggests that Kafka "creates a precursor" in Hawthorne; in a sense Fuentes creates his own precursor in Edgar Allan Poe. His allusions make characteristics of Poe's prose seem different now and suggest yet another way to "read" Poe.

NOTES

1. This chapter is a condensation of our article "Poe and Fuentes: The Reader's Prerogatives," *Comparative Literature* 36.1 (1984): 34–53.

2. In *La nueva novela hispanoamericana* (Mexico City: 1969), Fuentes says that certain authors "regresaron a las raíces poéticas de la literature y . . . cearon una convención representativa de la realidad que pretende ser totalizante en cuanto inventa una segunda realidad, una realidad paralela" (19). Referring to his own novel *Cambio de piel*, Fuentes said in an interview with Emir Rodríguez Monegal, "No pretende nunca al reflejo de la realidad. Pretende ser una ficción radical hasta sus últimas consecuencias" ("Situación del escritor en América Latina," *Mundo Nuevo* 1 [July 1966]: 10).

3. Luis Agüero, "Aura," *Casa de las Américas* 15–16 (1962–1963): 42. In a more recent discussion of the work, Fuentes traces his story line to an ancient collection of Chinese stories. See *Valiente mundo nuevo* (Madrid: Mondadori España S.A., 1990), pp. 153–154.

4. In "The Interpretation of 'Ligeia,'" *College English* 5 (April 1944): 363–372, Roy P. Basler argues that the struggle to overcome death — the struggle suggested by the motto of the tale — is the narrator's, not Ligeia's. A discussion of further ambiguities in the tale appears in Stuart Levine, *Edgar Poe: Seer and Craftsman* (Deland, Fla.: Everett/Edwards, 1972), pp. 28–37.

5. Herman P. Doezema, "An Interview with Carlos Fuentes," *Modern Fiction Studies* 18.4 (1972–1973): 497.

6. Carlos Fuentes, *Cambio de piel* (Mexico City: Joaquín Mortiz, 1967), pp. 131, 290, 404. "Ligeia," in *The Short Fiction of Edgar Allan Poe: An Annotated Edition*, ed. Stuart Levine and Susan Levine (Urbana: U of Illinois P, 1990), p. 79; hereafter cited as SF.

7. "Ligeia" is one of the stories in which the reader is given evidence that allows alternative interpretations of what actually occurs. Levine and Levine discuss this matter in SF 64, 104.

8. Perhaps a third of Poe's tales show multiple intention, as when a horror story, for instance, conceals literary satire. For examples of Poe's practice, see especially Section 12, "Multiple Intention," in SF, 471 ff.

9. See Carlos Fuentes, *Terra Nostra* (Mexico City: Joaquín Mortiz, 1975), p. 370; *Terra Nostra*, trans. Margaret Sayers Peden (New York: Farrar, Straus and Giroux, 1976), p. 364. Hereafter page references to *Terra Nostra* will be cited in the text as TN: the first refers to the Spanish original, the second (after a semicolon) to the English translation. See also SF 47–48.

10. Burton Pollin, "Poe's Use of Material from Bernardin de Saint-Pierre's *Etudes*," *Romance Notes* 12.2 (1971): 1–8.

# Horacio Quiroga

MARY G. BERG

One of the major Latin American fiction writers of the twentieth century, Horacio Quiroga (1878–1937) was born in Salto, Uruguay; attended school in Salto and Montevideo; and became interested at an early age in photography, chemistry, mechanics, and writing. A great admirer of Poe, he published numerous Poe-influenced stories and novels. His best-known works include the novel *Historia de un amor turbio* [Story of an obsessive love] (1908) and his collection of tales *Cuentos de amor de locura y de muerte* [Stories of love, madness, and death] (1917).

The stories, essays, and poems of Edgar Allan Poe were a major literary presence for all Latin American writers honing their skills around the turn of the twentieth century. It was a generation brushed by the wings of Poe's raven, as José Pablo Rivas remarked in 1916.[1] Rubén Darío's inclusion of Poe, whom he compares to Shakespeare, in *Los raros* [The exceptional ones] (1896) ensured attention. But few young writers apprenticed themselves to Poe quite as openly and obsessively as Horacio Quiroga. Years later, in his "Decálogo del perfecto cuentista" ["Decalogue of the Perfect Storyteller"] (1927), Quiroga advised beginning writers to "believe in a master — Poe, Maupassant, Kipling, Chekov — as in God Himself. . . . Resist imitation whenever possible, but go ahead and imitate if the influence is overwhelmingly strong. Above all, the development of personality is a lengthy process."[2] In Quiroga's case, Poe was his avowed master and lifelong soul mate, and many of his early stories flaunt this apprenticeship. His earliest fragments of imaginative prose (1896), his first stories published in *Revista del Salto* [Salto review] (1899), and his first book, *Los arrecifes de coral* [The coral reefs] (1901), published when he was only twenty-two, all reveal unassimilated borrowings from and imitations of Poe. Quiroga was obsessed with doubles, violent death, hallucination, monomania, neurotic guilt, and persecution anxiety. His readings of Poe would evolve as he matured as a writer, but his sense of intimate identification with Poe's topics and concerns endured. Ezequiel Martínez Estrada, one of Quiroga's close friends and his biographer, speaks in a memoir of how even in later years Quiroga remembered all of Poe's stories almost word for word and acknowledged their profound influence on him.[3]

Many of Quiroga's earliest known fragments of imaginative prose are stories of doubles, obsessions, hysteria, and split personalities that show clear awareness of such stories as "The Black Cat," "The Pit and the Pendulum," "The Tell-Tale Heart," and "William Wilson."[4] In "Fantasia nerviosa" ["Nervous Fantasy"], Quiroga's first published story, which appeared in *Revista del Salto* on October 2, 1899, the protagonist goes wild, rushes out and kills two women, then returns home to find one of them in his bed. Again in "Para noche de insomnio" ["For a Night of Insomnia"], published in the same magazine on November 6 of that year, a dead man comes horribly alive — alive in the same eerie, unreal sense as Poe's Ligeia, Mr. Shuttleworthy, or Morella. Quiroga even prefaces this story with an acknowledgment of his indebtedness to Poe, citing a long quotation about hallucination from Baudelaire's introduction to *Histoires extraordinaires*. The story itself is composed of a series of scenes of horror in which the narrator is grotesquely conscious of the presence of the dead body of his friend, who has committed suicide. Frozen in a dreamlike trance of horror, the narrator and his friends become aware that the corpse is watching them as they sit with it through the night. Tiny details and repetitions of description build up an unbearable tension and a sense that something dreadful is about to happen, the same sense of imminent nightmare Poe creates in such stories as "The Fall of the House of Usher" and "The Masque of the Red Death."

The first of Quiroga's two retellings of "The Cask of Amontillado" also has a dreamlike quality to it. In the 1901 version, which bears the title of the Poe story, Quiroga begins by summarizing Poe's tale, then switches abruptly to his own, paraphrasing and changing the Poe version, writing his story on top of the Poe text while his narrator chortles maniacally at the interplay. Quiroga's Fortunato and Montresor stand in front of a mirror watching their images (doubles) in the glass, trying on the images (doubles) of the Poe story. Fortunato tells the narrator about his adventures in the Poe story (with Poe in the role of Montresor), and as they get drunk together, that story is repeated with the characters switched around, as in a mirror image. The narrator is amused that his friend Fortunato is exactly like Poe's Fortunato until Poe's story is strangely reversed.

The narrator of "El crimen del otro" ["The Crime of the Other"] (1904) is also quite sure that he is sane and that it is his friend Fortunato who is mad. In both this story and "Los perseguidos" ["The Pursued"] (1905), the narrator goes to great lengths, just as do Poe's murderers, to demonstrate that he may seem a little nervous but is really altogether rational, while proving with his very self-defensive vehemence that the opposite is so. In "El crimen del otro" we are told that "Poe was the only writer I was reading at that time; that cursed madman had come to dominate me completely; every book on my table was by him. My head was crammed full of Poe. . . . Ligeia! How I adored that story! All of them and intensely: Valdemar, . . . Dupin, . . . the Espanayes, . . . Berenice . . . they were all familiar to me. But of them all, 'The Cask of Amontillado' had seduced me as though it were my very own."[5] He spends hours reading and rereading the story; he corners and reads to his friend Fortunato, who finally becomes even more obsessed with Poe than the narrator. In long arguments about the nature of insanity, each thinks the other quite mad. For Quiroga's narrator, Poe's stories become indistinguishable from reality; their identities become kaleidoscopic, encompassing Poe's characters and Poe himself. The story goes on to further explore the boundaries between sanity and insanity, the rational and the irrational, with continued references to Poe's stories.

Once Quiroga was past the early years of his apprenticeship, his explicit references to Poe are less frequent and not as extensive, but they continue to appear and are more deeply embedded in the narratives. The spiritual, emotional, and thematic affinities endure. It is as though Quiroga had internalized and assimilated Poe's texts so fully that nearly every story Quiroga wrote can be connected in some way to his mentor. His tales are fully his own but with an acute awareness of Poe's words. Quiroga's "Berenice" (1915) centers upon a ten-year-old girl so hypersensitive to music that she ages a lifetime during the first performance of the overture of Wagner's "Tristan and Isolde," then lives out the rest of her life as a wrinkled crone in a state of catalepsy, just as the beautiful child in Poe's "Berenice" is afflicted with a sudden disease that ages her beyond recognition. The narrator's obsession with teeth in Poe's "Berenice" is echoed in other Quiroga stories, such as "La lengua" [The tongue] (1906), where a vengeful dentist hacks out his enemy's tongue. The unwholesome Fortunato-Montresor relationship is apparent in "La lengua" and in dozens of other stories. The murderous orangutan of "The Murders in the Rue Morgue" is echoed in "La historia de Estilicón" ["Estilicón's Story"] (1904); traces of "The Mystery of Marie Rogêt" haunt "El triple robo de Bellamore" ["The Triple Robbery of Bellamore"] (1903); and qualities of "MS. Found in a Bottle" are conspicuous in "Los buques suicidantes" ["The Suicidal Ships"] (1906).

Poe and Quiroga shared a fascination with vampirism and a sadomasochistic preoccupation with death. In one of Quiroga's most famous stories, "El almohadón de pluma" ["The Feather Pillow"] (1907), in which a young wife is gradually drained of her life's blood by a parasite hiding in her pillow, her death is both a horror and a relief to her unloving husband, just as Morella's husband lets her fade away. Like Poe's "The Facts in the Case of Mr. Valde-mar," which reflects Poe's interest in mesmerism and the possibility that sheer will power can hold death at bay, as it does for Ligeia or Morella, Quiroga's "El vampiro" ["The Vampire"] (1927) reflects his fascination with the techni-cal advances of cinematography, his obsession with doubles, and his lifelong interest in the boundaries between life and death. Films, like mirrors, show images that both reflect and distort. Quiroga, like Poe, is deeply intrigued by pairs of doubles who destroy each other, often in a relationship with a third person, usually a narrator/witness, a destructive triangle. Other Quiroga sto-ries about photography and films, "El retrato" ["The Portrait"], "Miss Doro-thy Phillips, mi esposa" ["Miss Dorothy Phillips, My Wife"], "El espectro" ["The Spectre"], and "El puritano" ["The Puritan"], include explicit aware-ness of such Poe stories as "The Oval Portrait"; "El puritano" also ends with the death of the living woman so that the idealized image may "live" and be preserved.

Margo Glantz, in "Poe en Quiroga" ["Poe in Quiroga"], has discussed how Poe often describes a world fragmented into mind-filling yet miniscule ob-jects: Berenice's teeth, Usher's ear, the malign eye of "The Tell-Tale Heart," Ligeia's gaze — embodiments of an external world of solitude and destruc-tion. Turning in upon himself, Poe's narrator finds a similar horror, the de-mon of perversity. Glantz sees the same double horror in Quiroga, as he faces the succubi of irrationality and obsession within himself, while without, "his relationship with nature leads him to inexorable death."[6]

Many critics have commented, as did John Englekirk, that "no other His-panic prose writer has so vividly expressed the spirit of Poe's tales as has Horacio Quiroga."[7] Certainly Quiroga felt an extraordinary lifelong affinity with Poe, with his life story as well as with his topics, techniques, and emo-tions. From his early narrative exegeses of "The Cask of Amontillado" to his more complex later explorations of perversity, the irrational, the most extreme horrors and permutations of madness, and the balance (or imbalance) of sanity and insanity, acceptable and unacceptable behavior, or creativity and destructiveness, Quiroga incorporated what he learned from Poe about inci-sive drama and narrative immediacy and applied it to his own extraordinary stories of life on the frontiers of civilization and of sanity.

NOTES

1. José Pablo Rivas, "Rubén Darío," *Estudio* 13 (May 1916), 368–373; quoted in John E. Englekirk Jr., *Edgar Allan Poe in Hispanic Literature* (New York: Instituto de las Españas, 1934; rpt. New York: Russell and Russell, 1972) p. 168.

2. "Decálogo del perfecto cuentista" was first published in *Babel* (Buenos Aires), July 1927. This citation is from Horacio Quiroga, *Todos los cuentos*, ed. Napoleón Baccino Ponce de León and Jorge Lafforgue (Madrid: Colección Archivos, 1993), p. 1194.

3. Ezequiel Martínez Estrada, *El hermano Quiroga* (Montevideo: Editorial Arca, 1966), p. 73.

4. These early stories were published after Quiroga's death in the appendix of an edition of his 1900 *Diario de viaje a París* (Montevideo: Imprenta El Siglo Ilustrado, 1950).

5. Quiroga, *Todos los cuentos*, p. 872.

6. Margo Glantz, "Poe en Quiroga," in *Aproximaciones a Horacio Quiroga*, ed. Angel Flores (Caracas: Monte Avila, 1976), pp. 93–118.

7. Englekirk, *Edgar Allan Poe*, p. 340.

# Tanizaki Junichiro

NORIKO MIZUTA LIPPIT

The representative author of modern Japanese Aesthetic literature, Tanizaki Junichiro (1886–1965) built a self-sustained world of his own *monogatari*, a Japanese narrative genre of storytelling close to that of romance, exploring the realm of classical Japanese literature, folktales, and legends. He left behind thirty volumes of collected works which include novels, plays, tales, essays, and three versions of his translation into modern Japanese of the *Tale of Genji*.

Among the modern Japanese writers whose works reflect the influences of Poe, Tanizaki Junichiro stands unique. Tanizaki not only began his career under the influence of Poe but also developed his early Poesque world of the grotesque and arabesque into his own self-contained world of Romanticism in the Japanese literary tradition, with the pursuit of the unattainable supernal beauty as the major theme.

Critics of Tanizaki usually agree that although Tanizaki, like other Taisho writers, began his career under the spell of the West — with the influences of Poe, Baudelaire, and Wilde, among others, apparent in many of his early works — his main sources of influence were the Japanese literatures of the seventeenth and eighteenth centuries, especially the erotic and sadistic stories of *Kusazoshi* and *kabuki* plays. According to the orthodox view, the influence of Western writers, especially Poe, became superficial by the end of the Taisho period (1912–1926).[1] Drawn to both East and West, Tanizaki, after a period of severe internal conflict because of the two attractions, turned completely to the world of classical Japanese literature and made a conscious artistic effort to link his later works to his Japanese heritage. Tanizaki's Japanese- rather than Western-oriented works in his later period (beginning with his move to the Kansai area after the Kanto earthquake), however, even more strongly reveal the closeness to Poe's mythical world of supernal beauty, the original state reached only through destructive transcendence. In his later works Tanizaki, like Poe, integrates the grotesque into his Romanticism, turning the grotesque even more clearly into a positive although paradoxical symbol for ideal beauty, a tragicomic path of his heroes' search for the lost original home.

Tanizaki's creative works can be divided roughly into three periods: the first begins around 1910 and ends with *Tadekuu mushi* [*Some Prefer Nettles*] in 1928; the third starts with *Kagi* [*The Key*] in 1956.[2] It is in the first period that Western influences, including Poe's, are most evident. We can find many themes, expressions, descriptions, and stories reminiscent of Poe.

The major themes of Tanizaki's early works are the fear of death, the sadomasochistic pursuit of feminine beauty, the discovery of perversity or cruelty in human nature, and the relation of art to these themes. As a young man Tanizaki suffered from a strange nervous condition manifested in sudden seizures of fear, especially a fear of trains. In many of his tales, he describes this as a fear of persecution, a fear of madness and death. The narrator of "Kyofu" ["The Fear"] (1913) explains that his heart starts beating rapidly the minute he enters a moving vehicle. The drumming of his heart increases in speed and intensity, and he feels as if all his blood were rushing to his head, with his body about to burst into pieces or his brain into madness. This description immediately reminds us of Poe's in "The Imp of the Perverse" and "The Tell-Tale Heart," where the narrators burst into self-destructive confessions of their crimes, urged on by the ever-growing sound of their hearts.

In "Seishun Monogatari" ["My Adolescent Days"] (1932) Tanizaki said that he could not exalt death or madness as did Takayama Chogyu, a Romantic writer of a decade earlier. Instead, when he read Poe, Baudelaire, Strindberg, and Gorky, anxiety and fear permeated his nervous system, distorting his senses and his emotional responses to things. The fear of the explosion of his body and brain could be ignited at any time and place by the slightest sensory stimulus, for it had no concrete external source. These overwhelming feelings are repesented in Tanizaki's tales in terms of the dizziness experienced when standing at the edge of an abyss, a sensation of extreme fear and pain that might culminate in the total loss of his sanity.

The fear is clearly that of death and persecution, yet Tanizaki, unlike Poe, gives death itself a very small role in his works. Furthermore, the fear of death is actually the fear of his own urge toward self-destruction. The fear, therefore, can be called a "pleasurable pain," and its source is entirely internal. The protagonist's urge toward self-destruction is indeed what Poe called "the imp of the perverse." In fact, to evoke this state of pleasurable pain, of the abysmal terror of self-destruction, is the purpose of the protagonists' diabolic actions in almost all of Tanizaki's works and is their major theme.

Many of Tanizaki's tales were obviously inspired by Poe's crime and detective stories.[3] In Tanizaki's "Kin to gin" ["Gold and Silver"], "Zenkamono" ["The Criminal"], "Yanagiyu no jiken" ["An Incident at Yanagiyu"], and "Norowareta gikyoku" ["The Cursed Play"], we find many devices and techniques used by Poe, including the Dupin-narrator relationship. In most cases the criminals' extreme sadism, the analytical precision with which they murder and hide the corpse, and their observations on criminal psychology vividly reveal their fascination with evil and gratuitous cruelty and their concern with making murder a work of art. The discovery of one's own perversity is related to the theme of the double; Tanizaki wrote several tales, such as "A Story of Tomoda and Matsunaga," in which he deals explicitly with the double and doppelgänger.[4]

Yet the sadism of the Tanizaki's characters is often masochistic. In "Hakuchyukigo" ["The Devil at Noon"] (1918) the protagonist, after witnessing a grotesque murder carried out by a beautiful woman, offers to be murdered by the same woman. He asks a friend to witness the scene of his own cruel death. "Hokan" ["A Harlequin"] (1911), a masterpiece of the early period, is the story of a man who takes uncontrollable pleasure in humiliating himself and in pleasing others by allowing them to control and manipulate him. The protagonist feels a strong sense of himself, a unity of consciousness, by existing only in the other's image of himself.

Tanizaki's grotesque world of perversity is obviously similar to Poe's. In the latter's crime stories, the main characters commit sadistic, gratuitous crimes, which are often followed by self-destructive confessions. In "The Black Cat," for example, the main character perceives the ominous otherness in the cat's eyes and brutally murders it. The same pattern appears in "The Tell-Tale Heart," in which the hero is provoked to cruel murder by the old man's vulturelike eye. The act of evil for evil's sake is as masochistic as it is diabolic; the pure evil is directed against himself, to vex his own soul so that he can be immersed in the immediacy of pain and terror. In both Poe and Tanizaki, the diabolism is actually directed toward the protagonists themselves as a method of including pain and ecstasy and of intoxicating the reflecting consciousness in the immediacy of pain.

In Tanizaki's works the themes of the discovery of perversity in human nature and the masochistic desire for self-destruction are intertwined and are furthermore related to his other major theme, the pursuit of the femme fatale. In all of Tanizaki's stories in which the femme fatale is the main theme, the protagonists are involved in drawing out the diabolic nature of beautiful women, thus molding them into ideal women, black widow spiders that devour males after sexual ecstasy. The creation of the cruel, beautiful woman is the externalization of the hero's inner desire, and in actuality she is his puppet. This can be seen most readily in "Chijin no ai" ["A Fool's Love"] (1924). Tanizaki's characters, however, do not pursue beautiful women for the sake of erotic fulfillment. Rather, they pursue an unattainable absolute, the symbolic essence of feminine beauty. In his early period the beauty is typically revealed in human flesh, but it is human flesh as objet d'art which refuses normal erotic communication: Tanizaki's heroes find the essence of feminine beauty in women's feet.

For Tanizaki the eternal woman is first of all unreachable. In "Ningyo no Nageki" ["The Sorrow of the Mermaid"] (1919) he describes the mermaid's mysterious beauty, which absorbs the whole existence of the hero and is fully revealed in her immense, unfathomable eyes. Her "divine orbs" look as if they are gazing at eternity from the depth of her soul. The reader is reminded of Poe's description of Ligeia's eyes, which make the hero feel the approach of the full knowledge of eternity. The unattainable beauty gradually takes a more distinct form in Tanizaki's later works as both the beauty of eternal maternity, from which the hero is alienated, and that of the classical Japanese court lady hidden behind a thick screen.

Poe's supernal beauty is also unattainable. His myth of the poet's return to original unity presents a drama of the poet in search of the beauty that exists only in the original paradise, the origin of life itself. Poe's ideal woman is doomed to die. Both Ligeia and Eleonora, whose beauty symbolizes humanity's original state of harmony and the aspiration for it, die and thus become unattainable for the protagonists. They may even have existed only in the protagonists' dreams. Following this aspiration for supernal beauty, the main characters enter the path of self-annihilation, returning to the original condition of nothingness.

Supernal beauty is attained only through self-destruction. The grotesque in Poe is a symbol of decadent human nature and reality, the result of the Fall, as well as a symbol that points toward transcendence of the decadent. In Tanizaki, too, the grotesque serves not merely to induce sensuous pleasure but as a means of entering his dreamworld, of returning home. It is a means of the hero's assuring his sense of life, a sense which he cannot obtain in the modern, industrial world. The origin and function of Tanizaki's grotesque are also legitimized by this creation of a romantic world of dream.

The similarities and differences between the two authors' concepts of art can best be illustrated by comparing "The Domain of Arnheim" with Tanizaki's "Konjiki no shi" ["The Golden Death"] (1914), which is based almost entirely on Poe's tale. In both stories the narrator describes a friend, extravagantly rich and poetic in nature, who attempts the creation of an earthly paradise. In both cases the narrator's visit to the site produces the climax, and in both the narrator finds that original nature has been transformed by art, creating an extremely bizarre and bewildering earthly paradise. It was Poe's and Tanizaki's pleasure dome, which their art, by correcting nature, created. In "The Golden Death" the end of the hero's dream is also death. Yet the purpose of his art is not to cause death itself but to bring about a state of extreme sensuous intoxication, so extreme as to risk self-destruction. Tanizaki's paradise is more voluptuous and erotic than Poe's.

The narrators of both tales are "objective" observers who witness the heroes' grotesque endeavors to create their own paradises. While Poe's narrator gradually becomes involved in the drama of the hero and at the end becomes almost his double, Tanizaki's narrator remains a rational man who escapes from the intoxicating effect of paradise. Although he calls the hero a great artist, the narrator maintains the distance between the rational reader and the grotesque hero. In Tanizaki, too, the dual or ironic point of view that regards the hero both as absurd and mad and as a positive artist is present.

Tanizaki was fascinated by the Gothic themes presented in the writings of Baudelaire, Wilde, and Poe, such as the ties between love and cruelty, pleasure and pain, and domination and humiliation, and he tried to dramatize them in his own language and in the natural settings of Japanese life. The fact that he later turned to the world of classical beauty did not mean that he had discarded these themes and Western influences. On the contrary, he developed these same ideas more fully and uniquely within the tradition of Japanese culture. Poe's influence on Tanizaki is significant, especially Poe's concept of supernal beauty, his hero's tragicomic drama of the search for it, and the role of the grotesque in this drama.

NOTES

1. Edward Seidensticker acknowledges the similarity of Tanizaki's themes to those of Poe, although he dismisses Poe's influence on Tanizaki as insignificant. See *Tanizaki Junichiro*, ed. Nihon Bungaku Kenkyu Shiryo Kankokai (Tokyo: Yuseido, 1972), p. 95. Ohashi Kenzaburo points out Tanizaki's "deep empathy with the tradition of western Romanticism." He says, however, that Tanizaki's world is "different from both Poe's Gothic romance and Baudelaire's symbolism and Western *fin de siècle* decadence" and argues rather that Tanizaki's works are similar to Hawthorne's because of their ethical

qualities. See "Tanizaki to Poe," in *Tanizaki Junichiro kenkyu*, ed. Ara Masato (Tokyo: Yagi Shoten, 1972), pp. 434–445.

2. *Tanizaki Junichiro zenshu*, 30 vols. (Tokyo: Chuokoron-sha, 1981).

3. For a discussion of Tanizaki's detective and mystery stories, see Nakajima Kawataro, "Tanizaki to misterii," in *Tanizaki Junichiro kenkyu*, pp. 419–433.

4. For a discussion of Tanizaki's theme of the double and doppelgänger, see Hara Shiro, "Shoki no sakuhin o dokkai suru," in *Tanizaki Junichiro kenkyu*, pp. 119–141.

# Selected Bibliography

The notes to each chapter contain detailed references to sources in many foreign languages too numerous to list here. This selected bibliography gives the most important references in English (and a few in French) that deal with Poe's influence and reputation abroad. After the first two sections, the references are presented in alphabetical order by language groups, regions, or individual countries. For illustrated editions of Poe published in foreign countries, consult Burton R. Pollin's *Images of Poe's Works*.

## Poe Bibliographies with International References

Argersinger, Jana L., and Steven Gregg. "Subject Index to 'International Poe Bibliography': Poe Scholarship and Criticism, 1983–1988." *Poe Studies* 24.1–2 (1991): 1–48.

"Current Poe Bibliography" and "International Poe Bibliography," *Poe Studies. Poe Studies* began as *Poe Newsletter* (1968–1970), then was renamed *Poe Studies* in 1971. The journal is published by Washington State University.

Dameron, J. Lasley, and Irby B. Cauthen Jr. *Edgar Allan Poe: A Bibliography of Criticism: 1827–1967*. Charlottesville: UP of Virginia, 1974.

Hyneman, Ester. *Edgar Allan Poe: An Annotated Bibliography of Books and Articles in English: 1827–1973*. Boston: Hall, 1974.

## Books Dealing Wholly or in Part with Poe Abroad

*American Literary Scholarship*. Durham, N.C.: Duke UP. An annual volume with a chapter on Poe that includes sections on Poe's influence and studies by foreign authors.

Bandy, W. T. *The Influence and Reputation of Edgar Allan Poe in Europe*. Baltimore: F. T. Cimino, 1962.

Braddy, Haldeen. *Glorious Incense: The Fulfillment of Edgar Allan Poe*. Port Washington, N.Y.: Kennikat P, 1953; rpt. 1968.

Carlson, Eric W., ed. *The Recognition of Edgar Allan Poe: Selected Criticism since 1829*. Ann Arbor: U of Michigan P, 1966.

———, ed. *Critical Essays on Edgar Allan Poe*. Boston: G. K. Hall, 1987.

———, ed. *A Companion to Poe Studies*. Westport, Conn.: Greenwood P, 1996.

Fisher, Benjamin F., ed. *Poe and Our Times: Influences and Affinities*. Baltimore: Edgar Allan Poe Society, 1986.

————, ed. *Poe and His Times: The Artist and His Milieu*. Baltimore: Edgar Allan Poe Society, 1990.

Frank, Frederick S., and Anthony Magistrale. *The Poe Encyclopedia*. Westport, Conn.: Greenwood P, 1997.

French, John C. *Poe in Foreign Lands and Tongues*. Baltimore: Johns Hopkins UP, 1941.

Meyers, Jeffrey. *Edgar Allan Poe, His Life and Legacy*. New York: Scribner's, 1992.

Pollin, Burton R. *Insights and Outlooks, Essays on Great Writers*. New York: Gordian, 1986.

————. *Images of Poe's Works: A Comprehensive Descriptive Catalogue of Illustrations*. Westport, Conn.: Greenwood P, 1989.

Smith, C. Alphonso. *Edgar Allan Poe, How to Know Him*. Garden City, N.Y.: Garden City Publishing, 1921.

Wilson, Edmund. "Poe at Home and Abroad." *New Republic*, December 8, 1926; rpt. Carlson, *Recognition*.

## Arabic

Abdul-Hai, Muhammad. "A Bibliography of Arabic Translations of English and American Poetry, 1830–1970." *Journal of Arabic Literature* 7 (1976): 120–150.

## Brazil

Bellei, Sérgio Luiz Prado. "'The Raven,' by Machado de Assis." *Luzo-Brazilian Review* 25.2 (Winter 1988): 1–13.

## China

Ning, Sheng, and Donald B. Stauffer. "Poe's Influence on Modern Chinese Literature." *University of Mississippi Studies in English* New Series 3 (1982): 155–182.

## Croatia

Bašić, Sonja. "Edgar Allan Poe in Croatian and Serbian Literature." *Studia Romanica et Anglica Zagrabiensia* 21–22 (1966): 305–319.

## Czech

Babler, O. F. "Czech Translations of Poe's 'The Raven.'" *Notes & Queries* 192 (May 31, 1947): 235.

Škvorecký, Josef. "A Discovery in Capek." *Armchair Detective* 8 (1975): 180–184.

## Estonia

Sool, Reet. "Edgar Allan Poe in Estonian, Notes on Critical Reception and Method." *Uchenie Zapiski Tartuskogo Universiteta* 792 (1988): 77–86.

*France*

Alexander, Jean. *Affidavits of Genius: Edgar Allan Poe and the French Critics, 1847–1924*. Port Washington, N.Y.: Kennikat P, 1971.

Bachelard, Gaston. *La Psychanalyse du feu*. Paris: Gallimard, 1938.

———. "Introduction." *Aventures d'Arthur Gordon Pym*. Trans. Charles Baudelaire. Paris: Stock, 1944.

———. *The Psychoanalysis of Fire*. Trans. Alan C. M. Ross. Boston: Beacon P, 1964.

Bandy, W. T. "New Light on Baudelaire and Poe." *Yale French Studies* 10 (1952): 65–69.

———. *Edgar Allan Poe: Sa Vie et ses ouvrages*. Toronto: U of Toronto P, 1973.

Barthes, Roland. "Textual Analysis of Poe's 'Valdemar.'" In *Untying the Text: A Post-Structuralist Reader*. 1981, London: Routledge. 1987.

Baudelaire, Charles. *Baudelaire on Poe*. Ed. and trans. Lois Hyslop and Francis E. Hyslop Jr. State College, Penn.: Bald Eagle P, 1952.

———. "Edgar Allan Poe, His Life and Works." Trans. Jean Alexander. In Alexander, *Affidavits of Genius*.

Bonaparte, Marie. *Edgar Poe: Sa vie, son oeuvre — Etude psychanalytique*. Paris: Demoel et Steele, 1933.

———. *The Life and Works of Edgar Allan Poe: A Psycho-Analytic Interpretation*. Trans. John Rodker. London: Hogarth P, 1949.

Bonnet, Jean-Marie, and Claude Richard. "Raising the Wind; or the French Editions of Edgar Allan Poe." *Poe Newsletter* 1.1 (1968): 11–13.

Cambiaire, Célestin Pierre. *The Influence of Edgar Allan Poe in France*. 1927. New York: Stechert, 1970.

Caws, Mary Ann. "Insertion in an Oval Frame: Poe Circumscribed by Baudelaire." *French Review* 56.5 (April 1983): 679–787; 56.6 (May 1983): 885–895.

Chiari, Joseph. *Symbolisme from Poe to Mallarmé*. 1956. New York: Gordian P, 1970.

Cluny, Claude Michel, ed. *Le Livre des quatre corbeaux*. Paris: Editions de la Différence, 1985.

Eliot, T. S. "From Poe to Valéry." *Hudson Review* 2 (1949): 327-342; rpt. in Carlson, *Recognition*.

Forclaz, Roger. *Le Monde d'Edgar Poe*. Berne: Herbert Lang, 1974.

———. "Edgar Poe and France: Toward the End of a Myth?" Trans. J. Kelly Morris. In Fisher, *Poe and Our Times*.

Forgues, E.-D. "The Tales of Edgar A. Poe." Trans. and rpt. in Alexander, *Affidavits of Genius*.

Lawler, James. *Edgar Poe et les poètes français*. Paris: Julliard, 1989.

Lloyd, Rosemary. "Baudelaire's Creative Criticism." *French Studies* 36.1 (January 1982): 37–44.

———. *Selected Letters of Baudelaire: The Conquest of Solitude*. Chicago: U of Chicago P, 1986.

Lombardo, Patrizia. *Edgar Poe et la modernité*. Birmingham, Ala.: Summa Publications, 1985.

Mallarmé, Stéphane. *Oeuvres complètes*, ed. Henri Mondor and G. Jean-Aubry. 1945. Paris: Gallimard, 1961.

Muller, John P., and William J. Richardson, eds. *The Purloined Poe: Lacan, Derrida & Psychoanalytic Reading*. Baltimore: Johns Hopkins UP, 1988.

Quinn, Patrick F. *The French Face of Edgar Poe*. Carbondale: Southern Illinois UP, 1957.

———. *Poe and France: The Last Twenty Years*. Baltimore: Enoch Pratt Free Library, 1970.

Ricardou, Jean. "Gold in the Bug." *Poe Studies* 9.2 (December 1976): 33–39.

Richard, Claude. "André Breton et Edgar Poe." *Nouvelle Revue Française* 172 (April 1967): 926–936.

———. "Poe Studies in Europe: France." *Poe Newsletter* 2.1 (1969): 20–22.

———. *Cahier: Edgar Allan Poe*. Paris: Herne, 1974.

———. *Poe: Journaliste et critique*. Paris: Klincksieck, 1978.

Sprout, Monique. "The Influence of Poe on Jules Verne." *Revue de littérature comparée* 41 (1967): 37–53.

Valéry, Paul. *Leonardo, Poe, Mallarmé*. Trans. Malcolm Cowley and James R. Lawler; ed. Jackson Mathews. Princeton, N.J.: Princeton UP, 1972.

Vines, Lois Davis. "Dupin-Teste, Poe's Direct Influence on Valéry." *French Forum* 2.2 (1977): 147–159.

———. "Paul Valéry and the Poe Legacy in France." In Fisher, *Poe in Our Times*, pp. 1–8.

———. *Valéry and Poe: A Literary Legacy*. New York: New York UP, 1992.

———. "Edgar Allan Poe: A Writer for the World." In Carlson, *A Companion to Poe Studies*.

## Germany and Austria

Forclaz, Roger. "A German Edition of Poe." *Poe Studies* 9.1 (June 1976): 24–26.

———. "Poe in Europe — Recent German Criticism." *Poe Studies* 11.2 (December 1978): 49–55.

Hansen, Thomas S. "Arno Schmidt's Reception of Edgar Allan Poe: Or, the Domain of Arn(o)heim." *Review of Contemporary Fiction* 8.1 (Spring 1988): 166–181 (special issue on Arno Schmidt, ed. F. Peter Ott).

Hoffmann, Gerhard. "Edgar Allan Poe and German Literature." In *American-German Literary Interrelations in the Nineteenth Century*, ed. Christoph Wecker. Munich: Wilhelm Fink Verlag, 1983.

Hofrichter, Laura. "From Poe to Kafka." *University of Toronto Quarterly* 29 (1959–1960): 405–419.

Lyons, Nathan. "Kafka and Poe — and Hope." *Minnesota Review* 5 (1965): 158–168.

*Great Britain*

Hutcherson, Dudley R. "Poe's Reputation in England and America 1850–1909." *American Literature* 14.1 (1942): 211–233.

Kronegger, M. E. "Joyce's Debt to Poe and the French Symbolists." *Revue de Littérature Comparée* 39 (1965): 243–254.

Lawrence, D. H. "Edgar Allan Poe." *English Review* (April 1919). Rpt. in *The Symbolic Meaning: The Uncollected Versions of Studies in Classic American Literature*, ed. Armin Arnold. Fontwell, Arundel, Sussex: Centaur Press, Ltd., 1962; rpt. in Carlson, *Critical Essays*.

Menides, Laura Jehn. "There, but for the Grace of God, Go I: Eliot and Williams on Poe." In Fisher, *Poe and Our Times*.

Shaw, George Bernard. "Edgar Allan Poe." *Nation* (London), January 16, 1909; rpt. in Carlson, *Critical Essays*.

*Hungary*

Karatson, André. *Edgar Allan Poe et le groupe des écrivains du 'Nyugat' en Hongrie*. Paris: PUF, 1971.

Radó, György. "The Works by E. A. Poe in Hungary." *Babel* 12 (1966): 21–22.

*India*

Pavnaskar, Sadanand R. "Indian Translations of Edgar Allan Poe: A Bibliography with a Note." *Indian Journal of American Studies* (January 1971): 103–110. An expanded version of this bibliography by the same author but without notes is found in "Poe in India: A Bibliography, 1955–1969." *Poe Studies* 5.2 (1972): 49–50.

Ramakrishna, D. "Poe's *Eureka* and Hindu Philosophy." *Emerson Society Quarterly* 47.2 (1967): 28–32.

*Italy*

Cagliero, Roberto. "*Arthur Gordon Pym*'s Influence on Italian Literature." *PSA Newsletter* 15.2 (1987): 8.

Tani, Stefano. *The Doomed Detective: The Contribution of the Detective Novel to Postmodern American and Italian Fiction*. Carbondale: Southern Illinois UP, 1984.

*Japan*

King, James Ray. "Richmond in Tokyo: The Fortunes of Edgar Allan Poe in Contemporary Japan." In *Papers on Poe*, ed. Richard P. Veler. Springfield, Ohio: Chantry Music P, 1972.

Lippit, Noriko Mizuta. "Natsume Sōseki on Poe." *Comparative Literature Studies* 14.1 (1977): 30–37.

———. "Tanizaki and Poe: The Grotesque and the Quest for Supernal Beauty." *Comparative Literature* 29.3 (1977): 221–240.

Nakamura, Tohru. "Poe in Japan — 9: Bibliography 1978–1985." *Bulletin of the College of General Education*, Ibaraki University 19 (1987): 159–170.

## Poland

Kujawinski, Frank. "Leśmian and Edgar Allan Poe." *Polish Review* 33.1 (1988): 55–69.

## Portugal

Monteiro, George. "Poe/Pessoa." *Comparative Literature* 40.2 (1988): 134–149.

## Romania

Aderman, Ralph M. "Poe in Rumania: A Bibliography." *Poe Newsletter* 3.1 (1970): 19–20.

Carlson, Thomas C. "The Reception of Edgar Allan Poe in Romania." *Mississippi Quarterly* 38.4 (1985): 441–446.

———. "Romanian Translations of 'The Raven.'" *Poe Studies* 18.2 (1985): 22–24.

———. "Edgar Allan Poe in Romania, 1963–83: An Annotated Bibliography." *Bulletin of Bibliography* 44.2 (1987): 75–81.

Sorescu, Roxana. "Eminescu and Poe." *Romanian Review* 41.11 (1987): 62–67.

## Russia

Bandy, W. T. "Were the Russians the First to Translate Poe?" *American Literature* 31 (1960): 479–480.

Bidney, Martin. "Fire and Water, Aspiration and Oblivion: Bal'mont's Re-Envisioning of Edgar Allan Poe." *Slavic and East European Journal* 35.2 (1991): 193–213.

Burnett, Leon. "Dostoevsky, Poe, and the Discovery of Fantastic Realism." In *F. M. Dostoevsky (1821–1881): A Centenary Collection*. Colchester: University of Essex, 1981.

Dostoevsky, Fyodor M. "Three Tales of Edgar Poe." Trans. Vladimir Astrov. Rpt. in Carlson, *Critical Essays*.

Gogol, John M. "Two Russian Symbolists on Poe." *Poe Newsletter* 3 (December 1970): 36–37.

Grossman, Joan Delaney. *Edgar Allan Poe in Russia: A Study in Legend and Literary Influence*. Wurzburg: Jal-Verlag, 1973.

Harap, Louis. "Poe and Dostoevsky: A Case of Affinities." In *Weapons of Criticism: Marxism in America and the Literary Tradition*, ed. Norman Rudich. Palo Alto, Calif.: Ramparts P, 1976.

Yarmolinsky, Abraham. "The Russian View of American Literature." *Bookman* 44.1 (1916): 44–48.

Zakharov, Igor. "Edgar Allan Poe as We Have Seen Him." *Soviet Life* 8 (August 1989): 60–61.

## Scandinavia

Anderson, Carl L. *Poe in Northlight: The Scandinavian Response to His Life and Work.* Durham, N.C.: Duke UP, 1973.

## Spain

Del Vecchio, Eugene. "E. A. Poe and Antonio Machado: An Undetected Affinity." *Discurso Literario* 5.2 (1988): 395–400.

Englekirk, John E., Jr. *Edgar Allan Poe in Hispanic Literature.* 1934. New York: Russell and Russell, 1972.

Ferguson, John De Lancey. *American Literature in Spain.* New York: Columbia UP, 1916.

Franz, Thomas R. "Unamuno and the Poe/Valéry Legacy." *Revista Hispánica Moderna* 50 (1997): 48–56.

Inge, M. Thomas, and Gloria Downing. "Unamuno and Poe." *Poe Newsletter* 3 (1970): 35–36.

Pollin, Alice M. "Edgar Allan Poe in the Works of Llanos y Alcaraz." *Hispanofila* 79 (1983): 21–37.

## Spanish America

Bennett, Maurice J. "The Detective Fiction of Poe and Borges." *Comparative Literature* 35.3 (1983): 262–275.

———. "The Infamy and the Ecstasy: Crime, Art, and Metaphysics in Edgar Allan Poe's 'William Wilson' and Jorge Louis Borges's 'Deutsches Requiem.'" In Fisher, *Poe and Our Times.*

Englekirk, John E., Jr. *Edgar Allan Poe in Hispanic Literature.* 1934. New York: Russell and Russell, 1972.

Hernández del Castillo, Ana. *Keats, Poe, and the Shaping of Cortázar's Mythopoesis.* Purdue U Monographs in Romance Languages 8. Amsterdam: John Benjamins B.V., 1981.

Irwin, John T. *The Mystery to a Solution: Poe, Borges, and the Analytic Detective Story.* Baltimore: Johns Hopkins UP, 1994.

Kushigian, Julia A. "The Detective Story Genre in Poe and Borges." *Latin American Literary Review* 11.22 (1983): 27–39.

Levine, Susan F., and Stuart Levine. "Poe and Fuentes: The Reader's Prerogatives." *Comparative Literature* 36.1 (1984): 34–53.

Pollin, Burton R. "The Presence of Poe in Borges's Reviews in *El Hogar*." *Poe Studies* 25.1, 2 (June/December 1992): 39.

Woodbridge, Hensley C. "Poe in Spanish America: A Bibliographical Supplement." *Poe Newsletter* 2.1 (1969): 18–19.

———. "Poe in Spanish America: Addenda and Corrigenda." *Poe Studies* 4.2 (1971): 46.

# Contributors

Marcel Arbeit, assistant professor of American literature at Palacky University, Czech Republic, wrote the introduction to a new edition of Poe's poetry in Czech and has been an avid reader of Poe for many years. His main field of study is literature of the American South.

Tiina Aunin, professor of English and American literature at Tallinn Pedagogical University, Estonia, has published on Poe, Hawthorne, Melville, and Vidal. A board member of the Estonian Comparative Literature Association, she also serves on the editorial committee of its annual journal, *Interlitteraria*.

Massimo Bacigalupo, professor of American literature at the University of Genoa, Italy, has translated into Italian and prepared editions of works by Shakespeare, Wordsworth, Melville, Stevens, and Frost. An associate editor of *Paideuma* and *Poesia*, he contributes to many journals and has provided surveys for *American Literary Scholarship*.

Sonja Bašić, dean of the Faculty of Philosophy at the University of Zagreb, Croatia, has published on American authors, including Faulkner and Hemingway, and on Poe's influence on Croatian literature.

Mary G. Berg, who teaches Latin American literature at Boston University and Harvard, has written extensively about nineteenth- and twentieth-century Latin American authors, including Borges, Cortázar, Quiroga, Mújica, Peri Rossi, and García Marquez.

Eloise M. Boyle, lecturer in Russian language and literature at the University of Washington, is studying Vladimir Majakovskij and the creation of the Soviet myth. She is also coediting a book on Russian high culture and the ways it is manifested in the language.

Thomas C. Carlson, professor of English at the University of Memphis, spent two years in Romania on a Fulbright fellowship teaching and doing research on Poe. He has published three articles on Poe in Romania and numerous translations of contemporary Romanian poetry.

Carlos Daghlian, professor of American literature and theory of literature at the São José do Rio Preto campus of the Universidade Estadual Paulista, State of São Paulo, Brazil, is editor of *Estudos Anglo-Americanos*. He has published on Melville and Dickinson, among others.

Győző Ferencz, professor of English and American literature at Loránd Eötvös University in Budapest, was literary editor at Európa Publishers, where he translated into Hungarian "The Gold-Bug" in a collection of Poe's stories, poems, and essays, which he annotated.

Benjamin F. Fisher, professor of English at the University of Mississippi and former editor of the *University of Mississippi Studies in English*, has published and edited many works on Poe and on Victorian literature.

Roger Forclaz, independent scholar, has done research on and written about Poe's influence on German and Austrian literatures for the past twenty years. He is the author of *Le Monde d'Edgar Poe*.

Jan Nordby Gretlund, professor at the Center for American Studies, Odense University, Denmark, has done research on Poe and contributes to *American Literary Scholarship*. His most recent book on literature of the American South is *The Late Novels of Eudora Welty*.

José Antonio Gurpegui, professor of American literature at the University of Alcala de Henares, Spain, has contributed to *American Literary Scholarship*.

Thomas S. Hansen, professor of German at Wellesley College, is the author (with Burton R. Pollin) of *The German Face of Edgar Allan Poe, a Study of Literary References in His Works* and has published two articles on Poe and Arno Schmidt.

Elisabeth Herion-Sarafidis, associate professor of English at the University of Uppsala, Sweden, has published on contemporary fiction of the American South and contributes to *American Literary Scholarship*.

Gerhard Hoffmann, professor of American literature at the University of Wurzburg, Germany, wrote a chapter on Poe and Germany in *American-German Literary Interrelations in the Nineteenth Century*.

Frank Kujawinski, professor of Slavic and Baltic languages and literatures at Loyola University of Chicago, has done extensive research on Poe in Poland and is the author of "Lésmian and Edgar Allan Poe" published in the *Polish Review*.

Stuart Levine, professor emeritus of English at the University of Kansas, founded and for thirty years edited *American Studies*. Author of *Edgar Poe/Seer and Craftsman*, he has co-published with Susan F. Levine annotated editions of Poe's stories, articles on Poe and his ties to other authors, and the forthcoming annotated edition of *Eureka* and Poe's literary criticism.

Susan F. Levine, retired assistant dean of the Graduate School at the University of Kansas, has published on both American and Latin American literatures. She is coeditor with Stuart Levine of *The Short Fiction of Edgar Allan Poe: An Annotated Edition* and *"Eureka" and Essays on Literature and Prosody* (forthcoming) in *The Collected Writings of Edgar Allan Poe*.

Noriko Mizuta Lippit, president of Josai International University, Japan, and professor of comparative literature, has taught and published on American and comparative literatures for many years. Her numerous publications include a book on Poe and four articles dealing with Poe and Japanese writers.

F. Lyra, professor of American studies at Warsaw University, specializes in the relationships between Polish- and English-language authors. His *Edgar Allan Poe* was published in Warsaw in 1973.

Maria Leonor Machado de Sousa, professor of English literature and Anglo-Portuguese cultural and literary relations, served as vice-rector of the Open University. Her numerous publications include a book on Fernando Pessoa's prose fiction, which was strongly influenced by Poe. For six years she was in charge of the National Library of Portugal.

Björn Meidal, Strindberg scholar and professor of comparative literature at the University of Uppsala, Sweden, has published on Poe and Strindberg in Swedish.

George Monteiro, professor of English at Brown University, has done extensive research on Poe in Portugal and published an article on Poe's influence on Fernando Pessoa.

Sheng Ning, deputy editor of the *Review of Foreign Literature* at the Chinese Academy of Social Sciences, is the author of *Twentieth Century American Literary Theory* and *Postmodern Reflection of a Humanistic Dilemma: A Critique of Western Postmodernism*.

Devarakomda Ramakrishna, professor of English at Kakatiya University, India, and an active member of the American Studies Research Center in Hyderabad, founded the Indian chapter of the Edgar Allan Poe Society in 1993. He has published three books on Poe.

Hans H. Skei, professor and chair of the Department of Scandinavian Studies and Comparative Literature at the University of Oslo, Norway, has published articles on American writers and contributes to *American Literary Scholarship*.

Donald Barlow Stauffer, emeritus professor of English at the University of Albany, State University of New York, is the author of *A Short History of American Poetry* and essays on Poe and Whitman. He surveyed Poe scholarship for *American Literary Scholarship* from 1975 to 1982.

Graciela Tissera, professor of Spanish at the University of South Carolina, is general editor of *TEXTOS. Works and Criticism*. She has published articles on Borges, translated Poe's works, and done research dealing with Poe's influence on Latin American literature.

J. P. Vander Motten, professor of English literature at the University of Ghent, Belgium, is author of a book on the Restoration dramatist Sir William Killigrew and has published articles on seventeenth- and eighteenth-century English literature.

Lois Davis Vines, distinguished teaching professor of French at Ohio University, is the author of *Valéry and Poe: A Literary Legacy* and numerous articles on literature, the French media, and teaching. She was named Chevalier dans l'Ordre des Palmes Académiques by the French government in 1993.

# Index